The Articulate Voice

FOURTH EDITION

The Articulate Voice

An Introduction to Voice and Diction

Lynn K. Wells

Saddleback College

PEARSON

Boston ▪ New York ▪ San Francisco ▪ Mexico City ▪ Montreal
Toronto ▪ London ▪ Madrid ▪ Munich ▪ Paris
Hong Kong ▪ Singapore ▪ Tokyo ▪ Cape Town ▪ Sydney

Executive Editor: *Karon Bowers*
Editor in Chief, Social Sciences: *Karen Hanson*
Editorial Assistant: *Jennifer Trebby*
Marketing Manager: *Mandee Eckersley*
Editorial Production Service: *Whitney Acres Editorial*
Manufacturing Buyer: *JoAnne Sweeney*
Cover Administrator: *Kristina Mose-Libon*
Electronic Composition: *Omegatype Typography, Inc.*

For related titles and support materials, visit our online catalog at www.ablongman.com.

Between the time Website information is gathered and published, some sites may have closed. Also, the transcription of URLs can result in typographical errors. The publisher would appreciate notification where these occur so that they may be corrected in subsequent editions.

Library of Congress Cataloging-in-Publication Data

Wells, Lynn K.
   The articulate voice : an introduction to voice and diction / Lynn
K. Wells. — 4th ed.
      p.   cm.
   Includes index.
   ISBN 0–205–38032–8
   1. Voice culture—Exercises.   2. Diction.   3. Speech.   I. Title.
PN4162 .W45   2003
808.5—dc21

                                                        2002040872

Printed in the United States of America

10   9   8   7   6   5   4   3   2   1   08   07   06   05   04   03

CONTENTS

PREFACE

The human voice serves to communicate our ideas to others. Its distinctiveness in the sounds it produces creates an image in the ear of the beholder. Although the fields of linguistics, acoustics, and psychology can give us information about the perception of voice, it is the task of the textbook to give the student information about voice production and improvement. What we prefer to hear in another person's voice is (to some extent) subjective, but we do know that certain voices are thought to be more positively received than others. This text, then, serves to present as much information as possible in order to assist the reader in creating his or her best possible voice. In addition to all the information that we provide in this book, the student must also rely on the wise guidance of the instructor to assess and assist, and to serve as a role model.

The fourth edition of *The Articulate Voice: An Introduction to Voice and Diction* continues to stress the development of those skills necessary to creating a favorable vocal impression. The text continues to guide the reader in finding appropriate pitch and intonation, improving rhythm and rate of speech, supporting and placing the voice, and eliminating negative vocal qualities. The text takes the reader through a study of articulation and stresses exercises to improve lip, tongue, and jaw movement for crisper production of sounds. At a time when cultural identity issues and attendant identifying dialectal issues are in the headlines and because of the pervasiveness of radio and television, one may be required to be "bidialectal" in our society, or what has come to be called "code switching." The focus of this text is on the study of General American English as an "industry" or business standard.

Note that changes brought about by the IPA conference of 1989 are reflected or indicated in the text by means of footnotes. These include the clarification of the inverted [ɹ] as representative of the General American and General English sound and the upright [r] as representative of the trilled sound used in Spanish. This text will continue to use the upright "r" only for ease in reading and because of reader recommendations. The diphthongized vowels [eɪ] and [oʊ] supplant the pure vowel representations.

Suggestions provided by the text's adopters have resulted in the following changes:

- The chapter on language has become Chapter 3 at the behest of several reviewers who wished to see the information presented earlier.
- Information on vocal health has been amplified.
- A section on stage fright was included.
- Exercise materials have been added, including an extensive vocal warm-up.
- A list of commonly mispronounced words has been added, and Appendix Three provides a vocabulary builder list.
- Duplicate forms have been eliminated.

Reviewers made many other excellent suggestions, some of which can be found in the *Instructor's Manual,* for example, recommendations for audio, video, or online materials; a list of exemplary voices; further readings; and topics for discussion or research.

Many instructors and students have found this text to be a flexible tool for an introductory voice and diction class. It is designed for use by students in broadcasting, communication, and drama, and by ESL students, but is useful for other students as well. As always, readers may begin with any chapter after Chapter One as a starting point. Individual chapters discuss the vocal mechanism; language; the vocal components of pitch, rate, loudness, and quality, including a discussion of paraliguistics for each; and vowels and consonants. For student interest and for practice purposes, the drill material includes a wide range of formats, such as simple words and sentences, news articles, essays, literature, and poetry. Chapters Nine and Ten present the vowels and consonants and feature a simplified explication of each phoneme in a consistent format. Because mouth shape is important to vowels, we have continued to use photographs where possible. In addition, photographs are included for consonants for which mouth shape is important. These two chapters stress the individual phonemes of General American English and point out some common dialectal differences by indicating which speakers of other primary languages may have difficulty with a given sound. Drill words and sentences for each phoneme are designed to be particularly simple in order for students to concentrate on the sound under consideration. Advanced students, however, may find the pronunciation list in Appendix Three to be more challenging. Many students have commented positively on the opportunity to incorporate the list into their vocabularies. Because of the practical applicability of this material beyond the classroom, the entire book is perforated. Students can tear out lists and drill material for later use or reference. This is useful especially with the evaluation forms in Appendix Five, which can be used by the instructor and student to assess progress.

Several people deserve thanks for their contributions to this book in the form of assessment and suggestions. I want to thank the reviewers of the fourth edition for their insightful observations and helpful suggestions: J. D. Ragsdale, Sam Houston State University; Carol Saunders, Chipola Junior College; and Robert Westerfelhaus, University of Houston (downtown). My thanks also to the reviewers of previous editions: George Brown, Miami Dade University; Joe Chapa, University of Texas; Elaine Klein, Westchester Community College; John Modaff, Morehead State University; Mary Elizabeth Moody, George Washington University; Wendy Overly, Clemson University; John Payne, Florida State University; Joan Regnell, George Washington University; E. James Ubbelohde, North Dakota State University; and Kristin B. Valentine, Arizona State University. I sincerely appreciate the useful and kind assistance of these reviewers.

Special thanks to my daughter Laura Wells Schmidt for her photographs and to Walter Huntoon for artwork. Continuing thanks to Mark Nelson and my family and friends for their support.

The Articulate Voice

1 An Introduction

The articulate behavior I want everyone to master is an ability to put one's tongue on the most appropriate, effective, and beautiful way of saying what one means to a broad audience.

—Tom Shachtman

TERMS

Voice [vɔɪs] A good voice is clear, resonant, stable, well supported by adequate breath control. It is at a pitch level that is appropriate to the speaker and the message. Rate of speech is such that messages are clearly understood. A good voice has variety.

Diction ['dɪkʃən] Synonyms for diction are *articulation* or *enunciation*. Fine distinctions of these terms would be: *articulation*—producing individual sounds clearly; *enuncia-*

tion—producing linked sounds clearly and distinctly as in words; *diction*—producing both sounds and ideas clearly. The use of the term *diction* in this and subsequent chapters refers to clear production of the sounds of a language.

Paralinguistics [pærəlɪŋ'gʊɪstɪks] How we use certain factors such as pitch, loudness, rate, and quality to communicate messages beyond words.

Communication: A Discussion

The human voice is a powerful tool for communicating emotions, manipulating messages, and entertaining others. Command of your voice and command of the language you speak begins in infancy. It is a skill that requires fine-tuning and practice throughout our lives. With aging we may experience some degree of short-term memory loss because we do not practice memory work as we did when we were younger and in school. Your speech may suffer a similar effect. It may become corrupted by disuse, misuse, or simply the aging process. Thus it behooves you to make speech improvement a lifelong goal.

Many news or magazine articles are written to aid readers in improving their public speaking abilities, with advice to adjust pitch, modulate rate, or project voice. Writer Michael Phillips suggests, "Maybe it's time to reemphasize the training, the glory, the theatrical possibility of the human voice."[1]

Each year in the United States we spend billions of dollars and countless hours in order to improve our physical appearances. We exercise, diet, and go to health clubs. We buy clothing, cosmetics, and try new hair styles. We build muscle, engage in sports, and race cars. We spend this time and money because we hope that improving our appearance will make us happier and more successful and ultimately will get us good jobs, attractive partners, and interesting friends.

Our visual impact on others is one of the most important aspects of the impression we make on people. Experts agree that to a high degree visual features determine that impression. Yet, despite the predominance of our visual impact on others, we are all familiar with the cliché of the attractive man or woman who spoils that impression with a distracting voice. "Listen carefully. Words can lie, but the voice never does. . . . The voice can grab you like an arm, caress you like a hand, hypnotize you like eyes and walk all over you like feet. Its depth must match or heighten a man's physique: Is there anything more ridiculous than a german shepherd with a poodle's yap? Because even if a man can't always look like a movie star, he can at least make an effort to sound like one," notes one magazine advisor.[2] The auditory impression that we make can positively or negatively affect an impression we might have worked hard to achieve. In spite of this, many of us pay little attention to our voices. We fail to take care of our vocal mechanisms until something goes wrong. Many times we speak without thinking about or knowing how we sound.

Television, radio, and films provide our role models. Some educators view our media-saturated society as one that encourages replication of a certain style of speech, including both semantic constructs and manners of speaking. In other words, you may very well have grown up imitating those MTV veejays or those "cops and robbers" actors.

Learning to hear one's own voice objectively is the single most important step in a program of voice development. Personal testimony reported in news articles reveals how people feel about other's or their own voices: "After I heard myself in a radio interview sounding like a precocious 14-year-old, I began to look for a voice coach. . . ."[3] "Sometimes, I intentionally try to lose the accent totally, to assimilate . . . sometime, I'm like, what the heck, it's too much of an effort."[4] "When people have a very polished voice, I picture them as good-looking."[5] "A language teacher told me that a . . . friend thought she lost out on a job because she couldn't understand the interviewer's accented English—and she felt too awkward to ask the interviewer to repeat the questions or explain them."[6]

Our voices say a great deal about us. Some specialists consider communication to be a form of identity management or a way of telling others who we are. Vocal qualities indicate to others our moods, attitudes, states of health, self-image, and self-esteem. Concomitantly, our personalities may be so intertwined with how we sound so as to challenge our ability to change.

Because of our voices, we may be ignored, penalized, or even characterized as unintelligent. It seems ironic that we spend so much time and money grooming ourselves for the workplace or for our social lives and yet ignore our voices as an important tool for achieving success. Communication experts inform us that lasting first impressions are formed within minutes of an encounter. In direct encounters, we might have the advantage of an attractive face, firm handshake, or pleasant smile. On the telephone, we have only our voices to establish a positive impression. For example, one personnel director reports that in a matter of minutes she is able to reduce her list of potential candidates for management positions by interviewing them over the telephone.

Students learning English as a second language may find the sounds and music of English challenging. Often the pitch variations and stresses of the speaker's primary language are superimposed onto English. New English sounds may be approximated or substituted. For a non-native speaker, one's manner of speech may impress the listener as being too aggressive or even too shy.

Try this exercise for yourself. Smile broadly as you read the next paragraph. Then read the same paragraph again while you frown and tighten your jaw. Note how the superimposed "attitude" and facial expressions changed the sound of the message.

It may be that we pay so little attention to voice and to articulation because, in most cases, we are engaged in casual, interpersonal communication. Our friends seem to understand us easily and accept us for who we are and how we sound. Meeting new people and public speaking, however, require more attention to what we say and how we say it and therefore generate a great deal of apprehension for most people. James McCroskey, a professor of speech communication, proposes that individuals with high communication anxiety levels will try to avoid situations in which they are asked to speak. He suggests that some persons will avoid a job promotion if it means public speaking. Knowing that improving one's voice will better one's chances in the job market and social world is all the more reason to undertake a program for voice and articulation enhancement.

Communication is a complex process, and it involves some involuntary actions such as breathing. Because we learned to speak in our formative years, the act of producing connected, meaningful sounds probably no longer requires conscious effort. Let's examine the communication process. Communication involves five major steps: *encoding, transferring, decoding,* and *feedback* (see Figure 1.1).

Within this communication schema are multiple variables such as gender, culture, intellect, and so forth. Generally speaking, however, *encoding* involves

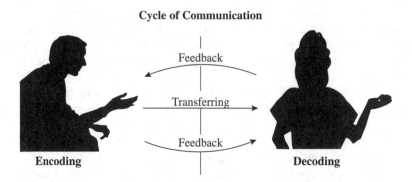

Cycle of Communication

FIGURE 1.1   The cycle of communication involves encoding, transferring, decoding, and feedback. Each participant in the cycle brings to the act of communication numerous factors, including gender, culture, education, religion, and physical and psychological components.

generating a concept and formulating that idea into a code or language. You might decide to send this message in either a verbal or nonverbal manner. That is to say, you may choose to gesture in some way in order to communicate an idea, or you may choose to sound out the words of a language. In encoding a verbal message, you must also decide what language and what words of that particular language you will use. We alter our manner of speech depending on our co-communicator, the situation, or the subject of our communication.

If you elect to send a verbal message, you will next *transfer* that message by means of an auditory channel. That is to say that you generate the specific sounds of the message by means of vocalization and articulation. Your listener or listeners will hear or *receive* your message and *decode* it. The decoding process itself is complex insofar as the listener needs to be able to translate or understand the message. He or she must have knowledge of the code used and be able to hear the message. Often a communication breakdown will occur at this point. *Feedback* takes place once a listener thinks he or she understands a message. This can be in the form of a nonverbal or a verbal response. In fact there are numerous ways we return information to one another; for instance, we can applaud, nod, frown, speak, or perform a variety of reactions. One aspect of feedback involves the regulation of interaction, sometimes called *back channeling*. This sort of communication behavior is learned regulatory behavior. Some examples are head nods while listening or the intentional use of a lower pitch to end a conversation.

This text is concerned with the vocal *transfer* step of the communication process. We engage in small cycles of communication on a daily basis. These points of verbal (and nonverbal) contact enable us to perform the simple and involved functions of our lives. Both the sounds of our voices and our manners of articulating messages affect the outcome of these daily encounters. Rarely do we receive complete, clearly articulated messages. Speech is temporal; that is, speech involves hearing and remembering just-vanished sound. For a brief moment we store in our minds what we have heard in order to sort out the message and respond properly. Though we may not hear complete words or sounds, we are still able to understand messages. Our minds fill in the missing pieces. As an example, you might think of what you do when you "read" cleverly devised automobile license plates. "1ST LUV" can readily be interpreted as "First Love." "FONECRU" could be construed as "Phone Crew." In the first instance the visual picture is completed by what we know to be the missing vowels. In the second example our auditory perception untwists the visual puzzle. Spoken and written language works in much the same way. When we only hear a spoken message, we depend heavily upon context to help us translate it.

> Read the following line: "Jeet foya came down heh?" Does it help to imagine that you are talking to someone in a restaurant? Author Tom Wolfe, in his novel *Bonfire of the Vanities,* goes on to provide the translation, "Did you eat before you came down here?"[7] Think about how you must slow down your reading and your communication process in order to translate the message.

Another aspect of social interaction involves adapting to our co-communicator. As we subtly assess the other's level of intelligence, ability, or willingness to understand us, we modify our voices to accommodate the situation. For example, we might increase loudness to accommodate someone who may be hard of hearing, or slow our speech if we feel someone cannot understand the language. Conversely, we must slow the communication process when we are trying to decipher the messages of persons with strong accents or dialects. There exist enormous implications for an increasingly multicultural society. In essence, we make adjustments in order to optimize the possibility that others will understand us.

In the course of daily conversation, speakers do omit, transpose, add, or distort sounds. A sales girl, ringing up a customer's purchase, is heard to say, "Spit?" "Pardon me?" replies the startled customer. "Wan an thin else?" the girl adds. The translation is, "Will this be it?"

We become used to the process of such translating. Perhaps we even no longer hear our own daily articulatory omissions, additions, transpositions, distortions, or substitutions. For example, the following is a list of common articulatory mistakes:

1. Omissions: *distrit* (for *district*), *libary* (for library)
2. Additions: *athalete* (for *athlete*), *didnent* (for didn't)
3. Transpositions: *alunimum* (for *aluminum*), *relator* (for realtor)
4. Distortions: *shomething* (for *something*) [as with a lateral lisp]
5. Substitutions: *pitchure* or *pikshure* (for *picture*)

See Appendix Two for a list of commonly mispronounced words.

Now that you know some common errors, you can begin to understand more about your voice and the verbal process of communication.

Speech As a Learned Process

Before considering how you might change your voice, you might wonder how you came to sound the way you do. By way of preface, we should consider that there has been a long running debate over language acquisition. This debate may have been fueled in October 2001 with the discovery of what scientists termed a "speech gene." In addition, ongoing brain studies continue to broaden our understanding of language and speech. Notwithstanding the potential ramifications of new discoveries, speech production is a unique act that you learned to perform. Though you were not born saying words, you probably produced sound very shortly after birth—crying, gurgling, and other infant sounds. In fact, you were born with the potential to speak any language on earth. If you had been born into a German-speaking family or a Japanese-speaking family, you would be speaking that language today. We learn the individual sounds of a language, and we learn the music or intonation of that language. Our teachers, in most cases our parents, also teach us to sound out the various nuances or subtleties of meaning inherent in language. (See p. 46 for further discussion.) Think, for example, of all of the possible meanings you can communicate with the simple word "oh."

Because of your imitation of a role model and for anatomical reasons, one day you may even hear yourself sounding like your parents or teachers. As a child, however, you had unlimited potential. Your muscles were free and flexible to produce all of the intricacies and complexities of all the languages in the world: the guttural sounds of German, the nasal sounds of French, the rolled [r] of Spanish. Yet many of us have been isolated within only one language. Our vocal structures have become used to making only the sounds of our native language. Consider having a broken arm that has been put into a cast. You may want nothing more than to straighten the bent arm. When the cast is removed, your urge to do so is thwarted by the rigidified position to which the arm became accustomed. Compare that rigidity to that of being cast in only one language.

Consider the "th" sound [θ], [ð] (see Chapter Ten), as in "think" or "this." If you speak English, you are used to producing this sound. However, this sound does not exist in many other languages. It does not exist in French or Italian for instance. No doubt an Italian or French baby makes the "th" sound during an early period of vocal play. Since that sound does not exist in either of those languages, the child is not reinforced for producing it. As the foreign speaker learns English, he or she may attempt to compensate. The tongue may hit as close to the "th" as possible, producing [s], [z], or [t], [d]. Conversely, this same principle applies to English speakers who try to learn another language in which a sound occurs that does not exist in English.

Wouldn't it be nice to simply read this book and experience overnight change? Wouldn't it be easy if all you had to do was go to class, listen to your professor, and then be able to transform your voice? It will take more work than that to improve. At least 52 hours is vital to work toward losing an accent, according to the Professional Voice Care Center of Long Island.[8] Length of time and learner's commitment, with other factors, are necessary elements in many language learning situations.

In the Basque region of Spain a government program teaching the native language estimates that it requires 20 hours per week for a year to teach good speech. Beverly Galyea, in *Language from Within,* contends that to achieve a second language one must hear it 150 times and say it 47 times in context. Martin Schwartz, in *Stutter No More,* notes that though he can effect an immediate noticeable change in a stutterer's speech behavior, it takes 12 weeks of dedicated practice to integrate the change into ordinary behavior. We would like to think that a magic wand will change us. We subscribe to the one-minute this or the five-minute that philosophy. However, **substantive change usually requires time.** Think back to how you learned any skill such as swimming, riding a bike, or playing golf. There were a series of processes that you went through to acquire that skill. Learning requires motivation, awareness, instruction, repetition, and time.

Scientists are discovering that motor stimulation enhances learning. It appears that there might be a window of opportunity in acquiring new skills as the brain perceives, stores the skill in short-term memory, and then shifts that skill to other areas of the brain. In addition to associating motor activity with learning, we can engage in mental exercise. In his book *A User's Guide to the Brain,* John J. Rainey says, "Even thinking the word 'cat' (silent naming) activates the motor speech areas."[9] Rainey goes on to point out that we store language information in different parts of the brain depending on when we learned the sounds of that language.

Motivation   At this point in time you may not realize what it is you know or don't know about your voice and diction. Many persons don't even realize how their voices sound, although they have been speaking for years. As you begin a course of study designed to make you more **aware** of your voice, you should have the occasion to
Awareness   tape yourself speaking. At this juncture students often remark, "I didn't think I sounded like that!" As you begin to learn the skills necessary to improve your voice you will learn that if you make a conscious effort you will be able to perform in an improved manner. You can consciously lower the pitch of your voice, slow down rate of speech, or produce the "th." The big question remains—What secret
Instruction   ingredient, what magic moment in time makes it all click into place so that a changed voice becomes part of your daily life, and you use this new voice without thinking? Bryant J. Cratty suggests that optimum learning takes place when we combine observation, mental rehearsal, and physical practice or repetition of a
Repetition   skill we are trying to acquire.[10] It would be nice if each step in this learning process took only a few minutes or a few classes to effect. The time frame and work process, however, will vary from person to person. So if improvement doesn't happen overnight, be patient. Change takes time. Realize that in the first place you didn't learn how to speak in just a brief session. The brain is required to create new
Time   neural connections, so the more one practices a new skill, the stronger the new connections become.

Although some people presuppose that one's voice cannot be changed, this is not true. You *can* revive flexibility of the vocal musculature. You *can* lower or raise your pitch level. You *can* alter your rate of speaking. You *can* increase support to your voice in order to be heard.

How many times do you have to record your answering machine message before you are happy with the way you sound? In order to improve your voice, you need to learn to listen to yourself discriminatively. The first step toward improvement is making yourself aware of your voice and articulation. Learning to listen to yourself will take conscious effort and objectivity. It may take the kind of distance and objectivity that can be achieved with the use of technology, such as tape or video recording. It is often more helpful to use video equipment so that you can hear your voice as well as see your manner of articulating. Your first reaction upon hearing or seeing yourself might be, "Do I really sound like that?" or "Is that really me?" It is difficult to separate our perceptions of how we sound or look from what we might hear or see on a recording. Try to gain some objectivity in listening to yourself (or viewing yourself) by imagining that you are analyzing someone else.

A dialect or accent may be part of your heritage and charm and is most probably closely linked with self-concept. There are sufficient role models available to suggest that acquiring a mastery of General American English may be advantageous to you professionally and economically. A dialect or regional accent will link you to any preconceptions your co-communicator may bring to the context in which you find yourself, whether it is a social or professional setting. To this end, most communication experts recommend the ability to *code switch* as a transactional and contextual process in order to gain an advantage in most situations. What this means is to have the capability of using Standard or General American speech in business settings and the ability to return to a dialect within familiar situations. This text will focus on helping you to become more marketable and perhaps even more comfortable in public settings. Presidential candidates and even U.S. presidents have been known to emphasize a regional accent when speaking in certain parts of the country. Your instructor should be able to identify several examples of public figures who have engaged in extensive training to rid themselves of accents.

Why Change?

Numerous indicators suggest viable reasons for you to improve your voice and articulation. Changing your own approach to vocalization can be rewarding. Here are a few good reasons researchers cite for doing so:

■ It is probable that vocal behavior influences others in such a manner that we are, in turn, affected both psychologically and physiologically.[11]

■ While a mobile society seems to be shifting accents in the United States, it appears that regional accents continue.[12]

■ Voice-recognition technology is fast becoming pervasive, indicating a need for clarity and consistency in articulation.

- A person with no accent appears to have an advantage in the business world over those with an accent.[13]

- Men in our society tend to speak at a lower pitch level and women at a higher pitch level than what would be most efficient for their vocal mechanisms. There is evidence that pitch is to a high degree an enculturated process.[14]

- Since women use a higher and more varied pitch than men, this implies, perhaps erroneously, that they are more emotional.[15]

- Odd pauses often indicate whether or not a person is telling the truth.[16]

- Sound distortions, such as a lisp, can lower a person's rating for intelligence and friendliness.[17]

- A person who relies on "restricted speech codes," which include slang or sound omissions, may be ill-equipped for the challenges of society, such as gaining an advancement in a job.[18]

- There are some indications that the dominant personality has a more energetic voice and the passive person a more lax voice.[19]

- The person who speaks at a faster rate is perceived as being more competent but, unfortunately, less kind.[20]

- A particular sound of voice is clearly associated in people's minds with a person's role in life.[21]

There are perceptual links between a particular voice and the age, gender, or occupation of the person speaking. Researchers have defined certain vocal characteristics of age such as "vocal fry," a type of breathiness characterized by a scratchy or popping sound. Though not all older persons exhibit these attributes, listeners tend to associate the distinctive sounds with age. Radio or television broadcasting has established certain listener expectations. For example the "voice of authority" delivering news or the voice used in voice-overs is a male sound or, if female, then pitched low. This text will focus on helping you to make the best of your voice.

The changes you wish to effect may be minor or extensive. Any improvement will take some degree of effort and a certain length of time. Your reward could be a sense of confidence about your abilities to express yourself with energy and clarity.

Communication Tenets

Since you use your voice every day, you probably haven't stopped in the middle of a conversation to assess what effect it has on others. By considering three general tenets of communication, you may begin to understand what occurs as you vocalize and articulate your thoughts.

Tenet One.   In an act of oral communication, a person makes two kinds of choices—*verbal* (e.g., linguistic and semantic in nature; having to do with words) and *paralinguistic* (e.g., having to do with pitch, loudness, rate, or quality). For example, if you were at the dinner table and you needed the salt, you might say, "Please pass the salt." Or you might say, "Yo! salt!" The words you have chosen to use are your verbal choices. If you choose to nudge the person next to you and simply point toward the salt, you have elected to use a nonverbal means of communication. If you said, "please pass the salt" so quietly that no one heard you or shouted, "Yo, salt!" in an angry manner, you have added the paralinguistic feature of the message. That is to say, you have communicated a message beyond words. You might have implied to your fellow diner, "I'm so insignificant that I don't really deserve your passing the salt to me," or, "Hey, I'm mean, so get me the salt right away before I punch your nose in." Frequently our messages are delivered so quickly that we are not even aware of the paralinguistic messages we send until someone says to us, "Hey, it's not what you said; it's how you said it!" How we use rate, loudness, pitch, and quality to add extra meaning or color our messages is vital to the impression we make on others. More will be said about paralinguistics later.

Tenet Two.   There are conditions over which a speaker may have no control. For example, illness or infection may alter the sound of your voice permanently or temporarily. Many conditions, for example, the weather, the degree of humidity in the air, your mood, or your psychological state, will affect your voice. Certain activities, such as smoking or drinking alcohol, also affect your voice.

Tenet Three.   The physical or social context in which an act of communication occurs may alter its delivery or perception. For instance, a large auditorium demands increased loudness; a bare, cement-walled room may distort the listener's perception of articulated speech. A good speaker adjusts to space and environment.

Influences on Your Voice and Speech

Friends

When you associate with a given peer group, you use the vocal and articulatory "sets" or behaviors of that group. For instance, when you are with a group of your friends you use your friends' and, of course, your own speech patterns. You no doubt say things like, "Hi, jeet jet?" (for "did you eat yet?") or, "Yeah, I gonna git goin' now." You don't speak with absolutely clear "stage diction," nor would you want to in those situations. However, you would no doubt want to make a better vocal impression if you were meeting with a potential employer.

Physicality

Various internal and external factors affect the way you sound. Your physical makeup plays a role in shaping your voice. You may have a wide gap between your two front teeth or an overbite, and this may be the reason for some sound distortions. The shape of your jaw, teeth, or lips determines, in part, the sounds you make, but you can work toward compensatory articulation, i.e., you can learn to compensate for an overbite.

Illness can affect the way you sound as well. All of us sound different when we have a cold. Consistent vocal abuse, such as yelling, screaming, or smoking, can temporarily or even permanently affect your voice. It is fairly common for athletic coaches, cheerleaders, some rock singers, and others who strain their voices to grow vocal nodules. Speech therapists are finding that more and more persons than ever before are developing these nodules or "callouses" on the vocal folds. These nodules can be removed, but if you continue to abuse your voice, they will grow back. This results in a very raspy sounding voice. Unfortunately, we often think of this sound as sexy; in fact, your body is communicating that something is wrong.

As we age, our vocal apparatus begins to deteriorate. Vocal folds or cords become thinner and tighter in men, thicker and loser in women, accounting for men's voices rising with age and women's lowering. Mucous linings become drier, which results in a hoarse sound. Flexibility is reduced with age. Diet and medications affect our voices by dehydrating the mucous linings and vocal cords.

Psychology

Your voice can reveal your psychological state. Listeners can tell whether you are anxious, depressed, or elated. How often has someone asked you, "What's wrong?" or said, "You sound depressed today." Attitude can be vocally transmitted. Psychologists tell us that our voices can say a great deal about us. If we are excited, we may speak at a higher level and more rapid rate. If we are tired or sad, we may speak more slowly. If we are lying, our voices may reveal the deception.

Stage Fright. Called by many names, such as anxiety, fear of performance, or just the jitters, stage fright manifests itself in a variety of physiological ways. Simply put, the brain perceives or translates danger and sends signals to glands to release hormones (adrenaline and epinephrine) that will give our bodies the energy to escape danger. Other bodily systems are put on temporary hold, and we experience the results we know of as stage fright. Heart rate speeds up from a resting rate of about 70 beats per minute to over 100 beats per minute. (Some people even exceed 150 beats per minute! Fortunately, this resolves within a few minutes.) The body sweats to cool down, but this leaves us with sweaty palms and armpits. We feel nauseous; we shake or tremble. There are numerous ways that this anxiety affects the voice.

Dry mouth. Shaky voice. Tight throat. Have you experienced any of these symptoms? Let's look at what happens. First, the salivary glands temporarily shut down, resulting in dry mouth. Muscles in the neck and jaw area tighten, giving us the feeling of a tight throat. We begin to breathe in a shallow manner, causing us to speak with a shaky voice. Tension results in trembling lips or chattering teeth.

What can you do to alleviate these symptoms? First, realize that, to a greater or lesser extent, everyone experiences stage fright. You will find many more suggestions and exercises in Chapter Two, but here are five tips to help you right away.

1. Visualize a positive outcome for whatever communication experience you are about to undertake.
2. Engage in regular, expansive breathing.
3. Practice relaxation techniques.
4. To temporarily relieve a dry mouth, press your tongue against your lower teeth and move it slowly from one side to the other. This should produce saliva.
5. Be careful to avoid spicy foods, caffeine, and milk products before speaking events.

Environment

Even the environment can affect our voices. Pollution, noise, even humidity, or lack of it, can alter our voices. Dry, smoggy air can give us a "scratchy" sound. We may try to speak louder over excessive noise without adequate breath support. Have you ever driven on an expressway or freeway for an extended period of time with the windows rolled down and at the same time tried to carry on a conversation? No doubt your voice experienced strain after a short time.

Because oral communication is such an integral part of our lives, we continue to vocalize even when illness or injury affects our voices, although this is potentially damaging. Surely you wouldn't continue jogging if you had pulled a leg muscle or sprained your ankle. A similar case can be made for protecting injured vocal folds or sore throats.

Improving Your Voice

Part of your individuality is the distinctiveness of your voice. A dialect, a special vocal quality, or pitch level can contribute to that uniqueness. This text can assist you in discovering what to do to become a better speaker. Keep in mind that there is a difference between description and prescription. In many instances this text will describe processes but in other cases will prescribe what it takes to achieve that description. That does not mean that you must change. As the "owner and operator" of your voice, ultimately you must decide how you want it to sound.

To achieve success in skills improvement, you must be willing to break habits, to do things differently. This is difficult because we all want to be part of a group and because people are used to us the way we are. No doubt the first time you attempt clearer diction or a lower pitch level among your family and friends, they will say, "Why are you talking so funny?" Consider what their reaction would be if you lost a great deal of weight. Hopefully, they will say, "Gee, you look great!" Whether it is your physique or your voice, you must realize that you are working toward positive change. To improve your voice, you must be willing to invest time and energy just as if you were trying to improve some other part of your body.

In the late 1800s, Maximillian Berlitz founded the now famous Berlitz Language School. Through a series of events, he learned that the student who became immersed in a language, who spoke it all day long, learned it faster and better than students who studied under any previously advocated method. That immersion technique is being revived in summer language camps for students around the country. Similarly, the person who employs proper vocal technique or clear articulation only for short periods of time cannot expect rapid improvement, if any at all.

You must immerse yourself in your project of developing a new vocal profile. Learn to hear yourself. An error in articulation is no sin as long as you can hear yourself make it and know how to produce the correct sound. For the student of English as a second language, it is most important to utilize the immersion method in practicing voice and articulation improvement. Listen to as much spoken English as possible. Try to speak English at all times.

Sequenced behavior can aid learning. Select a difficult sentence or passage that contains sounds or sound combinations that are difficult for you. For example, "Think of the things that are over there." There are five "th" sounds (often problem sounds) in this sentence. Place the tip of your tongue slightly between your teeth. Exhale air, then add vocalization. You have produced both sounds. Now add physical movement (snap your fingers, clap your hands, or take a step) each time you speak the sound.

What Is a Good Voice?

Because there is no single perfect vocal model, what should be your goal? A good voice is clear and strong. It should be well supported by adequate breath control so that it projects well. A good voice is one that communicates messages at an appropriate rate at a pitch level that is appropriate to the speaker and message. A good voice should be resonant and varied, articulating each sound clearly in connected speech. As a result of these qualities, a good voice makes a positive impression. In using such a voice, you will have altered for the better your self-image as you see people reacting more positively toward you.

Each chapter that follows will give you instruction and exercise for specific aspects of your voice. These areas of focus will be on the *vocal mechanism;* the *pitch, loudness, rate,* and *quality* of your voice; *language;* and the *articulation* of *vowels* and *consonants.* At the end of each chapter, a feature called "Focus Message" will address some concerns for people with specialized interest in English as a second language, acting, or broadcasting.

"I was waiting for the kind of solution where God reaches down and touches you with his magic wand and all of a sudden I would be fixed, like a toaster oven," writes Anne LaMott in her novel *Bird by Bird.* Is this your thinking? LaMott goes on to write, "But this was not the way it happened. Instead, I got one angstrom unit better, day by day."[22] You may have begun this course of study with some personal objectives in mind. Perhaps you feel your pitch level is too high or your rate of speaking so fast that no one can understand you. Perhaps you have been told that you mumble. The following steps will help you assess your voice and articulation needs and help you establish your goals.

- Begin by consulting with your instructor.

- Fill out the form at the end of this text. This vocal profile will help your instructor in evaluating your objectives.

- Identify the nature of the vocal change or changes you wish to effect.

- Learn to hear your voice.

- Try to select only a few things on which to work at a time.

- Realize that objectivity is important to undertaking such an evaluation.

- Now begin your program by learning how the voice works.

- Then try the relaxation and breathing exercises at the end of Chapter Two. Subsequent chapters will give you some suggestions for improving specific areas of your voice and your articulation.

- Engage in vocal play in order to discover all of the sounds that you are capable of producing.

- Commit to reading aloud every day for at least ten minutes.

- Practice every day, but remember: *Practice doesn't make perfect, practice makes permanent.* Be sure to seek out guided instruction as you work.

Chapter One Review

Review the following concepts:

- Terms: voice, diction, paralinguistics
- The communication process
- Speech as a learned process and advocacy for improvement
- Internal and external influences on voice and diction
- A program for voice improvement

Respond to the following:

1. What is paralinguistics? Give an example.
2. Explain the role of voice cycle of communication.
3. What role do parents, teachers, and friends play in vocal speech communication?
4. Discuss the following concept: "A particular sound of voice is clearly associated with the speaker's role in life."
5. What are the characteristics of a good voice?

APPLICATION

1. What roles have your parents, friends, teachers, or others had in influencing your voice?

2. How does your voice characterize you? Among your social group? At work? At school?

3. What is your plan for vocal improvement?

FOCUS MESSAGE

1. *ESL:* It is natural to speak your primary language when you are with friends and family. However, it may help you improve your English if you commit to speaking only English for the duration of this course. You might isolate yourself insomuch as possible or inform your other linguistic community that you are working on a special project. *Tip:* You need to know that there are four vocal factors that identify a dialect. (1) sound substitution (see p. 5); (2) intonation (see p. 56); (3) syllabic stress (see p. 76), and (4) resonance focus (see p. 24). In addition, word choice and word order will affect your English.

2. *Acting:* Think of your voice as a musical instrument that you must practice daily. Whether it is your script, a newspaper, or some other material, read aloud for ten to fifteen minutes each day with a special focus for each session. One day it might be breath support (see Chapter 2), on a different day, articulation (see Chapter 8). Another tip: Begin listening to the unique voices of others in order to practice vocal characterizations in the future.

3. *Broadcasting:* Many students are drawn into broadcasting because of their voices. The pitch and/or resonance may be attractive to others. Frequently articulation is weak for beginning students and, with weak diction, communication breaks down. Begin tape-recording yourself in a variety of situations—speaking on the phone, casual conversations, in public arenas. Begin to become more aware of your personal vocal habits.

> **Now turn to page 264
> and complete your Vocal Profile.
> Follow your instructor's directions.**

EVALUATION

SEE PAGES 264–265, where you'll find evaluation forms for this chapter. Follow your instructor's directions.

NOTES

1. Michael Philips, *Los Angeles Times*, June 4, 2000, p. 73.

2. Carol Schatz, *Mademoiselle*, June, 1990, p. 145.

3. Lauren Lipton, "Testing Her, Um, Totally New Voice." (*L.A. Times*, December 20, 1992).

4. Deborah Sontag, "Oy Gevelt! New Yawkese: An Endangered Dialect?" (*New York Times*, February 14, 1993).

5. Kathleen Doheny, "Making Those Sound Judgments." (*L. A. Times*, December 26, 1995).

6. Patt Morrison, "Easier Said Than Done." (*L. A. Times Magazine*, April 3, 1994).

7. Tom Wolfe, *Bonfire of the Vanities* (New York: Farrar, Straus, Giroux, 1987), p. 233.

8. Harper's Index (*Harper's Magazine*, 293, 1756, Sept. 1996), p. 15.

9. John J. Rainey, *A User's Guide to the Brain* (New York: Pantheon Books, 2001), pp. 178–179, 200–201, 269, 278.

10. Bryant J. Cratty, *Teaching Motor Skills* (Englewood Cliffs, NJ: Prentice-Hall, 1973), pp. 96–98.

11. Jeffery Pittam, *Voice in Social Interaction* (Thousand Oaks, CA: Sage Publications, Inc., 1994), pp. 78–79.

12. www.ling.upenn.edu/phono_atlas/home.html (2002).

13. John Tsalikis, Marta Ortiz-Buonafina, and Michael S. LaTour, "The Role of the Accent on the Creditability and Effectiveness of the Salesperson: The Case of Guatemala," *International Marketing Review*, 9(4), 1992; 57–72.

14. Philip Lieberman, *On the Origins of Language: An Introduction to the Evolution of Human Speech* (New York: Macmillan, 1977), p. 178.

15. R. Klaus Scherer and Howard Giles, *Social Markers in Speech* (Cambridge, Eng.: Cambridge University Press, 1979), p. 129.

16. Paul Ekman, *Telling Lies* (New York: W. W. Norton, 1985), p. 92.

17. D. E. Mowrer, P. Wahl, and S. J. Doolan, "Effects of Lisping on Audience Evaluation of Male Speakers" (*Journal of Speech and Hearing Disorders*, 43), pp. 140–148.

18. Robbins Burling, *Man's Many Voices: Language in Its Cultural Context* (New York: Holt, Rinehart, & Winston, 1970), p. 165.

19. Scherer and Giles, p. 159.

20. Ibid., p. 16.

21. Ibid., p. 52.

22. Anne LaMott, *Bird by Bird* (New York: Pantheon Books, 1994), p. 127.

2 Mechanisms for Speech

I was screamin' and suddenly…the voice was just gone. I've realized the most important thing an actor has is…voice.

—Nicole Kidman

TERMS

Breathing ['briðɪŋ]   The process of inhaling and exhaling air and, in this context, utilizing that air for producing voice.

Phonation [foʊ'neɪʃən]   The vibration of the vocal folds housed within the larynx.

Resonation [rɛzə'neɪʃən]   The amplification of vocalized sound that occurs in the pharynx, nasal cavities, and oral cavity.

Articulation [ɑrtɪkjə'leɪʃən]   The formation of the individual sounds of a language.

Imagine that you are not able to speak for whatever reason. If you have ever suffered laryngitis, you may already know the frustration of not being able to orally communicate your ideas. For those people who were born deaf or who might have had to undergo a laryngectomy, which makes them unable to produce normal speech, there are other methods of communication. American Sign Language, or ASL, is one method of nonverbally communicating. Esophageal speech has been used for years by those having undergone removal of the larynx, and other mechanical means of voice production are evolving technologically annually, such as the first successful laryngeal transplant in 1998 whereby Timothy Heidler, who was 40 years old at the time, received a new larynx. This text, however, will address the needs of those people who vocalize the language with attendant necessary organs intact.

Verbal communication separates us from the other species. Many species seem to use communication characteristics similar to humans. Researcher Jo Liska reports that groups or pods of killer whales each have a distinctive sound, and these differences are similar to human dialects. She goes on to note that, "parrots and magpies are special cases in that they can mimic the sounds of human speech so realistically that it is difficult to distinguish their sounds from those produced by humans . . . without the benefit of typical human vocal equipment such as a larynx."[1] The human anatomical structure and the physical processes involved in producing voice form an amazing interlocking system. It is valuable to understand how that system works in order to begin improving its operation.

Some persons call the act of voice production an *overlaid* process because the structures utilized are employed in basic life-sustaining functions. For example, the primary function of the lungs is breathing. The life-sustaining functions of the tongue, teeth, and palate are biting and chewing food. The secondary function is voice generation and support.

To examine the voice production system, we will discuss it in four parts: (1) *breathing*, (2) *phonation*, (3) *resonation*, and (4) *articulation*. Finally, we will examine methods of utilizing the system more effectively by means of relaxation and breathing exercises.

Breathing

Like any engine, the human body runs on fuel. Oxygen is an essential fuel for the body, and one of its functions is to sustain voice. It may seem a simple enough process to produce sounds, yet to sustain those sounds effectively requires education and practice. Let's first examine the structures involved in breathing (see Figure 2.1).

Your rib cage is connected by two sets of muscles called *intercostals—internal* and *external*. These muscles are, in part, responsible for the flow of air in and out of the lungs. Lung air capacity varies between approximately 4400 milliliters (ml) for females and 5900 ml for males. There is always a reserve of about 1200 ml of air in the lungs.

Taking air into the lungs is called *inhalation* or *inspiration;* expelling air is called *exhalation* or *expiration*. During relaxed breathing you usually inhale about a dozen times per minute, taking in about 500 ml of air with each inhalation. This rate is increased as your physical activity increases or as your stress level increases. Though you do not normally think about breathing, you can learn to increase your capacity and control of inhalations and exhalations for the purpose of producing vocalization. Posture is a vital component of effective breathing. Upright, expanded posture wherein the head is aligned over shoulders that are squared will enhance breath capacity. Because speaking can be stressful, good breath control enables you to use your vocal mechanism more efficiently.

The *diaphragm* is a dome-shaped muscle situated just under the lungs. In fact, the inferior (or lower) lobe of each lung rests on the diaphragm. Though you have no direct control in flexing the diaphragmatic muscle, you can indirectly control it with tension exerted by tangential muscles of the thoracic structure. By pulling the rib cage outward and upward, you are indirectly lowering the diaphragm.

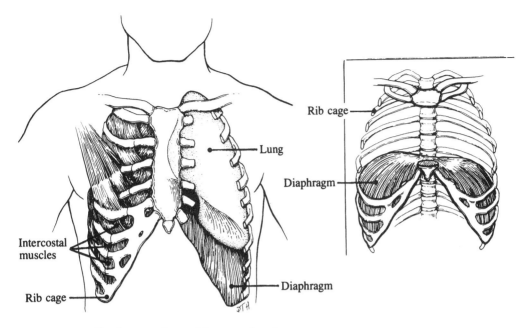

FIGURE 2.1   The human breathing mechanism.

During inhalation, two major structural changes occur. The external intercostals of the rib cage pull upward and outward, and the diaphragm contracts and flattens. This increases the space of the thoracic cavity, or chest cavity, and pulls air into the lungs. The greater the exertion, the greater the amount of air inspired.

During exhalation the internal intercostal muscles pull downward and the diaphragm relaxes upward, forcing air out of the lungs.

To understand better how relaxed and normal breathing occurs, you can perform two exercises. First, observe your breathing as you lie flat. Notice how your abdominal area rises with inhalation and falls with exhalation. Second, try breathing improperly: pull upward with your shoulders or clavicles, and at the same time suck in your stomach as you inhale. Note that in doing this, you will take in much less air. Yet a third manner of observing your own breathing habits is to lean over the back of a padded chair, being sure to rest on your diaphragm. Now inhale and exhale.

Stage fright tends to result in shallow breathing, the consequence of which is a shaky or quivering voice. While engaged in public speaking or in other public performances, you should become aware of your breathing in order to assess whether you are currently performing efficiently. If you are exhibiting the manifestations of nervousness, you can learn techniques for breath support.

In relaxed or quiet breathing, the time spent on inhalation and exhalation is about equal. For speaking, that ratio changes. The amount of time spent on inhalation is shorter. Exhaled air is utilized to produce and sustain voice over a longer period of time. Thus, an *effective* speaker learns to control exhalation. (Before continuing, you might wish to turn to page 32 to preview breathing exercises.)

> Sit quietly and simply inhale and exhale through your nose. Then tighten your jaw and clench your fists. What happened? You probably stopped breathing, right? Think about what happens when you are under stress.

Phonation

The *larynx,* commonly called the voice box, sits on top of the cartilage rings that form the trachea or windpipe. Cartilage is an elastic material in the human body and forms a large portion of the larynx. The *thyroid* cartilage, popularly known as your "Adam's apple," is the most prominent part of the larynx. It is this part that you might see protruding from a person's neck. In fact, because of its larger size, the tip of a male's thyroid cartilage may protrude more obviously in the neck than that of a female. You can feel the thyroid cartilage if you tip your head back and put your fingers to your throat. Both the composition and the position of the thyroid cartilage are important insofar as it acts like a shield. In fact, the word *thyroid* is derived from the Greek word for *shield.* Thus, it serves as the larynx's shield.

The larynx is suspended from a small U-shaped bone, called the *hyoid bone,* by ligaments and muscles. This bone is unique because it is not directly connected to other bones. The hyoid helps to elevate the larynx when you swallow or use high pitched sounds, particularly during singing, and then this small structure assists in performing the reverse function, that is, lowering the larynx when you sing in low pitches or when you yawn. A tongue-shaped flap of cartilage called the *epiglottis* projects above and behind the larynx and is responsible primarily for channeling food or other matter to the esophagus (see Figure 2.2). The epiglottis has no function in the production of voice. The esophagus is primarily used in the digestive process. When in January 2002, President George W. Bush choked on a pretzel while watching television (and, no doubt, cheering for his team while eating that pretzel), he demonstrated for us all the dangers inherent in eating and talking at the same time.

The larynx houses thin sheets of muscular tissue called the *vocal folds,* sometimes popularly called *cords,* which are attached in the front of the larynx to the thyroid cartilage (see Figure 2.3). In the rear of the larynx the vocal folds are attached to two small pyramid-shaped cartilages called the *arytenoids.* Other small muscles inside the larynx move the arytenoids in a pivotal manner. This action causes the vocal folds to abduct or come together. If the folds do not come together

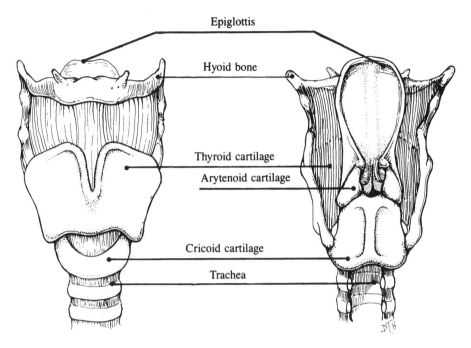

FIGURE 2.2   The larynx is composed of tough cartilaginous material and houses the vocal folds.

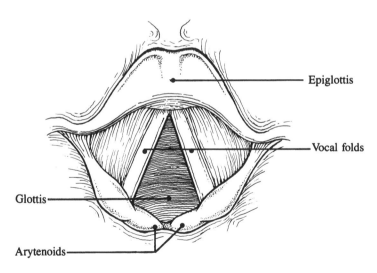

FIGURE 2.3   The vocal folds are stretched across the inner space of the larynx. The space between the vocal folds is called the glottis.

in the middle, or what is called *midline glottis* (the glottis is the space between the vocal folds), you may not produce a clear vocal quality. Thus the arytenoids are vital to vocal fold movement and voice production. A stroboscopic assessment of the vocal folds can determine the degree of fold closure a speaker achieves. Incomplete closure which results in a bowing or various other irregularities will create "airy" or "raspy" sounds.

Given your intent to vocalize, that is, as messages are sent from the brain to your larynx, air passing through the larynx provides the means for vocal fold vibration. This is the process of *phonation*. At this point, however, the sound produced is very much like the sound you can make by tensely vibrating your lips together.

Resonation

Resonation is the process of amplifying or modifying the fundamental vibrated sound that originated in the larynx. Because the space within the larynx is small—about the size of the tip of your index finger—only some amplification of vibrated sound occurs there. The *majority* of resonation occurs in three resonating cavities of the human body: the pharyngeal, oral, and nasal cavities (see Figure 2.4).

The *pharynx*, utilized by both the digestive and respiratory systems, is a tube of only four to six inches in length that extends from just above the larynx, past the rear of the mouth and to the rear of the nasal cavities. Lined with a mucous membrane, this muscular column transports food down to the esophagus and vibrated sound up to the mouth and nose. As that sound passes through the pharynx, it acquires new acoustical properties with added *formant frequencies,* which are sound characteristics resulting from resonance. You can better understand this concept if you will imagine a long rope lying on the ground. If you wiggle one end of the rope you will produce a movement. If the rope hits against a nearby object, the force will produce new movements in the waving motion. This same thing happens to sound as it travels in waves up the pharyngeal cavity. In a sense, the sound waves bump into one another to create new complexities of sound. Imagine that you initiate a vocal sound; as it travels through the cavity, it acquires new acoustical properties.

An increase in pharyngeal tension will alter the sound quality. For that reason it is important to maintain a relaxed neck and throat as you speak. As sound travels upward, it reaches a point at which it may pass through the oral or nasal cavities or both. The *soft palate,* which is the part of the roof of the mouth that seems to feel softer as you run your tongue backward along the roof of the mouth, becomes a projection called the *velum* (the tip of which is called the *uvula*). (See Figure 2.4.) Some people call it "that little punching bag" in the back of the throat, and it has often been mistaken for tonsils. This projection acts as a valve directing sound in one direction or the other. When the oral passage is closed off, as with closed lips for example, and when the velum is lowered, sound will be channeled through the *nose.* For speakers of General American English only three sounds are generally so directed. They are m [m], n [n], and ng [ŋ]. Sometimes, however,

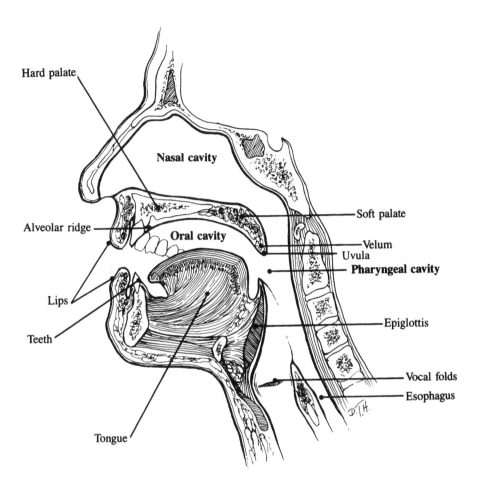

FIGURE 2.4 **The three resonating cavities are the pharynx, oral, and nasal cavities. This sketch also depicts the articulators.**

sounds adjacent to these nasals are partially nasally resonated. In some regions, generally eastern, of the United States or in some other languages, greater nasal resonance occurs.

The *oral cavity* is the most flexible of the three resonating cavities. With the velum raised against the pharyngeal wall, sound passes through the mouth and is further amplified. Because of the great degree of flexibility you have to alter the space available, you can orally produce a wide range of modified sound. You can discover this for yourself simply by producing the sound "ah" then changing the shape of the oral opening as you continue sounding.

For General American English, the center or focus of oral resonance is generally mid-mouth. For many people, focusing resonance a bit more forward of mid-mouth actually helps to promote greater lip activity, which can result in clearer, crisper sounds. Bringing it too far forward in the mouth, you will sound

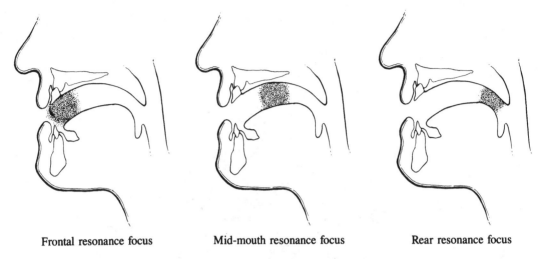

Frontal resonance focus   Mid-mouth resonance focus   Rear resonance focus

FIGURE 2.5   The resonance focus of General American English is approximately mid-mouth.

more British than American. If the center of resonance focus is too far in the rear of the mouth, you will sound guttural or even garbled (see Figure 2.5). As noted elsewhere in this text, studies inform us that persons whose resonance focus is rear mouth are frequently perceived as less intelligent and powerful than others.

As you grew up and learned new skills, you no doubt engaged in a series of trial and error attempts in order to improve them. You tried new kicks in swimming, or new ways of throwing that baseball, or new golf stances to correct that slice. As a baby, you engaged in vocal play while learning how to speak. For now, in order to acquire a sense of this concept, engage in a few moments of vocal play. The famous master of cartoon voices Mel Blanc playfully contorted his facial expressions to fit that of the cartoon character for whom he was speaking in order to find the voice for that character.

Lazy speech is characterized by rear-mouth resonance. Good speech is produced by placing that focus just a little bit forward of mid-mouth. For non-native

Try it for yourself. Scrunch up your face and introduce yourself to the person sitting next to you. You will hear a voice quite different from your usual one. Try to change old habits with play. Imagine putting a small ball in your mouth and pushing it into the pocket of your left cheek. Now speak around that ball as you introduce yourself. "How do you do? My name is . . ." Then push the imaginary ball into your right cheek. Repeat the introduction. Place the ball on the rear of your tongue. Repeat your line. Lastly, balance the ball on the tip of your tongue and repeat the same words. You should notice a distinct difference in the sound you produce.

speakers, you should note that you may be trying to produce the sounds of American English without adjusting your resonance focus. This concept is important for you to understand and acquire as you learn to speak English as a second language.

Articulation

The final step in voice production is the process of articulating meaningful connected sounds. *Articulation* is the process of producing the individual sounds or *phonemes* of any given language. Phonemes can be described as being made in a particular way if they are produced in isolation. That is not usually the case in speech. When we talk, sounds are combined with other sounds to create meaningful messages. This process is called *coarticulation*. When sounds occur together, or one right after another, they change each other. For example, the [t] in *tea* is slightly different from the [t] in *two*. The context in which a phoneme is articulated creates slight phonemic variations called *allophones*.

Your articulators are your *lower jaw, lips, teeth, gums, tongue, hard palate*, and *soft palate/velum* (see Figure 2.4). By juxtaposing these structures or by varying their positions and passing either vibrated (voiced) or unvibrated (voiceless) air through that configuration, you can create the sounds of English, French, German, Swahili, or any other language. Chapters Nine and Ten will focus in greater detail on the articulation of vowels and consonants.

Although we discussed the four parts of the vocal mechanism separately, each depends upon the efficient operation of the other. Two of the most important considerations for voice production are relaxation and breath support. Exercises at the end of this chapter will address those processes.

Hearing

Your ability to hear a sound is directly linked to your ability to reproduce that sound. Of course, hearing a sound and "listening," or paying attention, are not the same thing. Here is a brief explanation of the hearing process.

Sound waves traveling through the air are caught by the *concha* (see Figure 2.6) and channeled down the ear canal or *meatus* to the *tympanic membrane*, a thin diaphragmatic tissue at the end of the canal. These parts constitute the external or outer ear. As the sound waves strike the tympanic membrane, the tissue begins to vibrate much as would the surface of a drum when struck.

The vibration of this membrane sets up a chain reaction in the middle ear. On the inner side of the tympanic membrane are three tiny bones. Attached to the membrane is the *malleus* (hammer) that in turn is connected to the *incus* (anvil) and that to the *stapes* (stirrup). The oscillations set each tiny bone vibrating. The middle ear is connected to the pharynx by the Eustachian tube (which is why you can "pop" your ears when you yawn), and it is also connected to the sinus mastoidus. This small space is subject to calcium deposits, which can reduce hearing in some persons.

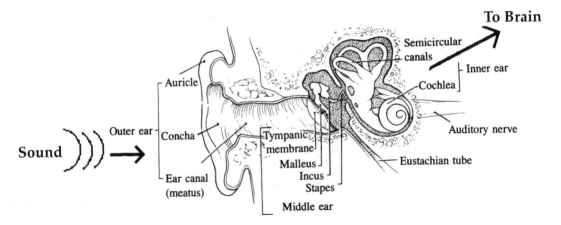

FIGURE 2.6   The human ear. The ability to hear is directly linked to the ability to speak well.

The inner ear is called the *cochlea*. This snail-shaped organ contains two "windows" called the *oval window* and the *round window*. The stapes is connected to the oval window. As the stapes vibrates, pressures push into the oval window of the cochlea. If you could unroll the coil of the cochlea you could see that along the middle of the fluid-filled cochlea lies a membrane called the *organ of Corti*. The vibrations displace the fluid along various points of this membrane touching upon tiny nerve hair cells contained therein. These nerve fibers in turn communicate impulses to the brain where they are translated into the sounds of language. Until recently, damage that occurred in this part of the ear was irreparable. Today, however, doctors are working with cochlear implants and auditory brain stem implants in order to aid hearing in some people with nerve deafness.

Whether you can hear acutely or have difficulty hearing may not matter if you don't want to listen to someone else or to yourself. Remember that (1) your ears are situated behind your voice; (2) your bones will reverberate with the sounds you make; and (3) you are busy processing messages as you speak. All three factors, and more, combine to make listening to yourself a challenge.

Vocal and Auditory Health

Improper stress and increased force on the vocal folds without proper breath support can be damaging. Vocal nodes or vocal fold lesions can result. Often those increased loudness levels occur at times of high emotion, such as when you are engaged in an argument or when you are excited. A football coach developed vocal nodules after several seasons of yelling at his team. Perhaps you have experienced a sore throat following what might be termed *vocal outbursts.* A rock music fan developed hearing loss and vocal fold lesions after screaming over the amplifiers' levels at rock concerts. Intense nervousness can produce vocal stress. A novice teacher experienced one paralyzed vocal fold after her first week teaching a new class. Continued stress can result in permanent damage. Here is a list of some common voice or speech disorders:

- *Laryngitis:* Inflammation of the vocal folds may be caused by illnesses such as a cold or flu and may result in hoarseness or even an inability to produce vocal sound. Screaming or shouting may cause laryngitis.

- *Laryngeal polyps, nodes, nodules:* While these terms seem synonymous, doctors often distinguish among the terms by cause. For example, polyps may be caused primarily by cigarette smoke and vocal abuse, whereas nodules or nodes may be caused primarily by excessive vocal abuse.

- *Laryngeal edema or swelling:* Gastric reflux, or gastroesophageal reflux disease (GERD), and allergies commonly cause swollen vocal folds that result in a hoarse voice or laryngitis. Diet and behavioral modifications are vital to mitigating or resolving the problem.

- *Spasmodic dysphonia:* Strained and choppy vocal sound is believed to be caused by neural impulses creating spasms in the vocal folds.

- *Stuttering:* We all experience normal speech hesitancies, but persons who stutter experience either blocking on initial sounds or repetition of initial sounds.

The following list provides guidelines for developing and maintaining healthy vocal and auditory systems.

Twenty Tips to Protect Your Voice and Hearing
1. Do not smoke anything.
2. Eat a balanced diet that is appropriate for your condition, and watch *when* you eat. (Late-night eating can be detrimental.)
3. Limit alcohol intake.
4. Hydrate by drinking plenty of water.
5. Get plenty of sleep, and evaluate how you sleep (on your back or left side may be best).
6. Avoid dry environments; use humidifiers.
7. Avoid polluted environments.
8. Apply individual relaxation techniques in stressful situations.
9. Employ breathing exercises to aid in relaxation and to develop adequate support for your voice.
10. Utilize oral resonance by opening your mouth more fully while speaking.
11. Avoid trying to talk over loud noises.
12. Consult with your instructor to determine your best loudness levels and the projective power of your voice.
13. Avoid prolonged exposure to loud sounds; wear earplugs or protectors if your work exposes you to noise.

14. Avoid wearing headphones to listen to loud music.

15. Be aware that certain prescription drugs may make you more sensitive to noise and may affect your voice.

16. Engage in regular exercise.

17. Do not scream or shout. If you must project your voice, use appropriate breath support.

18. Do not *clear your throat;* cough instead.

19. Rest your voice if you begin to experience an anomaly.

20. Warm up your voice before a speaking or performance event. (See p. 29 for suggested exercises.)

Vocal damage and some hearing loss are preventable. Though some people may lose hearing as the result of disease or aging, excessive noise has been identified as one of the main causes of hearing loss in our noisy society. Over 25 million people in the United States experience hearing loss, and 80 percent of those have a permanent loss. There is plenty in our environment to cause these loud levels—jackhammers, automobile horns, music, fire engines, inboard motors, subways, or power saws.

The ground crew at an airport wears ear protection for a good reason. The loudness level of an airplane engine is around 150 decibels (dB), loud enough to produce serious damage to anyone's hearing. In fact, any noise level over 100 dB can be harmful if listened to long enough. According to OSHA (Occupational Safety and Health Administration) standard 1910.95, exposure to noise at 120 dB for 7½ minutes can initiate a short-term hearing loss. Repeated exposures can add up to a permanent loss. That is why OSHA mandates that employees who are exposed to noise of 85 dB for 8 hours or more must be provided with an annual hearing exam and further mandates protective devices for various noise levels. As you work to protect your voice, also be conscious of protecting your hearing (see Table 2.1). You can access information on OSHA's guidelines on the Internet at http://www.osha.gov or, for information on hearing loss, http://www.hearnet.com.[2]

By working with a monitor, whether it is another person, a tape recorder, or video recorder, you can develop the input necessary to integrate loudness control and variation into your speaking habits. If you experience a persistent sore throat, unusual hoarseness, or decreased hearing you should consult a physician.

TABLE 2.1 Decibels levels of sounds and speech

Serious danger to hearing (jets, sirens)	140 dB
Danger zone (loud concerts, power tools)	120 dB
Stress zone (loud traffic)	80–100 dB
Conversation	60 dB
Whisper	20–30 dB

Exercises

Your first step in any exercise program is a warm-up. Just as athletes warm up their muscles, a speaker or singer should perform a vocal warm-up. This is particularly important if you are preparing to engage in extended and projected vocalizations. In addition, relaxation is vital to controlling your vocalizations. The exercises that follow should give you some directions for engaging in vocal warm-up, relaxation, and breathing for support. Remember this as you work: the imitative skill of learning to speak takes a surprisingly short time. The process of improving and implementing that improvement will require focus and repetition, which means more effort and time.

Ten-Step Vocal Warm-up

1. Begin with three full breaths. Release air slowly.
2. Inhale, then hum until you release as much air as possible. Repeat twice.
3. Count one to ten three times with a breath between each sequence. First use a quiet (personal space) voice; then use a medium (social space) voice; then use a projected (public space) voice.
4. Take three, slow, full breaths again.
5. Using a projected (public space) voice, count one to thirty on one breath. If you cannot achieve this on your first try, do not push your voice.
6. Repeat steps 3, 4, and 5.
7. Using a medium (social) voice, speak the alphabetic letters A through K. First employ a pitch beginning with a low to high pitch; then reverse the pitch from high to low on each letter. For example:
8. Take, three, slow, full breaths again.
9. Using medium (social) voice, speak the following sequences at a regular clip.

> mee, mee, mee, mee, mee, mee, mee, mee, mee, mee, mee, mee,
> ma, ma, ma, ma, ma, ma, ma, ma, ma, ma, ma, ma,
> mo, mo, mo, mo, mo, mo, mo, mo, mo, mo, mo, mo,
> mu, mu, mu, mu, mu, mu, mu, mu, mu, mu, mu, mu.
> pee, pee, pee, pee, pee, pee, pee, pee, pee, pee, pee, pee,
> pa, pa, pa, pa, pa, pa, pa, pa, pa, pa, pa, pa,
> po, po, po, po, po, po, po, po, po, po, po, po,
> pu, pu, pu, pu, pu, pu, pu, pu, pu, pu, pu, pu.
> tee, tee, tee, tee, tee, tee, tee, tee, tee, tee, tee, tee,
> ta, ta, ta, ta, ta, ta, ta, ta, ta, ta, ta, ta,
> to, to, to, to, to, to, to, to, to, to, to, to,
> tu, tu, tu, tu, tu, tu, tu, tu, tu, tu, tu, tu.
> kee, kee, kee, kee, kee, kee, kee, kee, kee, kee, kee, kee,
> ka, ka, ka, ka, ka, ka, ka, ka, ka, ka, ka, ka,

ko, ko, ko, ko, ko, ko, ko, ko, ko, ko, ko, ko,
ku, ku, ku, ku, ku, ku, ku, ku, ku, ku, ku, ku.
thee, thee, thee, thee, thee, thee, thee, thee, thee, thee, thee, thee,
tha, tha, tha, tha, tha, tha, tha, tha, tha, tha, tha, tha,
tho, tho, tho, tho, tho, tho, tho, tho, tho, tho, tho, tho,
thu, thu, thu, thu, thu, thu, thu, thu, thu, thu, thu, thu.

10. Take a deep breath and release a sigh. Repeat twice.

Relaxation

The two types of relaxation exercises that are most effective are *progressive* and *meditative*. Neither type is necessarily superior to the other. Each of us functions differently and may find that one method or a combination of the relaxation methods works best. The important point to remember here is that self-consciousness can be self-defeating. As you begin a relaxation program, be aware only of yourself. Try these exercises when you are alone, but if you can't, try not to pay attention to those around you in the classroom or the family room. Later, when you feel more confident, you may feel better performing in class.

Progressive. Progressive relaxation exercises are designed to work on actual physical tension.

Exercise 1   Perform this exercise standing with your feet about shoulder-width apart. Progressively tighten most of the muscles in your body. Begin by tightening your toes. Then, concentrating on each muscle group, work your way up: feet, calves, thighs, buttocks, abdomen, chest, back, shoulders, upperarms, forearms, hands, fingers, neck, scalp, face. This should take about 60 to 90 seconds. When all muscles are tensed, hold for a few seconds, then release. Repeat several times.

Exercise 2   Try the same progressive tensing again but this time release each muscle group in the order tensed. Do this slowly, focusing on the sensation of the relaxing muscle. Repeat.

Exercise 3   Raise your right arm over your head and slowly bend to the left, stretching the muscles along your right side. Hold the position; feel the stretch. Slowly return to an upright position. Repeat the stretch to the opposite side. Repeat twice.

Exercise 4   Isolate your shoulder and neck muscles by tensing and releasing. Repeat several times. Raise shoulders to ears, hold tensely to a count of 4. Release. Repeat.

Exercise 5   Head rolls should be performed slowly to the front, left, right, and around again. Avoid rolling your head to the rear in order to protect your cervical spine. Avoid abrupt and rapid movements. Continue for a minute or two, then reverse the direction. Remember, this is not competition, so go slowly and focus on releasing the tension of neck muscles. You might try massaging the muscles in your neck as you perform the exercise, particularly as you begin.

Exercise 6   Shoulder rolls can be a great form of self-massage. Roll both shoulders forward very slowly several times. Pause, then slowly rotate shoulders backward. As you do these rolls, stretch your muscles.

Exercise 7   Focus on facial muscles. Gently massage your face—under your jaw, cheekbones, and around your nose.

- Open your eyes widely, hold for a count of four, release. Close your eyes tightly, hold for four counts, release.

- Open your mouth as widely as possible. Hold for four counts. Release. Purse your lips tightly, hold, release.

- Puff out your cheeks by blowing air into them, keeping your lips compressed. Hold. Release the air and suck in your cheeks. Repeat.

Meditative.   Meditative relaxation utilizes the principle of tranquil mental states brought about by imagery and, in some cases, as used in transcendental meditation, the repetition of a given word or sound.

Exercise 8   Sit upright in as comfortable a position as possible. Maintain an upright posture. Close your eyes and mentally focus on the most pleasant sights, sounds, and smells you can imagine. The strength of your imagery will relate directly to the physical sensations you achieve. As you begin to experience a sense of relaxation, fix these sensations in your mind. Focus additionally on breathing through your nostrils. As you inhale, focus on the abdominal area. Think "up" as you inhale; think "down" as you exhale. Concentrate on the slow inhalations and exhalations of air. Focus means awareness, not forced control. Rid your mind of all other thoughts. Some people associate a sound, a word, a touch, or a posture with comfort and relaxation. You might use soft music or nature sounds in the background. Light a fragrant candle. Darken the room. These devices can be used simply to make you more comfortable. No one thing can work for everyone. Once you have achieved a relaxed state, it may be helpful to adopt some "talisman" to help you to associate with that state of relaxation. Music, a word, color, or a picture can become that focus. Use the talisman to carry over this relaxed state to times when you experience stress.

Exercise 9   Try a meditative focus on breathing as you walk in a slow methodical way.

Exercise 10   Combine the processes of tension, release, and visualization. Hold out either arm. Clench your fist tightly. Imagine that you are holding all the tensions of your day in your fist. Focus on both the physical and psychological tensions. Hold. Now, slowly open your hand, releasing the muscular tension and imagining that your stress is flying out of your palm. You might try to isolate your fears or stressors in this manner as you repeat the exercise.

Breathing

Deep and expansive breathing can lower your blood pressure and heart rate and can relax muscular tension. Practicing regulated breathing will assist you in engaging in good breathing habits under stress. Breathing under stress can result in *clavicular* breathing, which appears to pull up from your shoulders and clavicles. The times at which you breathe most naturally are just prior to sleep and when you are lying or sitting relaxed, as when you watch television or read. Learn the feel of that state of relaxed, quiet breathing.

Exercise 1   First, find a place where it is appropriate to lie down and wear loosely fitted clothing. Place one open palm just below your rib cage and the other open palm on your upper chest. Concentrate on a pleasant subject. In a moment you will begin to feel the rise and fall of your abdominal area as you breathe. Note how that area rises with inhalation and falls with exhalation.

If you are completely relaxed you should note that your hand on your chest is not moving.

1. Sit up. Repeat the process. You may perform the following exercises either sitting or standing, but standing may give you a better initial sense of movement.
2. Place a clock with a second hand in front of you (or a partner can time you by counting). Keeping your hands in place, inhale for 5 seconds. Exhale for 5 seconds. Repeat for 1 minute.
3. This time, inhale for 5 seconds, but exhale for 10 seconds.
4. Finally, inhale for 5 seconds, and extend the exhalation for 15 seconds. Note that with each instance of controlled exhalation, you had to *consciously* control your breathing. Practice until controlled exhalation can be implemented during moments of stress, such as when you are nervous.
5. Begin with a full exhalation until all of your breath seems to be gone. Do not strain, and do not roll your shoulders forward. Maintain an upright position. Note three actions: First your abdominal area naturally collapses with the exhalation, then your inhalation begins naturally, and finally your abdominal area expands with the inhalation.
6. Raising your arms from your sides to above your head as you inhale, engage in a series of three to five slow cycles of inhalation/exhalation.
7. Light a candle. Hold the candle about four inches from your mouth. Inhale and gently blow the candle flame so that it bends horizontally. With a steady exhalation, keep the flame in that position for ten seconds; try for 15 seconds.
8. Now add vocalization. Inhale and vocalize an "m" or a hum. Extend the sound for five seconds. Repeat, extending the sound for ten seconds. Continue your effort until you can hum steadily for at least 15 seconds.

9. Perform the same exercise using an ["f"] sound. Keep the air stream gentle but steady.
10. Do the same exercise using a vocalized sound, ["v"]. This requires more energy and control.
11. This time inhale for 5 seconds, exhale for about 5 seconds and then vocalize for about 5 seconds. Repeat several times.
12. Place the blade of your tongue against the sides of your upper molars. Slowly inhale and exhale through your nose three times. Add vocal sound on the next cycle.

    Place the tip of your tongue against you upper alveolar ridge. Inhale and exhale three times, then add vocal sound.

    Place the tip of your tongue between your teeth. Inhale and exhale slowly three times, then add vocal sound.

Increasing/Sustaining Breath Support

Exercise 2 It may be necessary for you to superimpose the abdominal sensations of expansion and contraction in order to work toward sustained breathing. As you inhale push your abdomen as far out as possible. Then exhale as you consciously pull in your abdomen. Try the following:

1. Perform the above described abdominal push/pull using a 5-second inhalation and a 10-second exhalation. Work for several minutes until you are able to build a 15-second exhalation.
2. Inhale for 5 seconds using the abdomen push. Exhale while pulling in for 5 seconds. Do it again, this time vocalize a hum for 5 seconds. Maintain an even sound.
3. If you have achieved the feeling of the push/pull by now repeat the same exercise, but this time use an "ah" sound for 5 seconds. Repeat this several times until your vocalization is even. Repeat trying the vocalization for 10 seconds.
4. Try counting one number per second. Inhale for 5 seconds. Begin counting. Stop the moment you begin to feel strain. Each number should be said at the same loudness level. Work toward counting to 30 or 40 without discomfort. If you cannot achieve this on your first try, don't be dismayed. Relax and continue breathing exercises until you are able.
5. Jog in place for about 30 seconds. Now perform the same counting exercise again. Work to maintain steady vocalization.
6. Inhale fully, then, using the sounds ["ho"] or ["ha"], release in short, strong bursts. Maintain as even a tone as possible until you are no longer able to do so. Inhale and repeat.
7. Fall forward at the waist allowing your arms to fall toward the floor and at the same time say ["ha"]. Swing up, pulling your arms toward the ceiling, again saying ["ha"]. Repeat about 5 to 10 times. Use an open mouth. Note the strong abdominal support you feel.

8. Inhale fully, vocalize a phrase. Try, "I can't hear you." Increase the volume as you repeat the message. Continue to increase loudness levels. Avoid strain. Maintain breath support. If you feel jaw or throat tension, stop and repeat breathing exercises from the start of this section.

9. Light your candle once again. With the candle about 4 inches from your mouth, try speaking the following sentences, which contain airy sounds.

    a. She sells seashells down by the seashore.
    b. Fractious Freddy met frivolous Freda at Friday's.
    c. Pompous Paul is happy to play patty cake at parties.
    d. Thinking thoughts like that can trip you up.
    e. Time and time again I tell you the time.

Did you note the degree of candle flicker you produced with such airy words? Try the sentences again, but this time try to reduce your degree of aspiration, or exhaled air.

Exercise 3   Try reading the following passages on a single inhalation, maintaining a strong, even sound while allowing for pauses or punctuation.

    1. Children should be seen and not heard.
    2. A good laugh is sunshine in a house.
    3. All will come out in the washing.
    4. Two is company; three is a crowd.
    5. I came; I saw; I conquered.
    6. In my youth, I thought of writing a satire on humankind; but now in my age I think I should write an apology for them.
    7. The best use of a journal is to print the largest practical amount of important truth—truth that tends to make humankind wiser, and thus happier.
    8. We should have a great many fewer disputes in the world if words were taken for what they are, the signs for our ideas only, and not for things themselves.
    9. The world is like a board with holes in it, and the square people have got into the round holes, and the round into the square.
    10. A vessel is known by the sound, whether it be cracked or not; so people are proved, by their speech, whether they be wise or foolish.
    11. The beginning is the most important part of the work.
    12. For extreme illnesses extreme treatments are most fitting.
    13. I know nothing except the fact of my ignorance.
    14. Haste in every business brings failure.
    15. Great deeds are usually wrought at great risks.
    16. It is better to be envied than pitied.
    17. Wisdom outweighs any wealth.
    18. Wait for that wisest of all counselors, Time.
    19. No act of kindness no matter how small is ever wasted.

20. People often begrudge others what they cannot enjoy themselves.
21. Poetry is simply the most beautiful, impressive, and widely effective mode of saying things, and hence its importance.
22. No matter how hard a man may labor, some woman is always in the background of his mind; she is the one reward of virtue.
23. People give us well-meant but miserable consolation when they tell us what time will do to help our grief; for we do not want to lose our grief, because it is bound up with our love.
24. How to save the old that's worth saving, whether in landscape, houses, manners, institutions, or human types, is one of our greatest problems, and the one that we bother the least about.
25. The teacher who can arouse a feeling for one single good action, for one single good poem, accomplishes more than he who fills our memory with rows upon rows of natural objects, classified with name and form.

Exercise 4 Try reading the following passages. There are numerous punctuation marks at which you may inhale. However, try stretching your control by taking fewer breaths than you might ordinarily.

1. The quality of mercy is not strained,
   It droppeth as the gentle rain from heaven
   Upon the place beneath: it is twice blest;
   It blesseth him that gives and him that takes;
   'Tis mightiest; it becomes
   The thronèd monarch better than his crown;
   His sceptre shows the force of temporal power,
   The attribute to awe and majesty;
   Wherein doth sit the dread and dear of kings;
   But mercy is above this sceptred sway;
   It is enthroned in the hearts of kings,
   It is an attribute to God himself;
   And earthly power doth then show likest God's
   When mercy seasons justice.
   —William Shakespeare, *The Merchant of Venice*

2. These are the times that try men's souls. The summer soldier and the sunshine patriot will, in this crisis, shrink from the service of their country, but he that stands it *now*, deserves the love and thanks of man and woman. Tyranny, like Hell, is not easily conquered; yet we have this consolation with us, that the harder the conflict, the more glorious the triumph. What we obtain too cheaply we esteem too lightly; it is dearness only that gives everything its value. Heaven knows how to put a proper price upon its goods; and it would be strange indeed if so celestial an article as *freedom* should not be highly rated.
   —Thomas Paine, *The American Crisis*

3. We shall go on to the end, we shall fight in France, we shall fight on the seas and oceans, we shall fight with growing confidence and growing strength in the air, we shall defend our Island whatever the cost may be, we shall fight on the landing grounds, we shall fight in the fields and in the streets, we shall fight in the hills; we shall never surrender, and even if, which I do not for a moment believe, this Island or a large part of it were subjugated and starving, then our Empire beyond the seas, armed and guarded by the British Fleet, would carry on the struggle, until in God's good time, the New World, with all its power and might steps forth to the rescue and the liberation of the old.

—Winston Churchill, Speech, June 4, 1940

4. You gain strength, courage and confidence by every experience in which you really stop to look fear in the face. You are able to say to yourself, "I lived through this horror. I can take the next thing that comes along."

——Eleanor Roosevelt, "You Learn by Living"

5. The sea lies all about us. The commerce of all lands must cross it. The very winds that move over the lands have been cradled on its broad expanse and seek ever to return to it. The continents themselves dissolve and pass to the sea, in grain after grain of eroded land. So the rains that rose from it return again in rivers. In its mysterious past it encompasses all the dim origins of life and receives in the end, after, it may be, many transmutations, the dead husks of that same life. For all at last returns to the sea—to Oceanus, the ocean river, like the ever-flowing stream of time, the beginning and the end.

—Rachel Carson, *The Sea Around Us*

6. A house divided against itself cannot stand. I believe this government cannot endure permanently half slave and half free. I do not expect the Union to be dissolved—I do not expect the house to fall—but I do expect it will cease to be divided. It will become all one thing, or all the other. Either the opponents of slavery will arrest the further spread of it, and place it where the public mind shall rest in the belief that it is in the course of ultimate extinction; or its advocates will push it forward till it shall become alike lawful in all the states, old as well as new, North as well as South.

—Abraham Lincoln, Speech, June 16, 1858

7. None of them knew the color of the sky. Their eyes glanced level, and were fastened upon the waves that swept toward them. These waves were of the hue of slate, save for the tops, which were of foaming white, and all of the men knew the colors of the sea. The horizon narrowed and widened, and dipped and rose, and at all times its edge was jagged with waves that seemed thrust up in points like rocks.

—Stephen Crane, "The Open Boat"

8. Rennie can't remember what people are supposed to think about. She tries to remember what she herself used to think about, but she can't. There's the past, the present, the future: none of them will do. The present is both unpleasant and unreal; thinking about the future only makes her impatient, as if she's in a plane circling and circling an airport, circling and not landing.

—Margaret Atwood, *Bodily Harm*

9. When you are a boy and stand in the stillness of woods, which can be so still that your heart almost stops beating and makes you want to stand there in the green twilight until you feel your very feet sinking into land clutching the earth like roots and your body breathing slow through its pores like the leaves—when you stand there and wait for the next drop to drop with its small, flat sound to a lower leaf, that sound seems to measure out something, and you cannot wait for it to happen and are afraid it will not happen, and then when it has happened, you are waiting again, almost afraid.

—Robert Penn Warren, "Blackberry Winter"

10. By what gets printed in some of the modern child-psychology books, you would think that girls to whom such a story had been told would never develop normally. Yet as far as I can remember what happened to the girls in that group, we all grew up about like anybody. Most of us married, some happily, some not so well. We kept house. We learned—more or less—how to live with our husbands, we had children and struggled to bring them up right—we went forward into life, just as if we had never been warned not to.

—Dorothy Canfield, "Sex Education"

11. From a distance New York seems a separate country, an international crossroads, different from other places where real Americans lead normal lives. It is an image New Yorkers love. In fact, the city faithfully reflects the rest of the United States. No generality about "Americans" is true, and yet hardly any is false. New York is the sum of all American traits and habits gone wild. Up close it is Middle America on speed.

—Mort Rosenblum, *Back Home*

12. To me, an astonishing thing about dreams is that we are not more astonished by them, and descend into them each night with so little fear and anticipation of their perils. In our dreams, without feeling a discontinuity, we become smaller or younger or even another person altogether, who leans up against our real self like a doleful contiguous bodyguard.

—John Updike, *Self-Consciousness*

13. It has often been said that a friendship is judged by whether or not we will stand by our friends in adversity. But there is an opposing, more subtle, point of view which argues that it is relatively easy to come through in times of adversity and that the tougher test of friendship is being wholeheartedly able to stand by our friends in their joys.

—Judith Viorst, *Necessary Losses*

14. A strong will to live, along with the other positive emotions—faith, love, purpose, determination, humor—are biochemical realities that can affect the environment of medical care. The positive emotions are no less a physiological factor on the upside than are the negative emotions on the downside.

—Norman Cousins, *Head First*

15. I was taught to swim by an instructor of the old school. He gave us two lessons. In the first we were allowed lifejackets and he showed us the movements of the breast-stroke; in the second he took away the jackets and pushed us into the deep end of the pool. That is where man is now. His first instinct is to turn back to the rail and cling to it; but somehow he has to force himself out and swim.

—John Fowles, *The Aristos*

Chapter Two Review

Review the following concepts:

- Speech as an overlaid process
- The structures of breathing: inhalation, exhalation, muscles, diaphragm
- The process of phonation: larynx, glottis, epiglottis, vocal folds, arytenoids
- The cavities of resonation: pharynx, formant frequencies, oral cavity, velum, nasal passages, resonance focus
- The process of articulation: tongue, lips, teeth, gums, hard palate, velum, lower jaw
- The structures of the ear—malleus, incus, stapes, tympanic membrane, cochlea, organ of Corti.

Respond to the following:

1. Explain why voice production is called an overlaid function.
2. Why does an effective speaker learn to control exhalation?
3. Explain how resonation gives quality to voice.
4. What is the difference between the terms *voice* and *voicelessness?*
5. Why should you work toward relaxing as you produce voice?

APPLICATION

1. Under what conditions or circumstances do you seem to be more breathless or does your voice seem to "tire"? Now that you understand breath control, how can you achieve better breathing during those times?

2. When does your voice seem to be tight, hoarse, or harsh? How can you produce a more relaxed sound? Keep a diary or journal. Set up a worksheet of exercises for yourself. You can build a set of exercises drawn from this chapter that specifically work for you.

3. What are the occasions when you seem to lose vocal control? When angry? At a sports event? A concert? What can you do to protect your voice during those times?

4. Assess the noise in your life. Do you wear headphones? Does your aerobics class play loud music? Is your car radio turned to maximum volume? What can you do to protect your hearing?

5. Select from the exercises in this chapter to design a program for yourself. Write these exercises on a "worksheet" so that you remember them.

FOCUS MESSAGE

1. *ESL:* Resonance focus is the concept that you need to master. Shifting the sound focus in your mouth to the center will help to give you an American English sound. (Just remember there is more to it than that, but this can be a start.) The two primary sounds you can work on right now are a mid-mouth sound called the *schwa* [ə], as in the article *a*, and a front of the mouth sound [ɪ], as in *it*, sometimes referred to as a short *i*.

2. *Acting:* While all vocal concepts are important to a good performance, relaxation and breath support are vital to a performance that may need to be sustained over many hours and projected to a large audience. Neck and throat tensions will inhibit voice production. An upright, expansive posture is important for effective vocalizations. Take time to understand your own mechanism. *Exercise:* Once you have a better understanding of your own mechanism, try jogging or walking a treadmill and speaking with breath support without laryngeal strain.

3. *Broadcasting:* Performance anxiety and lack of preparation time are two enemies of effective media presentation. Breath control is essential in order to avoid mic "popping," particularly on airy sounds (see Chapter Ten) such as [f], [s], [p], and [t]. Rehearse materials with varying styles and energy levels and focus on your breath control.

NOTES

1. Jo Liska, "Bee Dances, Bird Songs, Monkey Calls, and Cetacean Sonar: Is Speech Unique?" (*Western Journal of Speech Communication*, 57, 1, 1993), pp. 10–11.
   2. "Hearing Loss." http://www.hearnet.com (2002).

3 Language

The signs we inscribe or print should bow down to the sounds we utter.

—Anthony Burgess

TERMS

Linguistics [lɪŋ'gwɪstɪks]   The study of language.

Phoneme ['foʊnim]   An individual sound in any given language.

English ['ɪŋglɪʃ]   The name of a language generally spoken in the United States and several other countries, with all of its various dialects.

Dialect ['daɪəlɛkt]   A regional variation of a language characterized by differences from the overall language in vocabulary, grammar, and phonetic choices.

Voice is a tool for communicating meaning. Language is the medium in which we must work if we are to become articulate and communicate effectively. In his book *The Inarticulate Society,* Tom Shachtman notes, "Even though there is some evidence that the human species possesses certain innate abilities to comprehend language and especially that aspect of language known as syntax, it seems clear that advanced articulate behavior is learned, not inherited."[1] The United States has always opened its doors to people from many cultures. Coastal and border states serve as points of entry for worldwide immigrants. In some areas close to a fourth of the population is not fluent in English, and yet English is a global language. In our increasingly multicultural society we will continue to hear people struggling with the acquisition of a language that is not the easiest language to learn.

Add to that another stumbling block: English does not seem to make the most sense all of the time to those trying to learn it. Its colorful history has provided us with multiple linguistic resources that, for the uninitiated, can seem puzzling.

Consider the words *bough, cough, dough, rough,* or *though.* You might ask why aren't these words all pronounced similarly? Or try another list of words: *thumb, Wednesday, sign, mnemonic,* or *column.* All of these words feature "silent" letters. How *would* you know how to say these words? When trying to pronounce words, you might think about the visual representation of words with a series of vowels or consonants such as *queuing* and *facetious* or *nymphs* and *psychology.* How *do* you learn to pronounce such words?

In order to help you understand some of the complexities of English sounds, this chapter will provide a brief explanation of language and will examine the historical development of English. It will then explore the process by which an individual acquires language.

Language Defined

Language is a series of sounds which, when produced in a particular order, evoke meaning. A *word* is a significant series of sounds. These sounds, when joined in a particular way, serve to symbolize something. Words compose any given language.

Written language is a set of symbols. These symbols represent both meaning and sound. In English we use 26 written or orthographic symbols (letters of the alphabet) to represent words. We agree upon the ordering of these letters to form words, then we agree upon the ordering of words to form sensible messages. A current, but yet unproven, theory postulates that the alphabet as we know it today had its roots in 1500 B.C., when a Semitic scribe developed the alphabetical arrangement based on the place in the mouth a given sound was made. This has relevance to our later study of phonemes. The actual symbols, this theory contends, were handed down to us from the Egyptians to the Phoenicians, to the Greeks, Etruscans, and finally the Romans from whom we received our alphabet.[2]

Linguists—persons who study language—cannot agree on the exact number of languages in the world because they do not agree on what exactly constitutes a language. It is estimated, however, that between 2500 and 6000 languages are spoken in the world. In the English language alone, there may be as many as 1 million words made up of over 40 sounds or *phonemes.*

Language is in a constant state of flux because of the introduction of new words and new ways of saying old words. Generally, it takes hundreds of years for the sound values in a language to change or be lost. Still, changes can occur so slowly that we may not be aware of them. This process may be compared to the blooming of a flower: When we view this process naturally, change is hard to discern. But, when we watch it through time lapse photography, we can readily see the flower's development.

The following two principles should be kept in mind when considering language change and evolution.

Principle I

First, *language changes constantly.* For example, as foreign words are introduced into our vocabulary, we manipulate them so that we can say them more easily. A good illustration is the Spanish word *junta*. Introduced on a television news program to explain a South American country's military takeover, the word was at first articulated in the Spanish way, with the "j" sounding like an "h." However, since the "j" is not pronounced in such a way in English, it did not take long for news commentators to anglicize (to make English-sounding) the word by pronouncing the "j" as in *jump*. Technology introduces new words or new meanings for words. *Java* used to refer only to coffee but now this word is used to refer to language in the electronic information world.

Another example of change demonstrates the role of syllabic stress shifts in the pronunciation of words. Thirty years ago, primary syllabic stress in polysyllabic words was drifting toward the initial syllable of those words. Today there are new shifts of syllabic stress. The word *inquiry* was formerly pronounced with stress on the first syllable, " **'in** quiry." Today the stress has shifted to the second syllable, "in **'quiry.**" This, by the way, is the British pronunciation. On the other hand, this word may very well be shifting back to the prior pronunciation. Other words are undergoing this kind of change because of British pronunciation. Consider *formidable* or *lamentable*. Listen in coming years for a change with *contribute, applicable,* and *distribute.*

Principle II

Second, languages and sounds survive, but *survival* is rooted in common speech. Survival may depend on isolation. For example, the Native American language of Luiseno is fast disappearing because it is spoken today by only a few dozen persons. In South Africa the primary languages have been Afrikaans and English, yet a struggle continues to recognize one or the other as official. Ironically, for both Blacks and Whites, Afrikaans is the language most people speak at home. The Serbo-Croation wars resulted in linguistic splintering. Each faction now appears to refer to their own as a separate language: Serbian, Croatian, and so forth. Not too long ago in India, because news was broadcast in Urdu, a Muslim language, riots started that ended in several deaths in an area wherein the dominant local language is Kannada, a Hindi language.

To provide the impetus for language change, varying conditions need to exist. Among others, these conditions are (1) the conquering of one linguistic group by another, as in war, and the imposition of its language upon that conquered people; (2) the fading away of words, sounds, or stresses of a given language because people stop using them; or (3) the altering of the grammar of a language in such a way as to cause sound to be lost. Additionally, ongoing changes are responsible in part for creating and changing dialects or variations of a spoken language. In large cities in the United States, dialects are born and are changed as people with special linguistic needs band together. A dialect or language can reinforce one's heritage; thus in some communities enthusiasts may work to maintain cultural heritage by practicing a local dialect. In northern Holland, for example, over a quarter of a million people still speak West Frisian.

History of English

Approximately two dozen "family trees" identify the languages of the Americas, Africa, Asia, Europe, and the Mideast. English is derived from the Germanic branch of the Indo-European family of languages (see Figure 3.1). At one time Indo-European was thought to be a language in itself. However, we have no record of how it may have sounded. We do know that certain sounds, which must have been extant in Indo-European, continue through most languages of that family tree. For example, we know that Indo-European used an initial [p] sound, since linguists discovered it in the related languages of Old Slav, Greek, Latin, Sanskrit, etc., as *pro, pater, pita*. This initial [p] sound continues today in related languages and in some cases became, linguists believe, an [f] sound.

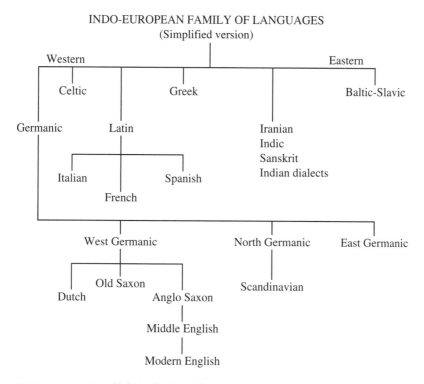

FIGURE 3.1   English is derived from the Germanic branch of the Indo-European family of languages.

Keeping in mind the principles and conditions previously discussed, it may be helpful to examine a condensed version of the development of English in order to better understand how we have come to speak the sounds that we speak.

The history of the English language is a colorful one and includes the intermarriage of many languages. To examine this history we must go back to the first century B.C. and the island that is today known as Great Britain but which around 60 B.C. was inhabited by a rural, agricultural people called the Celts. Since we have no written record of the Celtic language, the only way to determine its sound is to trace the linguistic "footsteps" of the Celtic people. Linguists undertake a painstaking and complex process called "phonological reconstruction" in order to discover how a language might have sounded and to trace the historical changes and evolutions of that language. This sort of linguistic reconstruction is complex and requires much skill and background in languages and history. Such language reconstruction involves comparing the roots, suffixes, and other parts of words in order to draw parallels among them.

For the Celtic people, hundreds of years of invasions and geographical relocation determined the sounds their language assumed or lost as time passed.

England

In 55 B.C. the Romans, who had conquered most of the known world, invaded England, conquered the Celts, and settled down for about a hundred years. The Romans left their mark on the countryside, people, and language. They built camps, streets, baths; they married Celtic women and raised children. Though troops were eventually called back to Rome, no doubt many Romans stayed on in Britain, contributing a Latin influence on the language and culture.

In A.D. 449 England was again invaded, this time by Germanic tribes—the Angles, Saxons, Jutes, and Frisians. Each of these tribes spoke a distinctly different Germanic dialect. These warring invasions forced the Celts into Ireland, Scotland, and Wales (which may give you some idea of the sound of the Celtic language). Then, each of these Germanic tribes settled in a different area of England. During the next several hundred years, influences on and changes to the native language were constantly in force until the Germanic Anglo-Saxon became the dominant means of communication. In fact, today the predominance of words in the English language is derived from Anglo-Saxon, such as the parts of speech: pronouns, conjunctions, and prepositions. From A.D. 450 to 1150, known as the Old English period, the language was almost all Germanic. By the end of that period, little remained of Celtic and less than 500 words were Latin. Endings were dropped. For example, the ending of the Old English word *findan* was dropped to create *to find*.

In this same period, an additional force was at work. Between the sixth and seventh centuries, the Vikings conducted many assaults upon the European continent and began raids on England around A.D. 790. When the Saxon King Alfred finally brought this Scandinavian plunder to an end, many Danes and Norwegians settled in England primarily in the northeast area. True to historical precedent, another condition for change in language was established. Sounds such as [g], [l], [r], and sound combinations such as "sc" were introduced by the Scandinavians.

In A.D. 1066 the Normans invaded England and pushed the English language in yet another direction. With the Normans came the edict that French be spoken for sermons and legal cases. In other public arenas Latin was the acceptable language. However, the Normans had little control over what language was spoken "behind closed doors." The occupied English still spoke Anglo-Saxon at home. So, although the aristocracy spoke Latin and French and the English language received specialized words derived from those languages, Anglo-Saxon predominated.

In the fourteenth century, when the Black Death killed half the population of England, the farmers, who spoke Anglo-Saxon, became highly valued because they were responsible for food production. Once again Anglo-Saxon gained favor as the spoken language.

Two other historical events had a profound influence on the English language. First, the Gutenberg printing press, invented in Germany in 1456, enabled words to be affixed in permanent and tangible form for mass consumption. Prior to that time uniformity and continuity did not exist. This event occurred during the period we identify as Middle English, from A.D. 1150 to 1500. We usually identify Chaucer as the representative writer of this period. However, by looking at the first two lines of Chaucer's *Canterbury Tales* (circa 1387), note how much our spelling has changed from that period:

Whan that Aprill with his shoures soote

The droghte of March hath perced to the roote

Loosely translated, Chaucer is saying the dry-spell or drought of March is broken by the sweet showers of April. Clearly time and the printing press had altered what was before a primarily oral tradition.

Second, in 1755 the introduction of the first English language dictionary, produced by Samuel Johnson, served to fix words in a particular manner of spelling and form from which we have never completely escaped. Johnson worked for almost 10 years with many scholars to compile his dictionary and based many spellings and pronunciations on Old French, Latin, and Greek. Today we can trace several word origins back to those earlier languages, which may help to explain some seemingly incongruent word spellings and pronunciations. For example, with the word *debt,* the spelling was Latin-based, *debitum,* and the pronunciation was French-based, *dette.* The spelling of *nation* comes from the Latin *natio* but our pronunciation is Middle English, *nacioun.*

This fixation of spelling and pronunciation took place during the period we identify as Modern English, from A.D. 1500 to the present. It is clear that English has passed through many more subsequent stages of change since the sixteenth century.

United States

For Americans, the period of Modern English is most important since the United States was established during that time. Settlers from the British Isles, speaking sixteenth-century British English, arrived, settled, and eventually migrated west, intermingling with immigrants from other European countries. History books invariably point out that America is a "melting pot," which certainly describes the intermingling of languages in this country. As people traversed the land and established towns, they took with them dialects that, given both isolation and intermarriage, took on nuances of change. Those people who remained near the eastern seaboard of our continent generally maintained more contact with England and thus tended to tune their dialects to British English, whereas those who moved west tended toward isolation in language. With the influx of peoples from Italy, Germany, Scandinavia, France, and Spain and with the manifest social clusterings of these people, language changed.

Though we identify three to four *major* distinctions in dialect in this country, Eastern, Southern, Midwestern, and General American, it is obvious to any listener that there are dialectal variations within each of these areas. The Georgian sounds different from the Alabaman. The New Yorker sounds different from the person from Maine. Dialectal variations occur in every language. When people move from one dialectal community to another, they often wish to learn the standard dialect of the new community simply because they do not wish to sound too different. This is an individual matter. Often, it is desirable to maintain the dialectal integrity of one's heritage. The ability to utilize a General American dialect, as well as to speak in one's own dialect, is what makes a person "bidialectal."

Media Influences.   Today, television and radio play an enormous role in shaping our language and the articulation of that language. With national networks reaching into the homes of almost every person in the country, we can't help but be influenced by the standard set by media spokespersons. While many linguists believe that the media may produce a leveling of dialects, researcher William Labov has found that just the opposite effect seems to be occurring, that there is an increase rather than a decrease in dialectal diversity.[3]

Language Development in the Individual

Even more wondrous than the history of a changing language is the evolution of language within the individual. Emerging studies are suggesting that even before birth we are imprinted with our capacities to understand and speak language and that that imprinting may be linked to gender. Our understanding to date has been that in the left hemisphere of the brain lie two areas specific to language and speech. Wernicke's area is that which processes language, and Broca's area deals with the mechanisms for speech production. New findings reveal that the brain has an even wider capacity for language storage, sorting, and retrieval.

Whatever these studies determine, we acquire language in a miraculously short period of time. By age five most people have acquired the language skills necessary to function, and we do so primarily by means of imitation. Of course the process is refined as we attend school, but at that very young age, we have already learned the subtle rules of sounds, meanings, and structures of language.

How does this happen? How, in so short a time, can one person, sometimes in spite of handicaps, learn what would take many specialists several years to accomplish from scratch? Imitation is the key word.

First, a child must have a role model/co-communicator or someone to talk to. In most cases that role model is the child's mother. In *The Miracle of Language,* Charlton Laird says, "The great arbiters of language are the women who speak it in the presence of children . . . there is no question as to who preserves the language. . . What women pass on to the next generation is 'right' and what they do not bother to pass on to their children sooner or later becomes 'wrong.' "[4] In the few instances in which children were raised in isolation, without anyone to communicate with and imitate, it was discovered that these children had not acquired language.

Second, a child must have access to a constructed language. Structure—phonemic, semantic, and grammatic—is one of the means by which a child acquires language. In a simplistic sense, we can say that (1) sounds, when put together, form words, (2) words represent meaning, and (3) rules order those words in order to communicate meaning. To illustrate, consider the following: "Serlo ho glain," twists the listener's phonemic sense. We simply do not use sounds in that order in the English language. "Ringing boards depress gastronomically," makes no semantic sense. That is to say that those words are not used together in that way, ever. "Classes discussioned the wordagely," makes no phonemic, semantic, nor grammatic sense.

Imagine what life would be like if one morning you awoke to find that all grammatical rules were gone. The result would be one big language "traffic" accident. Thus, the learner of language must have access to an ordered code.

A child progresses through several stages while learning to speak the English language. He or she passes through stages of playing with sound until reaching a babbling stage. By 6 months a child can tell the difference among sounds. Later a child becomes more selective of the sounds used. Eventually sounds are combined in such a way as to form words. Following that, the child passes through the one-word stage, then a two-word stage. Ironically, from there he or she jumps to a stage called "telegraphic speech." In such a stage there are no functional words, so that a child might say something like "Me like cat" rather than "*I* like *the* cat." Finally refinements are added, such as articles, prepositions, and adverbs.

As a child differentiates words, he or she also processes individual sounds. The first sounds learned by most English-speaking children are [m], [b], and [ɑ]. It takes time for a child to learn the difference between some sounds such as [k] and [g]. Then there are sounds that are not incorporated into speech until later because these are difficult sounds to produce, such as [ʤ], [ʃ], or [θ], as in *j*ust, *sh*ip, or *th*ink. (See Appendix One for IPA Guidelines, showing corresponding sounds to these symbols.) By the time we are adults, our articulation is distinctly culture-bound. We have a hard time distinguishing and producing sounds not commonly used in our own language.

Very early in life, in fact even before a child learns specific words, he or she has learned the music of a language and can reproduce the pitch variations and modulations peculiar to that language. This occurs even prior to mastery of sound combinations. Often a caregiver will think a child is speaking simply because the child, in vocal play, may hit upon a combination of phonemes that sounds familiar or intelligent. That, combined with a familiar intonation pattern, sounds sensible to an anxious and hopeful parent.

Researchers are continually gaining greater insights into the process of speech acquisition and behavior, and have found that even young children learn to modify speech with regard to pitch and rate when speaking to a child who is younger than they are, just as adults appear to do when speaking to children. It seems apparent that there is some unidentifiable cue to the sounds of language that helps us in both learning it and using it, and that cue seems to reside in rate and intonation. Just about the time a child has achieved a high degree of comprehension and control over the sounds and structures of language, puberty and the teen years come along. By the time a child is 5 or 6, he or she has acquired a functional vocabulary of about 1500 to 2500 words; by the age of 10 there are about 7000 words; by 14 years there are around 15,000 words. Peer group influences with their attendant slang and varying manners of speech have an impact on the development of clear speech. Braces on teeth and lack of self-confidence also play a part in shaping speech delivery. This period may last for 6 to 8 years. By age 18 or 20, a person is then expected to function in an articulate, "adult" manner.

In spite of the apparent ease with which we are able to acquire language, English is a difficult language to master because of its complex history. Yet for all of its complexity, mastering English can give us one of the most powerful tools of communication available to us, since the English language has become the official language of the international business world. For example, it is the official language of air controllers worldwide and the language most commonly used on the World Wide Web.

It is not uncommon for persons in other countries to study English, whereas in the United States it is the exception to study a foreign language. Statistics tell us that between 1915 and 1976 U.S. students studying a foreign language dropped from 36 percent to 17.9 percent, and that only 17 percent of those who study a foreign language in the United States can speak it with ease. Of those who study abroad, 63 percent can speak the foreign language with ease.[5] Whether it is an American trying to learn French or an Argentinian trying to learn English, the act requires an ear for the music of the language and a facility for producing the sounds of the language coupled with continuous exercise in speaking that language.

The chapters that follow address various components of the human voice, such as pitch, rate of speech, volume, quality of voice, and the individual sounds of the English language. Chapter Eight provides an overview of these sounds. Chapters Nine and Ten explain the individual vowels and consonants and present drill material for articulation improvement.

Chapter Three Review

Review the following concepts:

- Terms: linguistics, phoneme, English language, dialect
- A definition of language
- Two principles of language—change and survival
- British English history
- Modern English and the United States
- Language acquisition for the individual

Respond to the following questions:

1. How would you define "language"?
2. What manifestations of change might a language experience and why?
3. How can a language survive?
4. How do linguists figure out how languages are related?
5. How does the individual acquire language?

APPLICATION

1. How would you assess your grasp of the English language?

2. What sounds or words are problematic for you?

3. What words have changed pronunciation over the time you have been speaking English?

4. What dialect of English do you use? What obvious differences do you notice between your dialect and that of General American English?

FOCUS MESSAGE

1. *ESL:* Not only must you acquire the sounds of a new language, but you must also learn new words and meanings. You should understand that English is one of the most flexible languages because of its rich heritage. Speakers of English manipulate the language by twisting meaning with colorful images. For example to "kick the bucket" does not mean to literally strike a bucket with one's foot, but rather it is a colorful way to say someone died. There will also be a number of sounds with which you are not familiar. The following chapters should help you target those sounds. *Tip:* Both "th" sounds [θ] and [ð] are two sounds you can begin to master.

2. *Acting:* Because an actor usually speaks the words of others, it behooves you to understand the nuances of meaning that language can evoke in order to fully use your voice to communicate that meaning. Work to extend your vocabulary by reading widely and looking up meanings.

3. *Broadcasting:* You will often encounter words or names that are unfamiliar to you. The media provides its announcers with written pronunciations, but without a broad knowledge and understanding of language, a speaker can mangle words. Develop a broad vocabulary by listening and reading in a wide variety of fields.

NOTES

1. Tom Shachtman, *The Inarticulate Society: Eloquence and Culture in America* (New York: The Free Press, 1995), p. 13.

2. Bill Billiter, *L.A. Times,* June 4, 1987. The newspaper reports that University of California-Irvine Professor William Watt has developed this theory, which appears to hold promise for general acceptance among linguists.

3. William Labov, "The Organization of Dialect Diversity in North America" (paper), ICSLP4, October 6, 1996.

4. Charlton Laird, *The Miracle of Language* (Greenwich, CT: Fawcett, 1965), p. 213.

5. Paul Simon, *The Tongue-Tied American: Confronting the Foreign Language Crisis* (New York: Continuum, 1980), pp. 2–5.

CHAPTER

4 Pitch

Voilá, here was the famous voice, a bass baritone with a beautiful grain to it . . . What an asset!

—Norman Rush

TERMS

Pitch [pitʃ] The perception of frequency, which defines the number of vibrations of a sound wave. Pitch is perceived as high or low.

Inflection [ɪnˈflɛkʃən] An upward or downward change in pitch. Sometimes this occurs on a single vocalization, and sometimes there is a slight break in vocalization.

Intonation [ɪntoʊˈneɪʃən] The overall pitch movement or pattern that characterizes a language or a person's speech.

Variety [vəˈraɪətɪ] The employment of upward and downward pitch in order to avoid monotone or a narrow pitch range.

When you listen to music you may be aware of the highs and lows of the sounds you hear. When we speak of singers we call them soprano, tenor, alto, or baritone depending on the "key" in which they sing. Human voices and animal sounds also have a "key." We call it pitch. *Pitch* is the psychological perception of the highness or lowness of a sound. Scientists are discovering that in the animal kingdom pitch differences communicate subtle messages. For example, a lower pitch in a certain kind of male fish indicates larger size and thus greater possibilities for protection for a female and her fertilized eggs. Elephants communicate in a pitch so low as to be inaudible to the human ear, and the variations used may be maternal or sexual.

The physical component of pitch is *frequency,* which defines the number of vibrations or cycles a sound wave makes per second, sometimes called *cycles per second* or *cps* (measured in *hertz* or *Hz*). The lowest frequency we hear is about 20 Hz and the highest we hear is about 20,000 Hz, but generally adult hearing is between 100 and 12,000 Hz. If you read music you may be able to understand the cycles of frequency if you know that middle C on the piano vibrates at around 262 Hz. If you don't read music, then try to compare your vocal folds to the strings of a guitar. The thinner, more tightly pulled strings vibrate at a higher frequency than do those thicker, more loosely stroked strings. Whereas comparisons with music can be somewhat helpful in visualizing the concepts of pitch, *understand that there is a difference between speech and singing. If you attempt exercises to determine pitch range or to work toward extending your pitch range, take care to speak pitch changes rather than sing those changes.*

Pitch is the vocal component that most distinguishes children from adults and men from women. Until puberty, the sizes of the vocal tracts of most children are about the same. During the teen years the larynx grows. Though all of us undergo some vocal change, young men experience a more dramatic transformation than do young women. By maturity typical vocal fold length is about 23 mm, or about 9/10 of an inch, for men and about 17 mm, or about 3/5 of an inch, for women. In vocalizing, men generally use a pitch *range* of 80 to 700 Hz and women generally use a range of 140 to 1100 Hz. As we age, our pitch levels continue to change. For men, pitch lowers until about age 40, and between 60 to 80 years it rises. For women, pitch continues to lower with age and rises only with extreme age. As an average, men generally vocalize around 120 Hz, and women usually vocalize around 225 Hz. If you are at all familiar with a piano keyboard (see Figure 4.1), you can understand the sound placement on a musical scale. You might note that going up an octave doubles frequency, and going down an octave halves the frequency.

Though there are some physiological reasons for most men to have lower-pitched voices than women, there is evidence that the determination of pitch is an enculturated process.[1] Comparisons of men and women from diverse cultures indicate that if the vocal tracts of two persons are equal in size, one person may nevertheless utilize a lower or higher pitch level than the other person.

In fact, men in our society tend to speak as if their vocal tracts were larger than they are, which results in a lower pitch level[2] and, for many, a more positive audi-

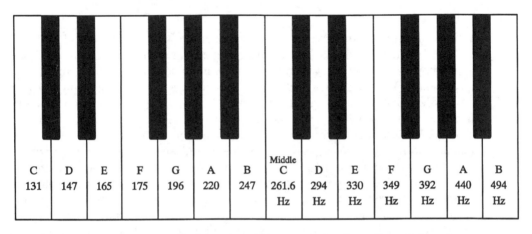

C	D	E	F	G	A	B	Middle C	D	E	F	G	A	B
131	147	165	175	196	220	247	261.6 Hz	294 Hz	330 Hz	349 Hz	392 Hz	440 Hz	494 Hz

FIGURE 4.1   Two octaves each side of middle C (on a keyboard) and showing approximate hertz rating.

tory perception. Women in our society generally use a higher and more varied pitch than is dictated by their mechanisms, which in turn may result in the stereotypical impression that women are more emotional.[3] Generally, for both men and women pitch levels and the use of pitch to convey meaning vary from culture to culture.

A simple explanation may help you to better understand the concept of pitch and your own use of it. As explained in Chapter Two, the passage of air over the vocal folds provides the means for vibration. Given your specific anatomical structure, you will produce a fundamental frequency, or basic pitch level (see Figure 4.2). Messages from your brain direct your vocal folds to tighten or to relax, which in turn creates pitch variations as you speak. You also receive information pertinent to language and meaning which tells you to use certain pitch variations at specific points in a given conversation.

As you mature, you adjust to a given pitch level, which becomes what is called *habitual pitch*, your *usual* pitch, or that level at which you most frequently initiate vocalization. You have probably come to use a given pitch level as the result of imitation, socialization, and enculturation. However, this pitch level may not be the best one for you. You may not be able to project well, or use a public voice effectively at this level. You may sound childlike and weak or far too low. You may even frequently suffer hoarseness. For a woman the habitual pitch level may be several notes (compared to the notes on a musical scale) above her best pitch level. Often called *optimum pitch*, it is the level that is the best for your particular vocal

Width measures frequency (pitch)

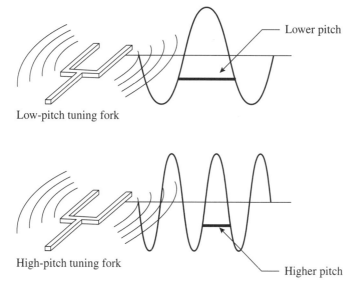

Lower pitch

Low-pitch tuning fork

High-pitch tuning fork

Higher pitch

FIGURE 4.2   The frequency (or pitch) of a sound wave is measured in cycles per second or hertz. The more Hz the higher the pitch.

structure and the one that projects well. It is the pitch level you use when relaxed; it is comfortable, projects clearly, commands greater authority, and seems more pleasant to the ear. In everyday life you may have heard the differences in people around you. When a colleague speaks to coworkers he or she may use habitual pitch, but in an important business meeting or in giving orders to a subordinate, that colleague probably uses optimum pitch. When you speak among your friends, you will no doubt use habitual pitch; when you are engaged in an interview, you will need to use optimum pitch.

Your optimum pitch level is already in the range you now use. However, the ratio of "notes" may not be distributed in a balanced manner. It is important to note, however, that specialists inform us that there is little indication that speaking at the improper pitch level, unless it is extreme, does us physical harm. The consideration, then, is a social one and depends on the impression you wish to make.

Inflection: The Paralinguistics of Pitch

Though you may begin to communicate an idea at a given pitch level, you usually change that level as you speak. That is to say, your voice level goes up and down. Pitch change is called *inflection*.

Inflection is one of the means by which we communicate meaning beyond the dictionary definition of a word. This is one of the paralinguistic features of voice. For example, the word *yes* is defined as an "affirmative reply." Yet many times we have said *yes* to someone while still implying "we would rather not."

TRY THIS

Try saying *yes* in the following ways:

1. As if you really can't wait.
2. As if you don't know.
3. As if you would hate to do the job.

You have just employed a paralinguistic device of language by changing the inflection of the word *yes*. You have given your listener a message beyond words. In English, the meanings of words and sentences are reinforced by or changed by subtle pitch variations. Consider the following sentence:

I didn't say I would go with you.

If you speak the sentence eight times, using a pitch variation each time on a different word, you will alter the meaning of the sentence.

There are several ways to alter meaning through the use of vocal inflection. Let's examine those ways.

Rising or Upward Inflection

When you vocalize, moving from a lower pitch to a higher pitch on a continuous vocalization, you are using *rising* or *upward inflection*. In the English language, this type of inflection has several functions. Rising inflection is generally used for the following:

1. To stress a syllable in a word or the most important word in a sentence.
   "I did_{n't} think you would do <u>that</u> today."
2. To ask questions requiring a "yes" or "no" response.
   "Would you like to <u>go</u>?"
3. To connect incomplete ideas such as lists.
   "I took flo<u>wers,</u> can<u>dy,</u> a bo<u>ok,</u> and a magazine to her."
4. With dependent clauses.
   "When I first entered the <u>room,</u> I saw you there."
5. To suggest uncertainty.
   "This is the pl<u>ace</u>?"

Women or children may employ upward inflection more often than men and often add a *tag* question to what could be a positive statement. This has popularly come to be known as *upspeak*. For example, rather than saying, "This is the pl_{ace}," some people often say, "This is the pl<u>ace,</u> isn't <u>it</u>?" In this way they have used rising inflection twice as if to reinforce doubt. Even if that tag question is omitted, the speaker often continues to employ rising inflection at the end of the statement:

"This is the pl<u>ace</u>?"

Falling or Downward Inflection

When you move from a higher pitch to a lower pitch level on a continuous vocalization, you are using *falling* or *downward inflection*. This is most often used for the following:

1. To make positive statements.
   "I'm leaving <u>now.</u>"
2. To ask questions beginning with interrogatives—who, what, when, where, and why.
   "When did you get <u>here</u>?"
3. To finish lists and ideas.
   "I bought a baseball, a mitt, and a <u>bat.</u>"

A speaker can employ downward inflection to give an impression of certainty. For example:

BOSS: "When will that report be <u>ready</u>?"

EMPLOYEE: "I will have it to you by this after_{noon}."

Circumflex Inflection

Both the upward and downward pitch inflection used on a single vocalization is called *circumflex inflection*. An example might be, "G^{e}e, you should have ^{s}e^{e}n that $_c$^{a}r!" Excessive use of circumflex inflection can cause you to be perceived as excited or overly emotional. Excessive use of inappropriately placed circumflex inflection may cause you to be perceived as less confident.

Step Inflection

The foregoing explanations of rising or upward, falling or downward, and circumflex inflection are those pitch variations that occur during an *unbroken* vocalization, during which we may change the pitch levels of different words within sentences. *Step inflection* is defined as pitch change, either upward or downward, characterized by a *break* in vocalization. Examples are:

"Stop $_{it.}$" "Please $_{go.}$" "^{I} said $_{no.}$"

You will find material for inflection exercises at the end of this chapter.

Intonation

A syndicated cartoon "The Family Circus" by Bil Keane depicts Mom and Dad greeting guests while the children peek from behind a corner. "Dear me! It's been *ages!* How've you been?" Mom is shown to say almost singing. Dad chimes in with, "We're delighted to *see* you guys! Hey! Pull up a chair." The son observes, "Why does everybody have a different voice when we have company?"

All languages are characterized by the music of rising and falling inflection. This is called *intonation*. Most languages feature distinctive intonational patterns; some languages have characteristic intonational patterns that are unique to that language alone. This is particularly true of Chinese, in which tonal change on a word will alter the meaning of the word. One translator of Chinese literature has said that when he is indecisive about a translation, he reads the selection aloud. In that way he is better able to grasp the nuances of meaning. Speakers of English, however, are noted for a free ranging use of pitch. In addition, some individuals develop distinctive patterns of intonation. This often occurs in public speaking or reading situations; for example, former President Jimmy Carter speaks with a distinctive intonational pattern. We might hear such patterns when we hear "responsive readings" in churches or when we listen to a group of people pledging allegiance to the flag.

We learn the nuances of a given language very early in life. Psychologists studying language and speech examine the difference in the speech we direct toward infants and that we direct toward adults. "Motherese," as some call it, is characterized by broad intonational variations and rhythms.[4] With age we rely more heavily on intonational patterns in order to understand the meaning of messages when we might not hear the entire content.

Try these additional examples:

1. [*As if you doubt that a person can*] If you complete this job by Friday, you'll be lucky!
2. [*As if you would hate it*] Of course, I would love to have lunch with you.
3. [*As if you find the person dull*] He seems to be a pleasant enough man.
4. [*As if you had nothing else to say about a theater performance*] How do they do it night after night?
5. [*As if you don't feel well*] Oh sure, I feel just fine.

Spoken English offers us a high degree of pitch flexibility, allowing us the opportunity to manipulate meaning. This is the highly paralinguistic nature of our language. (Remember that paralinguistics simply means what we imply beyond words.)

Changes in tone have functional uses in communication. We use a higher pitch, usually on a single word or sound, to enter or interrupt a conversation. Through the use of tonal changes you can indicate your attitude toward an idea. A person from another culture or for whom English is a second language may not readily grasp these paralinguistic indicators of attitude. Thus it may appear that speakers of American English are using a special code. Conversely non-native speakers may carry over the intonational pattern from a primary language. This intonational carryover is another factor that makes a person sound "foreign."

It is difficult to record here examples of these tonal changes since they may be only subtly perceived. A quick reference resource for you is your television. If you have access to many channels, you may be able to observe a variety of intonational patterns. Listen to the differences among speakers on foreign language channels, evangelical channels, news networks, or shopping channels. Imagine that you are asked by your instructor to remain after class. He says to you, "You know, your term paper was interesting." Reading that, one might infer that the instructor was praising you. If, however, the instructor employed certain pitch changes on the word *interesting* (ᶦⁿter_esting) and at the same time stretched out the word a bit, you might feel that your authorship was being questioned. Your response would be determined by the pitch changes you heard.

Pitch levels may also provide clues as to your mood or emotional states. Whether you are relaxed and in control or tense and lacking control is often evidenced by your pitch level and management of its variations. These variations may be individual, but they are usually decipherable. For example, it was once believed that nervousness caused a rise in pitch; now we know that in a stressful situation many people experience instead a lowering of pitch.

Pitch change is an integral part of spoken language. American English is characterized by a few "rules" of intonation, but as a whole English is a relatively flexible language that enables its speakers to imply much meaning beyond the spoken word. Some general guidelines are:

1. Pitch change occurs on the stressed syllable of a word.
2. Pitch change occurs on the most important word or words in a message.
3. Pitch change occurs at the end of a message.

Extralinguistic Features

Vocal features that are termed *extralinguistic* are those that indicate to others the condition of the anatomical structure. For example, with regard to pitch, if you have strained your vocal folds, grown vocal nodules, developed vocal fold lesions, or are a heavy smoker, your pitch level and resulting quality of voice will be altered. If you are extremely tired, your pitch may change. If you have a cold or the flu, phlegm may alter vocal fold vibrations. It is also the extralinguistic characteristic of pitch that suggests to a listener whether the speaker is a man or a woman.

Pitch Variety

A student reported that he was bored in his Economics class because his professor spoke in a "moan-a-tone." (You and I would say "monotone," but for this student the sound was a "moan.") Teaching, reading reports or stories, sharing jokes or experiences, conducting interviews or other business, or any other act of verbal communication can be enhanced by appropriate and varied pitch levels. Few of us can remain alert to communication that is delivered in a monotone. If your speech is perceived by your instructor and others to be intonationally patterned or monotoned—that is, lacking appropriate pitch variation—you can work to employ pitch changes. In achieving an appropriate pitch level and variety you will be on your way toward being perceived as a more confident speaker who can better hold the attention of your listeners. The exercises that follow can help in your program for improvement.

Exercises

Pitch Range

Exercise 1   You will need to perform this exercise next to a piano or keyboard. To assess your *pitch range*, begin with your basic note, the one with which you most frequently begin to vocalize, and count (1, 2, 3, etc.). You can also use letters of the alphabet, names of states, streets, or any other list with which you are familiar. For each number or word raise your pitch level one note. **Do not sing**—singing extends sound and blends sounds together without a break. It may help you to actually feel the physical action of the larynx if you place a finger on the projection of the cricoid cartilage. You will feel the cartilage rising with each increase in pitch. Write down the number of notes you were able to vocalize without strain. Return to your basic note.

Once again count or say your list. This time lower your pitch level one note with each word or number. Again, write down the number of notes you were able to vocalize. Add the two figures. This is your pitch range. If it is less than sixteen notes, you may wish to work toward widening your pitch range. The following exercises address that need. They deal with raising, lowering, and widening the pitch levels.

Raising and Widening Pitch Range.   Should you find that you are unable to vocalize more than a few notes below your usual pitch level, you may wish to work toward raising that level. In this case your pitch level may be too low. You may also need to work toward widening your pitch range.

Exercise 2   Once again, using a piano or keyboard, try this: First say, "one" at your usual pitch level. Then begin counting using a higher pitch with each number. When you have reached the number "three" repeat "three" several times. Listen to the sound. If possible, use a recorder. Using that pitch level, read the following sentences and passages:

1. My wife had a baby!

2. I'm so happy about that.

3. The bells are ringing.

4. Aren't you cute!

5. He's very young.

6. Let's have a party.

7. Come join the fun.

8. I have the time if you have the money.

9. Where do you work?

10. Mornings are shorter.

11. We only have an hour.

12. Look at that sky!

13. Don't drive so fast!

14. They are having a sale.

15. Rise and shine!

16. There are only so many hours in a day.

17. I'll go if you will.

18. You caught me!

19. Thank you again.

20. We won the race.

21. Play the music.

22. Do it over and over again.

23. Speak the speech.

24. Can it be avoided?

25. Ask him what's new.

26. Remember to vote.

27. How can it not be?

28. We'll talk again sometime.

29. Things began slowly.

30. Business is picking up.

Exercise 3   Read the following news stories at an appropriate pitch for the message. Pay attention to inflection within and at ends of sentences.

News

1. The state supreme court issued a ruling today on the meaning of the common exclusion in life insurance policies for "suicide, whether sane or insane." In a case from San Diego County, the court ruled that the exclusion can apply to someone who was insane when he killed himself. But if he did not know what he was doing, legally the death should not be considered a suicide and the insurance company must pay benefits. The court said benefits can be denied even if the victim was insane, in the sense of not being able to distinguish right from wrong. But if he did not understand the physical nature and consequences of his actions, the court said, he did not intentionally commit suicide. The court also said it is up to the insurance company to prove an intent to commit suicide.

2. On the American stock exchange, sales totaled six million, eight hundred and eighty thousand shares, compared with seven million, two hundred and twenty thousand the previous session. In all, seven hundred eighty-seven issues were traded; there were two hundred thirty-six advances, two hundred ninety-one declines, and two hundred sixty remained unchanged. There were ten highs for the year and ten lows. The Amex estimates that a share of common stock was down one cent. The American Exchange Index was down zero point twenty-two at two hundred twenty-six point eighty-five.

3. Record breaking heat has gripped the southern two-thirds of California for a second day during the Easter break. However, riptides and cold water are resulting in many beach rescues. A record high of 89° was set today in Santa Maria. The thermometer reached a national high of 94° in Palm Springs before noon.

4. The President of Cochise College in southeast Arizona says four of his students who heroically saved two children from drowning in Hemet will be properly recognized. The four students were in Hemet for a flying competition when they saved the lives of two children found at the bottom of a motel swimming pool Sunday. The students pulled the children from the pool and got them breathing by the time city firefighters arrived.

5. House and Senate tax committees have rejected a proposal that would have extended federal unemployment benefits for 3 months. The benefits program is to expire Saturday. The panels today also approved a phase-out of the program for those already receiving payments.

6. Six buildings in the downtown area are crawling with potentially dangerous spiders from South America, and health officials want to know how they got there. The spiders belong to the South American violin spider family. They were found March 24th during a routine county health department inspection for rats. A bite from the brown spider, which derives its name from the violin-shaped pattern on its back, can cause permanent scarring. No bites have been reported from the current infestation.

7. A new study projects the nation will have more doctors per capita by the turn of the century, but the increase will contribute to the rising costs of health care. Researchers at the University of San Francisco say that by the year 2000, the number of doctors will have increased 22 percent from 1986. That translates to a physician-to-patient ratio of 176 per 100,000, up from 144 per 100,000.

8. A three-alarm blaze destroyed a half dozen business firms in the city today, forcing the evacuation of eighteen people. There are no reports of injuries and the cause of the fire is under investigation. Firefighters were called to the scene shortly after 4 A.M. There is no immediate damage estimate.

9. It's crunch time today for millions of Americans rushing to get their income tax returns in before the midnight deadline. The postal service and the IRS say they expect to receive around 27 million returns this week. Many of them will be dropped into collection boxes close to the deadline.

10. Spring hasn't sprung in the Rockies and Midwest, where heavy snow and high winds are snarling traffic and closing schools. In Utah a ski area reports 30 inches of snow since Wednesday evening, and a traffic death is blamed on slippery road conditions. The national weather service in Kansas clocked a record wind gust of 82 miles per hour.

Exercise 4 With the following announcements, pay attention to pitch and inflection, but try to announce each as if you were a rock and roll disc jockey, a classical d.j., a museum guide, and a commercial announcer. You will find that you need to employ varying intonational patterns.

Announcements

1. You are invited to a community open house and student orientation at Webster College on August 14th. Activities begin at 9 A.M. and include campus tours, discussions, food, fun, and entertainment. There is something for everyone at Webster College. For information about our August 14th open house, call: (800) 555–4530.

2. Expand the world for yourself and others by becoming a volunteer tour guide at the Bowers Museum. Give tours related to exhibits on art and anthropology or become part of the museum's outreach programs to local schools. No special education or background is required. Training classes begin this fall.

3. Enroll now in the continuing education program at Midline College. Earn degree credit, or take courses just for fun or for professional advancement. Courses are scheduled evenings and weekends and are taught by regular faculty and staff at the school. Courses in business, arts, literature, and applied technology are available. Call 555–2356 for further information.

4. The works of composer Wolfgang Amadeus Mozart will be featured in a special concert in the Whitman Auditorium this weekend. Two performances have been scheduled for 8 P.M. on both Friday and Saturday. Tickets are being sold at the Whitman Auditorium Box Office from noon to 5 P.M. daily. Adults' tickets are $12, children's tickets are $9.

5. "American Art: the Last Hundred Years," works by famous American artists including Winslow Homer and Thomas Eakins, will be on display in the New York Museum of Art beginning July 10. The display ends on the first of August. Museum hours are from 10 A.M. to 6 P.M. daily.

Lowering and Widening Pitch Range. You may find that you wish to lower your usual pitch level. In this case your pitch level may be too high.

Exercise 5 Try this: Begin at your usual pitch level and count, using a lower pitch level with each number. When you have reached 3 or 4, sound the number several times. At that level practice with the following materials.

1. That's a heavy load.

2. He's in a quiet mood.

3. Go make the phone call now.

4. This job is very important.

5. Please keep the noise level down.

6. It's been a long trip.

7. Everyone is finally gone.

8. Maybe it will rain.

9. Try, try again.

10. Nothing is ever hopeless.

11. It was a disaster.

12. I demand you pay me.

13. You did that job well.

14. "I pledge allegiance to the flag."

15. The game will end in five minutes.

16. This has been a tiring day.

17. Just give me one good reason.

18. That story saddens me.

19. No man is an island.

20. You can't go home again.

21. It is time to buy.

22. There will be early morning low clouds.

23. Don't miss this show.

24. It's a small price to pay.

25. We made a deal.

26. I thought you were gone.

27. That was quite enough.

28. It's the newest thing to do.

29. Don't drink and drive.

30. The supply is limited.

Exercise 6 With the following selections, read with your own voice, and then try to read as if you were a professor, gospel preacher, weather forecaster, parent, announcer, or lawyer.

News

1. Deficit reduction negotiations between the White House and Senate Republican leaders may be snagged. While both sides have indicated they're making progress on a compromise plan, sources say they stalled today over sharp cuts in education programs. The American Association of State Colleges and Universities

says hundreds of thousands of low-income students would lose a lot of federal aid under the president's proposed budget. The association says its analysis refutes the president's claim that only middle-income students would be affected.

2. A 4-hour siege at a Detroit schoolhouse is now over. Police say a gunman who took three elementary school students hostage is in police custody, and the children have been released unharmed. The man was picked up soon after a police car drove up to a side entrance to the Loving Elementary School on the city's near north side, and two officers rushed into the school. The man was brought out in handcuffs and shoved into the car, which then drove off. Police said the man was armed with a "sawed-off rifle" and had been demanding a car and money.

3. Two environmental groups say the danger of exposure to toxic substances in the home and workplace is greater than people realize. The National Environmental Law Center and the U.S. Public Interest Research Group estimate that American industries produce at least 50 times more toxic chemicals than are reported nationwide as emissions or waste. They're pushing for state and national laws requiring companies to reduce their use of dangerous chemicals.

4. State lawmakers are beginning to feel the heat of a projected $13 billion dollar budget shortfall. Many are welcoming a plan to direct some of that heat to county officials. Under the plan, a significant portion of the tax increases needed to balance the budget may be imposed by counties rather than the state. Many legislators say they're finding that an increasingly attractive option.

5. Fire prevention experts say March rains have reduced the potential for fire for now. But they also say that weather patterns on the whole are conspiring to make a difficult summer. The rain may have intensified the fire hazard by allowing quick growth of grass. Experts say the same low pressure system that brought the rain could also bring thunderstorms and lightning that could ignite blazes.

6. A report in the journal *Psychosomatics* says a woman faked terminal cancer for 2 years to get sympathy after her fiance broke off their engagement. She fooled co-workers and even a cancer support group. The 35-year-old woman shaved her head to mimic hair loss from chemotherapy, dieted away 20 pounds, and acted listless. She had what psychiatrists term a *factitious disorder,* in which a person consciously fakes an illness for some psychological gain.

7. New research confirms mom was right when she told you to eat your oatmeal. A study published in the *Journal of the American Medical Association* says oat bran and oatmeal have passed additional tests that prove they're effective agents in reducing cholesterol. People with high cholesterol, on a low-fat diet with 2 ounces of oat bran daily, experienced a drop of up to 15 percent in cholesterol levels.

Announcements

1. How do you get to the Olympic Games? Now you can take a bus. During the two weeks of the games, RTD bus shuttles will be given preference over many streets, and will have special unloading zones right next to the events. Remember, riding the bus ensures that you see the games. Purchase a reserved seat at selected Ticketron outlets or call RTD at (800) 555–4455.

2. If you would like to discover the services and resources available to the deaf in Cook County, a free seminar is being held on a variety of deaf assistive devices and programs. This free seminar will be at the Providence Speech and Hearing Center in Cook County on Saturday, April 4th. A sign language interpreter will also be provided.

3. Calling himself an environmentalist, the Secretary of the Interior said today that he expects the department's Bureau of Reclamation to avoid poisoning any more wildlife refuges or other bodies of water. Hodel also said he expects to re-orient the Bureau to deal with declining water tables and less receptivity to its irrigation and dam projects in the West. In an interview with news agency correspondents, Hodel stated that there are difficult technical issues to be resolved before physical work can be done.

4. Police say one man was killed and two others were wounded today in a Salt Lake City courthouse when a woman handed an inmate a gun in an apparent escape attempt. The inmate was one of those wounded in the shooting.

5. The annual summer jazz festival will be held in Atlantic Amphitheatre on June ninth and tenth. Tickets are being sold now at authorized agencies. There is a different lineup of jazz greats for each day. So, buy tickets for both sessions. Pack a picnic lunch and spend the day.

Inflection

Material for Rising or Upward Inflection. In the sentences that follow use rising or upward inflection in order to emphasize the underlined words or syllables.

Exercise 1   *Important word or syllable*

1. Heaven gives almonds to one who has no teeth in his mouth.
2. He is so poor that he could not keep a dog in his house.
3. A weed is no more than a flower in disguise.
4. Delay is ever fatal to those who are prepared.
5. Boldness is a mask for fear.
6. A poem should not mean but be.
7. Weaknesses are often necessary to the purposes of life.
8. Injustice is relatively easy to bear; what stings is justice.
9. National honor is national property of the highest value.
10. Nothing is stronger than habit.

Exercise 2   *Yes/No questions*

1. Will you leave now?
2. Is the sky darkening?

3. Do you think I <u>care?</u>
4. Is it to the strong the prizes <u>go?</u>
5. Will it please you to see the roses <u>bloom?</u>
6. Does this train always go so <u>slowly?</u>
7. Were you born in New <u>York?</u>
8. Should I write you a <u>letter?</u>
9. Did you hear the <u>news?</u>
10. Would you go to <u>dinner?</u>

Note: If you use downward inflection on these questions, you are no longer asking a question but stating an attitude.

Exercise 3   *Incomplete ideas*

1. We first <u>endure</u>, then <u>pity</u>, then embrace.

2. It's a great <u>wide</u> beautiful, <u>wonderful</u> world!

3. They are the <u>books</u>, the <u>arts</u>, the academes, that <u>show</u>, <u>contain</u>, and nourish all the world.

4. You've <u>played</u>, and <u>loved</u>, and <u>eaten</u> and drunk your fill.

5. Like <u>mother</u>, like daughter; like <u>father</u>, like son.

6. The sweetest <u>joy</u>, the wildest woe is love.

7. He is an <u>experienced</u>, <u>industrious</u>, <u>ambitious</u>, and often quite picturesque liar.

8. A time like this demands strong <u>minds</u>, great <u>hearts</u>, true <u>faith</u>, and ready hands.

9. The <u>true</u>, <u>strong</u>, and sound mind is the mind that can embrace equally great <u>things</u> and small.

10. Nothing is more estimable than a physician <u>who</u>, having studied nature from <u>youth</u>, knows the prospectus of the human <u>body</u>, the diseases that <u>assail it</u>, the remedies that will <u>benefit it</u>, exercises the art with <u>caution</u>, and pays equal attention to the <u>rich</u> and the poor.

Exercise 4   *Dependent clauses*

1. If all the <u>world</u> and <u>love</u> were <u>young</u>, these pretty pleasures might me move to live with thee and be thy love.
2. <u>Speech</u> is a mirror of the soul: as a man <u>speaks</u>, so is he.
3. As it <u>happens</u>, I like football.
4. In the scale of the <u>destinies</u>, brawn will never weigh so much as brain.
5. When they are <u>kissed</u>, some women blush.

6. As for me, all I know is that I know nothing.
7. If the law is upheld only by government officials, then all law is at an end.
8. If the blind lead the blind, both shall fall into the ditch.
9. Where the spirit of the Lord is, there is Liberty.
10. To make good use of life, one should have in youth the experience of advanced years, and in old age the vigor of youth.

Material for Downward Inflection. In the sentences that follow use falling or downward inflection in order to emphasize the underlined words.

Exercise 5 *Positive statements and complete ideas*

1. The true art of memory is the art of attention.
2. It is best to rise from life as from a banquet, neither thirsty nor drunken.
3. A fool and his money are soon parted.
4. Necessity makes even the timid brave.
5. What is valuable is not new, and what is new is not valuable.
6. All I know is what I see in the papers.
7. Obedience alone gives the right to command.
8. Do not suppose opportunity will knock twice at your door.
9. Originality is nothing but judicious imitation.
10. Patience is a necessary ingredient of genius.

Exercise 6 *Interrogative questions*

1. What will Mrs. Grundy say? What will Mrs. Grundy think?
2. What will you say when the world is dying?
3. Who lost Mark Anthony the world?
4. Who knows the thoughts of a child?
5. When shall I hear news of you again?
6. Who shall decide when doctors disagree?
7. As long as I count the votes, what are you going to do about it?
8. If men are so wicked with religion, what would they be without it?
9. Why are you worrying?
10. Where would you send me?

Step Inflection. Step inflection is characterized by speaking words at different pitch levels with a break in vocalization.

Exercise 7 The short sentences that follow may be used for drill in step inflection. The sense of the sentence should tell you in which direction the inflection should go (upward or downward), or you can experiment with varied pitch movement.

1. Talk is cheap.
2. It is a twice-told tale.

3. <u>Go West</u>, young man.
4. The <u>game</u> is <u>up</u>.
5. I <u>think</u>; therefore, <u>I am</u>.
6. He is a <u>wise man</u>.
7. <u>Reason</u> <u>reigns</u>.
8. <u>Neat</u>, not <u>gaudy</u>.
9. By <u>hook</u> or <u>crook</u>.
10. <u>Stop</u> it.
11. <u>Don't go</u>.
12. <u>Please</u> <u>call</u>.

Pitch Contrasts

Exercise 8   The following are short sentences that require upward inflection in one instance and downward inflection in the other. Non-native speakers may find this list to be a helpful drill.

1. The sun is rising. Is the sun rising?

2. Is she coming home? She is coming home.

3. The coffee is ready. Is the coffee ready?

4. Did you let the cat out? You let the cat out.

5. Your homework is done. Is your homework done?

6. Can you swim? You can swim.

7. She has written you a letter. Has she written you a letter?

8. Can he play the piano? He can play the piano.

9. They have just moved into the house. Have they just moved into the house?

10. Is he appearing in a play at school? He is appearing in a play at school.

11. Cake is her favorite dessert. Is cake her favorite dessert?

12. Did you write the date on your calendar? You wrote the date on your calendar.

13. The firetruck sped by our house. Did the firetruck speed by our house?

14. Is he a disk jockey on the radio? He is a disk jockey on the radio.

15. She took our wedding portrait. Did she take our wedding portrait?

16. Can the mechanic fix my car? The mechanic can fix my car.

17. The book is easy to read. Is the book easy to read?

18. Did you see the movie version? You did see the movie version.

19. We need to clean the house. Do we need to clean the house?

20. Does the game begin at noon? The game begins at noon.

Circumflex Inflection and Variety

Exercise 9   The following material may be used to employ circumflex inflection and pitch variety.

1. The old house was divided into two dwellings by a thin wall that passed on, with high fidelity, sounds on either side.

On the north side were the Leonards. On the south side were the Hargers. The Leonards, husband and wife and eight-year-old son, had just moved in. And, aware of the wall, they kept their voices down as they argued in a friendly way as to whether or not the boy, Paul, was old enough to be left alone for the evening.

—Kurt Vonnegut, "Next Door"

2. The machineries of joy, is that one of them in front of us? And is that another, sitting there, the rocket on its stand? It could be tonight, if the thing goes up, and the man in it, all around the world, and him still alive, and us with him, though we just sit here. That would be joyful indeed. The rocket was getting ready. Voices from far Canaveral were crying in a wind of time. Strange phantom powers loomed upon the screen. Father Brian sat back in his chair and closed his eyes. He waited for the thunder, he waited for the fire. He waited for the concussion and the voice that would teach a silly, a strange and wild and miraculous thing: how to count backward, ever backward . . . to zero.

—Ray Bradbury, "The Machineries of Joy"

3. I try to explain to Margaret why I'm taking this trip, that I'm looking for something I lost a long time ago. I don't remember when, some moment in my life that slipped away, the moment in which I should have turned around, reached out, made my move, stepped forward, gone the other direction, taken hold of the life that was meant for me. Do you know what I mean? That little space in time? Someone says, "Love me!" but you're busy, preoccupied, and you go on laughing, polishing the glass and arranging the furniture, and you don't suppose you heard right anyway, "Love me!" and you'll have to dry your hands and get the weather report before you pick up the moment, answer the knocking at the door, and nothing matters very much, so you say, "They'll be back tomorrow," but the moment's gone, slipped away.

—Winston Weathers, "Now, Voyager"

4. Something must be radically wrong with a culture and a civilization when its youth begins to desert it. But the plain, unpalatable fact is that in America today that margin of freedom necessary for expression has been reduced to a vanishing point.

—Harold Stearns, "America and the Young Intellectual"

5. In the country, one snowy night of some seventeen years ago, a friend of his had given a small tea party in his honour. There was a young lady alone near the mantel-shelf who looked round the room with a small vague smile, discreet, a disguised yearning which seemed somehow at odds with her isolation. He looked at her a moment. Miss Caroline Spencer was not quite a beauty, but was none the less, in her small odd way, formed to please.

—Henry James, "Four Meetings"

6. "After all everybody, that is, everybody who writes," said Gertrude Stein, "is interested in living inside themselves in order to tell what is inside themselves. That is why writers have to have two countries, the one where they belong and the one in which they live really. The second one is romantic; it is separate from themselves, it is not real but it is really there."

—G. A. Harrison, "Gertrude Stein's America"

7. On the particular evening in question, the scene was of a more-than-typical picturesqueness. Anton Cul, the blind gypsy violinist, was weaving iridescent harmonies in one corner, despite the unbridled enthusiasm of the neighboring spectators who showered him with hundred franc notes, which were cleverly collected by a cocker spaniel furnished by the management, and deposited in the musician's by-no-means-microscopic hat. On another part of the hilltop, a group of diners were applauding the prowess of Ziss, the Fire-bird, who—having climbed on a somewhat rickety table—proceeded to balance upside-down on an ordinary champagne glass and at the same time to swallow lighted cannon crackers, pinwheels and even—to the horror of Marianne Moore, whom I particularly remarked—a roman candle.

—George Firmage, *E. E. Cummings: A Miscellany Revised*

8. It was a matter of chance that I should have rented a house in one of the strangest communities in North America. It was on that slender riotous island which extends itself due east of New York—and where there are, among other natural curiosities two unusual formations of land. Twenty miles from the city a pair of enormous eggs, identical in contour and separated only by a courtesy bay, jut out into the most domesticated body of salt water in the Western Hemisphere, the great wet barnyard of Long Island Sound. I lived at West Egg—the, well, less fashionable of the two.

—F. Scott Fitzgerald, *The Great Gatsby*

9. Just inside the door was a big trash barrel. On top of the barrel were stacks of soggy newspapers and magazines, moldy and damp. A thick stench of decay issued from them as Charles began to move them around. Spiders dropped onto the cement. He crushed them with his foot and went on looking. The sight made him shriek. He managed to turn the beam down into the barrel. The father thing had stuffed it down in the very bottom of the barrel among the old leaves and torn up cardboard. It still looked a little like his father, enough for him to recognize. He had found it . . . and the sight made him sick to his stomach.

—P. K. Dick, "The Father Thing"

10. The bystanders began now to look at each other, nod, wink significantly, and tap their fingers against their foreheads. There was a whisper, also, about securing the gun, and keeping the old fellow from doing mischief, at the very suggestion of which the self-important man in the cocked hat retired with some precipitation. At

this critical moment a fresh, comely woman pressed through the throng to get a peep at the gray-bearded man. She had a chubby child in her arms, which, frightened at his looks, began to cry.

—Washington Irving, "Rip Van Winkle"

11. He walked into the day as alertly as might be, making a definite noise with his heels, perceiving with his eyes the superficial truth of streets and structures, the trivial truth of reality. Helplessly his mind sang, *He flies through the air with the greatest of ease; the daring young man on the flying trapeze;* then laughed with all the might of his being. It was really a splendid morning: gray, cold, and cheerless, a morning for inward vigor; ah, Edgar Guest, he said, how I long for your music.

—William Saroyan, "The Daring Young Man on the Flying Trapeze"

12. In the station the train was puffing. Nearly everyone in Victory was hanging around waiting for it to leave. The Victory Civic Band was scattered through the crowd. Ed Newton gave false signals to start on his bass horn. Everybody wanted to see Lily all dressed up, but Mrs. Carson and Mrs. Watts had sneaked her into the train from the other side of the tracks. The two ladies were going to travel as far as Jackson to help Lily change trains.

—Eudora Welty, "Lily Daw and the Three Ladies"

13. I walked the long block east from the movie house. The street was empty, black, and glittering. The water soaked through my coat at the shoulders, and water dripped down my neck from my cap. I began to be afraid. I could not stay out in the rain, because then my father and mother would know I had been wandering the streets. I would get a beating, and, though Caleb was too old to get a beating, he and my father would have a terrible fight, and Caleb would blame it all on me and would not speak to me for days.

—James Baldwin, *Tell Me How Long the Train's Been Gone*

14. Miss Amelia listened with her head turned slightly aside. She ate her Sunday dinners by herself; her place was never crowded with a flock of relatives, and she claimed kin with no one. She had had a great-aunt who owned the livery stable in Cheehaw, but that aunt was now dead. Aside from her there was only one double first cousin who lived in a town twenty miles away, but this cousin and Miss Amelia did not get on so well, and when they chanced to pass each other they spat on the side of the road. Other people had tried very hard, from time to time, to work out some kind of far-fetched connection with Miss Amelia, but with absolutely no success.

—Carson McCullers, "The Ballad of the Sad Cafe"

15. Her decision had been indicated in an instant, but it had been made after days and nights of anguished deliberation. She had known she would be asked, she had decided what she would answer, and, without the slightest hesitation, she had moved her hand to the right.

The question of her decision is one not to be lightly considered, and it is not for me to presume to set up myself as the person able to answer it. So I leave it with all of you: Which came out of the opened door—the lady or the tiger?

—Frank Stockton, "The Lady or the Tiger"

Chapter Four Review

Review the following concepts:

- Terms: pitch
- Inflection: the paralinguistics of pitch
- Rising inflection
- Falling inflection
- Circumflex inflection
- Step inflection
- Intonation
- Extralinguistic features of pitch
- Pitch variety

Respond to the following:

1. Discuss the cultural implications of vocal pitch.
2. When might you use circumflex inflection?
3. What are some general "rules" of intonation?
4. Discuss the extralinguistic vocal features that are related to pitch.

APPLICATION

1. Identify the various social and business contexts of your life. When you are visiting with friends, what seems to be the general pitch level of your voice? In business situations does that pitch level change? How has it changed over the last several years?

2. Does your pitch level change depending on whether you are speaking to someone of the opposite gender? How do others react?

3. How varied does your pitch level become: When you are excited? When you are afraid? When you are bored? When you are reading aloud? When you are speaking?

4. Do you frequently end declarative sentences with upward inflection?

5. How has your pitch level changed during illness?

FOCUS MESSAGE

1. *ESL:* Imitation can be an effective tool for learning another language or for improving one you are currently working on. Try to focus on the inflectional patterns of English. For some Middle Eastern and Asian cultures, work toward achieving a lower pitch level. Listen closely to the "music" of English and try to imitate those sounds. Avoid adopting "upspeak" (see p. 55).

2. *Acting:* Pitch levels and intonation will help you portray characters. However, remember that a higher pitch level may not project as well as a lower pitch. Actors need to develop a wider pitch range in order to achieve performance flexibility. Learning the intonational patterns of other languages will help an actor in developing a dialect repertoire.

3. *Broadcasting:* A low pitch and variety should be the focus for the broadcaster. Learning and practicing appropriate inflections and intonation is the key to sending messages. Take care that as your delivery rates increase, you do not also raise pitch levels.

EVALUATION

SEE PAGE 268, where you'll find an evaluation form for this chapter. Follow your instructor's directions.

NOTES

1. Klaus R. Scherer and Howard Giles, eds., *Social Markers in Speech* (Cambridge, Eng.: Cambridge University Press, 1979), p. 9.

2. Philip Lieberman, *On the Origins of Language: An Introduction to the Evolution of Human Speech* (New York: Macmillan, 1977), p. 178.

3. Scherer and Giles, p. 129.

4. Helle Bering-Jensen, *Insight,* May 9, 1988, p. 50.

CHAPTER

5 Volume

*If you are an actor and you can't make yourself heard in a thousand seat house,
you're doing something wrong—you should get off the stage and go home.*

—David Mamet

TERMS

Loudness ['laʊdnəs]   Refers to the degree of intensity of vocal sound. Amplitude is its physical component, used interchangably with volume.

Projection [proʊ'ʤɛkʃən]   The ability to support the voice in order to place vocal sound to appropriate points or distances.

Stress [strɛs]   In this chapter, stress is used in two ways: (1) The emphasis on a given syllable or word and (2) as in strain or tension due to too much intensity.

A theater director used to say that loudness is the least effective means for indicating a character's intensity. By this she meant that often a novice performer shouted culminating or angry dramatic lines that very well could have been more effectively delivered at a quieter, more intense level.

Conversely both performers and conversationalists are often directed to "speak up" in order to be heard. Writer Dorothy Parker was said to speak intentionally in such a quiet voice that people had to lean toward her in order to hear her clever comments.

Loudness is the perceived *amplitude* of a sound. Amplitude, measured in decibels (dB) gauges the force of a sound wave (see Figure 5.1). We may whisper at around 15–20 dB, hold ordinary conversation at around 65–70 dB, and may experience damage to hearing at 90–100 dB.

When subjected to sound over 130 dB (see Table 2.1) for extended periods, we may even experience visual distortion. Such exposure may even alter your reaction time. You may wish to consider the ramifications of driving in an auto-

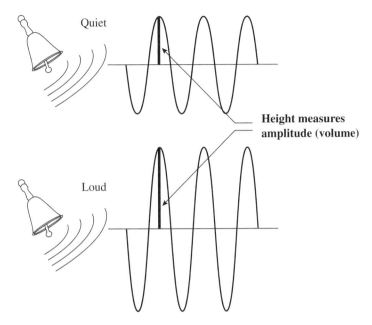

Quiet

Loud

Height measures amplitude (volume)

FIGURE 5.1 **The amplitude (or loudness) of a sound wave is measured in decibels. Greater force increases the height of the sound wave.**

mobile with loud music blaring, for possible distorted vision and delayed reactions can occur. Mice that have been subjected to continuous discordant loud music were found to have developed actual brain cell deterioration that resulted in learning difficulties.

Generally, it is easier to detect pitch change than loudness change. It takes at least a five percent increase in loudness for a listener to perceive the change. For the speaker this means that a distinct force must be exerted on the vocal mechanism in order for a listener to hear the change. In addition, your ability to perceive the loudness level of a sound at all is directly related to the pitch level (or frequency) of a sound, since pitch levels exist that cannot be detected by the human ear.

Two other factors contribute to your ability to hear the sound of another person's voice: (1) the acoustical properties of the room you are in and (2) the decibel level of nearby sounds. For instance, if you are in a gymnasium with cement walls, a voice will echo; if you are in a small, thickly carpeted room with velvet drapes, a voice will be absorbed. If a jet flies overhead while you are speaking, your listener may not hear you.

The loudness level of the human voice is determined by a series of factors: *force, support,* and *amplification.* The *force* of air vibrating the vocal folds initiates the sound that in turn must be adequately *sustained* and *amplified* by the resonating cavities. You may imagine yourself speaking more loudly (or softly) than you actually are simply because you "live" within the mechanism. Sounds are vibrating within your chest, throat, and head as you produce them, so they may seem louder to you. Further, your ears are situated behind your vocal output. Thus, you may not be your best judge when it comes to evaluating how loudly you are truly speaking. It is important to have the loudness level of your voice assessed objectively by your audience, which, in your case, may be your class and instructor.

The Paralinguistic Factors of Loudness

The force with which you speak may characterize your personality. A dominant person probably uses a more energetic voice, a passive person a more lax voice. Studies suggest that both men and women speak louder when speaking to members of the opposite sex.[1]

Consider under what circumstances you might use a more forceful voice. Try a few experiments yourself. Go to a counter in a busy department store and attempt to get the salesperson's attention first using a quiet, lax voice and then a more assertive or forceful voice. Experts suggest that it is the customer who sets the tone of such encounters and not the salesperson! Try the same experiment in a meeting wherein you wish to present a proposal or in a social setting wherein you wish to share an experience. You will, no doubt, readily observe a variety of reactions.

In addition to characterizing your mood or attitude, loudness levels can convey emotional *meaning* beyond the words you use. Changes in loudness of words play an important role in suggesting affection, anger, compassion, or a host of other feelings to listeners. The degree of force with which you speak a word or phrase can amplify or alter the meaning you intend.

TRY THIS

> To illustrate, try the following:
>
> First, speak each sentence softly. Then, using the size values of each word in the sentence as a guide, increase loudness with word size. Note changes in meaning that occur.
>
> 1. I didn't say that!
> 2. Leave me alone.
> 3. Give it to me.
> 4. Get out of here.
> 5. I love you.

Syllabic Stress

Life is composed of rhythms like heartbeats, breathing, or walking. Spoken language has rhythms, too. Changes in loudness levels are important to the English language in areas other than conveying meaning and making ourselves heard. Small units of loudness level change called *syllabic stress* identify the most important syllable in a polysyllabic (more than one syllable) word, for example, " **'syl** la ble." In monosyllabic words (one syllable) the relationship of that word to the rest of the sentence determines the degree of stress you give it. "He is **my** dog." In some word combinations, such as **"White House,"** nearly equal stress is given each syllable. In polysyllabic words there may be primary stress, as in "a **'bout**"; secondary stress, as in " **'ex** tri · *cate*"; or tertiary stress, as in " · *tin* tin · *nab* u **'la** tion." Where the syllabic stress is placed in a word may alter the phonemes or sounds used to produce the word. For example, if you say *inquiry* with the stress on the first syllable you say [INKWIRI]; if you stress the second syllable, you say [INKWAIRI].

Where primary stress falls in some words is somewhat of a linguistic phenomenon. Over a long period of time there occurs what linguists call a syllabic drift or shift. As an example, again consider the word *inquiry.* Some people may say " **'in** quiry." Others may say "in **'quiry.**" Consider these other words currently experiencing syllabic shifts: *ambiguous, applicable, confluence, formidable, profitable, contribute,* or *distribute.*

As with pitch, emphasis with increased loudness enjoys a high degree of flexibility in the English language. Though there are syllabic stress "rules," there is still a great deal of variety. The rhythms of other languages, of course, differ. Non-native speakers frequently impose on English stress patterns from their native language, thereby reinforcing their so-called accent.

Projection

We normally apply the concept of *projection* or *voice placement* to actors and public speakers. However, the ability to support and project one's voice in order to be heard applies to everyone. A listener should never have to think about listening; rather he or she should think about the ideas being presented. If people consistently respond to you with "huh" or "what did you say?" it is time to develop your ability to project your voice; that is, to increase the loudness level sufficiently to place your voice just behind your intended listener.

Breath support, a relaxed pharyngeal cavity, and open mouth are vital to adequate projection. Continued work on breathing, relaxation, and lower jaw exercises will aid you in developing more adequate control over the loudness level of your voice. Another important consideration is your audience. Are you speaking to one person in a confined space or to many in a large area? Where you "place" your voice will depend on your audience.

The technique of voice placement is difficult to describe, but it may help if you compare it to the concept of "guided imagery." To understand this idea, imagine yourself on a golf course or tennis court. In either sport you wish to hit your ball in such a way as to achieve a particular objective. In golf you want to drive the ball so that it reaches or comes close to the green; then you want to putt it into the hole. In tennis you hope to hit your ball with such a degree of force and angle that it will land in your opponent's court in such a way or place that your opponent is unable to return it. This seems quite simple in both sports. Why then are we not all excellent golfers or tennis players? You might argue that those sports require physical dexterity, skill, and practice, and to an extent you are correct. There is, however, one more ingredient that completes the package. By relaxing, centering, and visualizing the act, the player is better able to achieve the goal. When he or she is tense, and perhaps not concentrating, errors occur. This may be fairly obvious, for surely we have all experienced a wide slice, an errant lob, or any of a number of errors in all sorts of games.

Guided imagery is the process wherein we imagine and actually visualize the successful performance and completion of an act. It is a kind of rehearsal in the mind. How does this concept apply to voice projection? Imagine yourself at the tee of a 350-yard hole on a golf course. You know from previous experience that you cannot drive the ball 350 yards. But at one time, having hit the ball 200 yards, you can recall the feeling of that stroke. You relax, recapture that feeling, and imagine the club hitting the ball squarely, following through with your swing, and watching the ball flying straight down the fairway. Most golfers can tell you they have had that experience, though they may not be able to explain it.

You may have had the experience of attempting to vocalize an idea, of breaking into a conversation, or of getting someone's attention but failing. No one even heard you. You know, perhaps only viscerally, that you did not speak loudly enough to be heard. Space and the acoustical variables of that space are great detractors from the human voice. What you need to apply to your own voice is the principle of "guided imagery." In this instance rather than hitting a ball to a particular spot, you will lob your voice to a given point.

Sociologist Edward Hall first described a series of spaces within which human interaction occurs. For our society these are defined as (1) *intimate space* (within inches), (2) *personal space* (arm's length), (3) *social space* (around ten feet), and (4) *public space* (beyond ten to twelve feet).[2] With regard to voice, we alter the loudness levels of our voices given these spatial parameters. When you are in a small room with one other person whom you know well, and given that you are not engaged in an argument with that person, you obviously speak more quietly than you do when addressing an auditorium of 400 people without a microphone.

When you are faced with a public speaking situation, you need to use *public voice*. Most persons are not used to employing public voice because their stations in life do not require speaking beyond the distance of a few feet. For public voice, increased breath support becomes important. Rather than focusing your energy on your larynx, you must concentrate on abdominal control and force.

Depending on the spatial parameters in which you are speaking, you need to make vocal adjustments. For instance, if you are in a large space, you will need to increase the degree of vibratory force upon the vocal folds and open your mouth wider than you would if you were in an intimate space. You need to think about where you are trying to send your voice. You need to be able to mentally guide or place your voice for your listener.

In order to practice this, try the following exercise:

Place your open palm just under but within inches of your mouth. Keeping your head up, say this line: "I'll be leaving you now. Goodbye." Do not whisper. Speak the line directly into your hand as though you were tossing your voice there. Now hold your palm at arm's length. Repeat the line again placing your voice into your hand. Next focus on a point about 12 feet away. Repeat the process. Lastly, pick a spot at least 50 feet away. Although pitch may rise slightly when you increase loudness, try to maintain the same pitch. Repeat.

You should have noticed several things with this exercise. First, you probably required a great deal more energy and concentration to speak the line toward the farthest point; second, your diaphragm may have seemed tighter and your mouth more open; and third, you had to concentrate on that point. Like the "guided imagery" used to direct the golf ball to a specific point, you may employ a similar imagery to impel your voice toward a specific listener. Learn to put these things together. You need to know the actual physical process, then to feel the process— the physical tightening in the abdominal area, the lower jaw opening wider, and to coordinate that with the visualization process.

People often use the cliché that learning a physical activity is "as easy as riding a bike." When you were a child, learning to balance on that bike as you steered and pedaled may not have been that easy. As an adult who has not ridden a bike in a great many years, you might now get on one to find that, albeit shaky at first, you are quickly able to recapture the skill. Once you have put together the elements involved in achieving certain vocal skills, such as projection, you will have captured them forever. Right now you may be consciously aware of each step, but as you practice and develop skill, you will push those skills into the unconscious part of your mind, thus converting them to habit—hopefully a good habit.

Try the palm exercise again. Feel the diaphragmatic pressure changes involved. Note the degrees of jaw and lip movements as you envision the placement of sound. Think of the sound as if it were a tangible object. Place the sound at various distances. If it is easier for you, use a partner and play with the vocalized sound as if it were a ball. Physically move to varied distances. You can use the following words and phrases or make up your own.

1. Oh!
2. Don't go.
3. You can do it.
4. Thank goodness it's Friday.
5. I want you to know I care.

6. The telephone is ringing.
7. It's time to come in.
8. Shut the door.
9. Are you coming?
10. I can't hear you.

There are additional exercises for projection and vocal support at the end of this chapter. Use them daily. Build them into your exercise repertoire.

Variation

Have you ever been speaking to a group when you sensed that some of your listeners were drifting? Perhaps you were a part of an audience that had begun to fall asleep. It may have been that your voice or the speaker's voice had fallen into a loudness lull. In Chapter Three we discussed the avoidance of monotone through pitch variation. Variety in loudness levels is important in projecting a positive vocal profile. If everything you say is delivered at the same loudness level, your messages are as monotonous as if you used no pitch variation. Again, mood and meaning are conveyed through loudness variations. To illustrate, try the following: Say the sentence that follows as loudly as you can without strain. "I am very angry with you." Now repeat the sentence as though you want no one to hear you except the listener who is 2 feet away from you. Then, speak the line raising the loudness level on the word *very*. Do the same for the word *you*. By vocalizing in these ways you have varied loudness levels in such a way as to alter first mood and then meaning. Language and its intended meaning demand such loudness variations.

Exercises

General Stress Rule

Nouns may receive stress on the first syllable of two-syllable words, and *verbs* may receive stress on the second syllable, although there are frequent exceptions.

Noun	*Verb*
'con duct	con **'duct**
'com mune	com **'mune**
'in crease	in **'crease**
'in sult	in **'sult**
'in dent	in **'dent**
'ob ject	ob **'ject**
'per mit	per **'mit**
'pres ent	pre **'sent**
'rec ord	re **'cord**

Examples of exceptions:

Stress always on first syllable:

distance, **pur**chase, **prom**ise, **punc**ture, **rea**son, **sea**son

Stress always on second syllable:

de**mand**, re**sult**, re**lease**, re**mark**

Equal Stress

In compound, two-syllable words or special two-word combinations, both syllables or words receive equal stress. Examples: roadblock, postmark, roughneck, ringworm, scoreboard, White House, wishbone, no show, red ball, World's Cup, top dog, Mount Black, last days.

Multisyllabic Words. Obviously, many words in the English language are made up of more than two syllables. Some may have three, four, five, or more syllables. It would be nice to be able to say that the stress is always on the first or second syllable, but there are no general rules regarding syllabic stress in multisyllabic words. You will note in the following examples that the stress may occur at different places in words.

Three syllables	*Four syllables*	*Five syllables*
accident	appli**ca**tion	audi**tor**ium
e**la**tion	conver**sa**tion	ex**plor**atory
hesitate	im**pos**sible	in**tell**igible
relative	me**chan**ical	organi**za**tion
under**stand**	relax**a**tion	vo**cab**ulary

Stress in Sentences

Exercise 1   Generally, in English the following parts of a sentence receive stress: *nouns; verbs; adjectives; adverbs;* and some *pronouns,* such as "this," "that," "who"; or some *interrogatives,* such as "when" and "why." Parts of a sentence that do not receive stress are words that are functional in nature, such as *articles, prepositions, pronouns, conjunctions,* and *auxiliaries* (helping verbs). Using these general guides, read the following sentences. Identify the words that should receive stress and emphasize those words with an increase in loudness.

1. The pedals on the bike turned around and around.
2. After the plane took off, the passengers relaxed against their seats.
3. When he retired from his job, he announced his candidacy for the office.
4. Over the long weekend, the weather will be fair.
5. She had a job at the bank during the school year.
6. It was the final round of the tennis match.
7. We have been shown a better way to exercise.
8. It is the one on the left not the one on the right.
9. The donations will be used for student scholarships.
10. I may catch you off your guard if you are not careful.
11. After a long pause, he spoke with authority.
12. A report was sent to the Senate from the White House.
13. Pop art has taken a back seat to a new kind of painting.
14. It may be her sense of timing that makes her a good musician.
15. You said that as if it were my fault.

16. At one point I was ready to quit.
17. If you don't believe me, call someone else.
18. We will all meet together at ten so that I can have a chance to talk.
19. He has, for the moment at least, given up hopes of getting a raise.
20. It was a great book to read, but it never made the bestseller list.

Projection and Support

Exercise 1   Since you have no direct control over your diaphragm, it is impossible to suggest that you work to flex it as you could your bicep. You can, however, simulate the muscular tightening necessary by doing the following.

Stand about two feet from a sturdy wall. Place both palms against that wall and try to shove it over. Become aware of all the muscular movements engaged at that moment. Relax, then try it again until you are confident you know the feelings involved in the activity. At that point, once again shove against the wall, but this time vocalize, "I am going to push this wall over." If you tried to say the sentence quietly, you no doubt felt a degree of abdominal relaxation. What you should achieve as you speak is an increased vocal force. Now step back from the wall and deliver the line in the same manner. Without a rise in pitch level, try achieving the same force and support with these sentences:

1. Hit him again, harder.
2. Can you hear me back there?
3. I hope you haven't lost it.
4. My car won't start.
5. Let's get out of this place.
6. Don't go now.
7. Look around for it.
8. Please come help me.
9. Run a little faster.
10. Add one more.
11. Seize the day!
12. Hoist the mainsail.
13. Try to speak up.
14. Here's a toast to you.
15. Push down on the accelerator.
16. Throw it to the outfielder.
17. Try your five iron.
18. Gentlemen, start your engines.
19. I said, clean up the garage.
20. Can you speak up?

Exercise 2   Use the following materials to build projection and variety in loudness. Deliver the following passages to the four distances described in this chapter: within inches, about four feet, ten to twelve feet, and beyond that as if in a large auditorium. Use variety as you read.

News

1. Hearings were held this week in Congress to examine the disclosure of foreign lobbying under the Foreign Agents Registration Act. Congress apparently has growing concerns that laws and regulations governing lobbying, both foreign and domestic, need an overhaul. On the basis of testimony and a General Accounting Office report, a specially appointed subcommittee has concluded that FARA is not working and that lobbyists either don't understand the act or ignore it. The subcommittee will continue hearings throughout the month.

2. The administration has presented Congress with sweeping banking reforms. If adopted, the reform effort will be granted new powers and will be permitted to branch out across state lines. The most important aspect involves deposit insurance. Many opponents to the reform measures view the plan as flawed. However, the administration will continue to push hard to get the act through Congress.

3. A local activist group has formed to influence legislative change in county nursing homes. In recent years, numerous cases of elder abuse and neglect have surfaced giving rise to increased concern over the plight of the elderly in nursing homes. The state assembly is currently considering a bill that would force nursing homes to pay punitive damages when physical abuse has been inflicted by an employee.

4. A suspected gang member died early this morning of a gunshot wound received during a gang fight last evening. Police said the man was shot once in the chest in a fight involving about a dozen people. No suspects are in custody, and the investigation is continuing.

5. It may not always be necessary for doctors to prescribe an anti-inflammatory drug for certain pain and injuries. According to a study reported in the *New England Journal of Medicine,* an over-the-counter pain reliever will work just as well for knee pain. Prescription drugs often carry the risk of side effects such as ulcers or gastrointestinal bleeding. In the case of marked inflammation, doctors reported that prescription drugs may be in order.

6. The city council tonight is scheduled to announce two vacant seats on the planning commission and four vacant seats on the parks and recreation commission. The terms of current commissioners expire today. There are several applicants for each of the vacant seats including the incumbents. The seats are appointed by the city council. An announcement will be forthcoming by the end of the week.

7. A public hearing scheduled for last week on a proposed shopping mall for the northwest sector of Crescent City was postponed for one month. The City Council hearing was delayed to give developers and city staff extra time to work out differences in plans to build the large commercial development. The 15-acre site is planned to include three major stores, smaller retail shops, a service station, a movie theater, and a drive-through restaurant. A new hearing has been scheduled for August tenth.

8. A report in the *Journal of the American Medical Association* reported that a small dose of aspirin can reduce hypertension in pregnant women and decrease a risk to the fetus from high blood pressure. In the reported study, the risk of developing pregnancy induced hypertension dropped by 65 percent among those taking about one-half an aspirin daily. The researchers found no risk to the infants from the low doses of aspirin.

9. The Springfield City Unified School District has been awarded a $200,000 federal grant to fund a language program for 350 students who are not literate in English or their native languages. The program is designed to develop reading, writing, and speaking skills in the student's native language and to prepare students for English instruction. The program will begin with the fall opening of school and continue through spring.

Poetry

> Beat! beat! drums!—blow! bugles! blow!
> Through the windows—through doors—burst like a ruthless force,
> Into the solemn church, and scatter the congregation,
> Into the school where the scholar is studying;
> Leave not the bridegroom quiet—no happiness must he have now with his bride,
> Nor the peaceful farmer any peace, ploughing his field or gathering his grain,
> So fierce you whirl and pound you drums—so shrill you bugles blow.
>
> —Walt Whitman, "Beat! Beat! Drums"

> There was a roaring in the wind all night;
> The rain came heavily and fell in floods;
> But now the sun is rising calm and bright;
> The birds are singing in the distant woods;
> Over his own sweet voice the Stock-dove broods;
> The Jay makes answer as the Magpie chatters;
> And all the air is filled with pleasant noise of waters.
>
> —William Wordsworth, "Resolution and Independence"

> That with music loud and long,
> I would build that dome in air,
> That sunny dome! those caves of ice!
> And all who heard should see them there,
> And all should cry, Beware! Beware!
> His flashing eyes, his floating hair!
> Weave a circle round him thrice,
> And close your eyes with holy dread,
> For he on honey-dew hath fed,
> And drunk the milk of Paradise.
>
> —Samuel Taylor Coleridge, "Kubla Khan"

Prose literature

1. The hoofs clattered again; and the voices, talking so strangely in the empty air, passed on through the forest, where no church had ever been gathered or solitary Christian prayed. Whither, then, could these holy men be journeying so deep into the heathen wilderness? Young Goodman Brown caught hold of a tree for support, being ready to sink down on the ground, faint and overburdened with the heavy sickness of his heart. He looked up to the sky, doubting whether there really was a heaven above him. Yet there was the blue arch, the stars brightening in it.

   —Nathaniel Hawthorne, "Young Goodman Brown"

2. The engine did not wake him—he had slept with the noise of heavier ones for years. Nor did the boat's list. Before the engines was the forgotten sound of a woman's voice—so new and welcoming it broke his dream life apart. He woke thinking of a short street of yellow houses with white doors which women opened wide and called out, "Come on in here, you honey you," their laughter sprawling like a quilt over the command. But nothing sprawled in this woman's voice.

   —Toni Morrison, *Tar Baby*

3. In the distance he heard the approach of a train. It jarred him back to a sharp sense of danger. He ran again, his big shoes sopping up and down in the dust. He was tired and his lungs were bursting from running. He wet his lips, wanting water. As he turned from the road across a plowed field, he heard the train roaring at his heels. He ran faster, gripped in terror.

   —Richard Wright, "Big Boy Leaves Home"

4. Rainsford sprang up and moved quickly to the rail, mystified. He strained his eyes in the direction from which the reports had come, but it was like trying to see through a blanket. He leaped upon the rail and balanced himself there, to get greater elevation; his pipe, striking a rope, was knocked from his mouth. He lunged for it; a short hoarse cry came from his lips as he realized he had reached too far and had lost his balance. The cry was pinched short as the blood-warm waters of the Caribbean Sea closed over his head.

   —Richard Connell, "The Most Dangerous Game"

5. From the kitchen porch below came the sound of splashing water, the creaking of the pump handle, and the stamping boots of men. I sat in the window watching the darkness come on slowly, while all the lamps were being lighted. My own small lamp had a handle on the oil bowl, like a cup's. There was also a lantern with a frosted chimney hanging by a nail on the wall. A voice called to me from the foot of my stairs and I looked down into the face of a dark-skinned, flaxen-haired young woman, far advanced in pregnancy, and carrying a prosperous year-old boy on her hip, one arm clutching him to her, the other raised above her head so that her lantern shone upon their heads. "The supper is now ready," she said, and waited for me to come down before turning away.

   —Katherine Anne Porter, "Holiday"

6. "Wait a minute! You men wait a minute!" he cried. His words cut out above the clamor of the mob like an electric spark.

"You'll gain nothing, you'll help nothing if you do this thing!"

They tried to drown him out with an angry and derisive roar. He shot his big fist up into the air and shouted at them, blazed at them with that cold single eye, until they had to hear.

—Thomas Wolfe, "The Child by Tiger"

7. It blew day after day: it blew with spite, without interval, without mercy; without rest. The world was nothing but an immensity of great foaming waves rushing at us, under a sky low enough to touch with the hand and dirty like a smoked ceiling. In the stormy space surrounding us there was as much flying spray as air. Day after day and night after night there was nothing round the ship but the howl of the wind, the tumult of the sea, the noise of water pouring over her deck. There was no rest for her and no rest for us.

She tossed, she pitched, she stood on her head, she sat on her tail, she rolled, she groaned, and we had to hold on while on deck and cling to our bunks when below, in a constant effort of body and worry of mind.

—Joseph Conrad, "Youth"

8. Then she swept into the bedroom and threw herself on her knees by the bed. She moaned when she saw the gash over my eye. In the kitchen Sonny set up a loud bawl on his own, and a moment later Father appeared in the bedroom door with his cap over his eyes, wearing an expression of the most intense self-pity.

—Frank O'Connor, "The Drunkard"

9. Tessie Hutchinson was in the center of a cleared space by now, and she held her hands out desperately as the villagers moved in on her. "It isn't fair," she said. A stone hit her on the side of the head.

Old Man Warner was saying, "Come on, come on, everyone." Steve Adams was in the front of the crowd of villagers, with Mrs. Graves beside him.

"It isn't fair, it isn't right:" Mrs. Hutchinson screamed, and then they were upon her.

—Shirley Jackson, "The Lottery"

10. The shaft of umbrella swung violently around and knocked the silk hat from Professor Irving's head. His white hair was caught by the wind. Lashed in another direction, the shaft now struck the Professor's glasses, and they flew away. Now he could see little or nothing. He became bewildered.

Great glaring headlights broke upon him, passed him, and then immediately other glaring lights flared up toward him out of the sheets of water. He couldn't see because of his lost glasses and because of the stinging rain.

He rushed between two cars. He slipped. . . . The chimes on the Metropolitan Tower rang out, in wails of wild sound, the half-hour after four.

—O. F. Lewis, "Alma Mater"

Variety

Exercise 1 The passages that follow contain varying emotional levels. Read these for variety in loudness.

Prose Literature

1. Doubtful as to his proper conduct, he decided at last to murmur: "Fine morning!" and was passing on, when Mr. Tandram answered: "Beautiful for this time of year!" Detecting a slight nervousness in his neighbor's voice, Mr. Nilson was emboldened to regard him openly.

   —John Galsworthy, "The Japanese Quince"

2. I felt myself bombarded with punches. I fought back with hopeless desperation. I wanted to deliver my speech more than anything else in the world, because I felt that only these men could judge truly my ability, and now this stupid clown was ruining my chances. I began fighting carefully now, moving in to punch him and out again with my greater speed. A lucky blow to his chin and I had him going too—until I heard a loud voice yell, "I got my money on the big boy."

   —Ralph Ellison, "Battle Royal"

3. On the slope he began to run, he could not help it. Just as he reached the road, where his car seemed to sit in the moonlight like a boat, his heart began to give off tremendous explosions like a rifle, bang bang bang. He sank in fright on to the road, his bags falling about him. He felt as if all this had happened before. He covered his heart with both hands to keep anyone from hearing the noise it made.

   —Eudora Welty, "Death of a Traveling Salesman"

4. Exultation beat up in him. Half a mile now. The crew's bodies, sheeted in sweat, gleamed strangely in the twilight. The line of yachts was opening on either side. They were in, Kip thought. "Pick it up," he called. "Pick it up!" They drove the blades deep, the great bodies bent. "We're in!" he kept thinking in time with the beat of his tiller grips. "We're in! We're in!"

   —Harry Sylvester, "Eight-Oared Crew"

5. But on this particular morning, the first morning, as he lay there with his eyes closed, he had for some reason *waited* for the postman. He wanted to hear him come round the corner. And that was precisely the joke—he never did. He never came. He never had come—*round the corner*—again. For when at last the steps *were* heard, they had already, he was quite sure, come a little down the hill, to the first house; and even so, the steps were curiously different—they were softer, they had a new secrecy about them, they were muffled and indistinct; and while the rhythm of them was the same, it now said a new thing—it said peace, it said remoteness, it said cold, it said sleep.

   —Conrad Aiken, "Silent Snow, Secret Snow"

6. For weeks Ramelle lay in the hospital, dying of lung cancer. She wanted to get it over with. A spike through her lungs pinned her to the bed. Fierce pain would not let her go. She lay there, observing fluttering nurses tiptoe around her. She saw the faces of Juts, Louise, Fannie, and Spotty every day, but she could barely speak. Sometimes she thought of Curtis, too, but then she remembered he had died four months before of a heart attack.

—Rita Mae Brown, *Six of One*

7. The Montana sunset lay between two mountains like a gigantic bruise from which dark arteries spread themselves over a poisoned sky. An immense distance under the sky crouched the village of Fish, minute, dismal, and forgotten. There were twelve men, so it was said, in the village of Fish, twelve sombre and inexplicable souls who sucked a lean milk from the almost literally bare rock upon which a mysterious populatory force had begotten them. They had become a race apart, these twelve men of Fish, like some species developed by an early whim of nature, which on second thought had abandoned them to struggle and extermination.

—F. Scott Fitzgerald, "The Diamond as Big as the Ritz"

8. People spoke of them as the Kunkel twins. Mostly nobody tried to tell them apart. Homely corkscrew-twisty girls you wouldn't know would turn up so quiet and solemn and almost beautiful, perfect little dolls' faces with the freckles powdered over, touches of rouge on the cheeks and mouths. I was tempted to whisper to them, kneeling by the coffins. Hey Rhea! Hey Rhoda! Wake *up!*

—Joyce Carol Oates, "Heat"

9. The loud groaning of the hydraulic valves swallowed up the pilot's song, and there was a shrieking high in the air, like automobile brakes, and the plane hit flat on its belly in a cornfield and shook them so violently that an old man up forward howled, "Me kidneys! Me kidneys!" The stewardess flung open the door, and someone opened an emergency door at the back, letting in the sweet noise of their continuing mortality—the idle splash and smell of a heavy rain.

—John Cheever, "The Country Husband"

10. 'O Tiger-lily,' said Alice, addressing herself to one that was waving gracefully about in the wind, 'I WISH you could talk!'

'We CAN talk,' said the Tiger-lily: 'when there's anybody worth talking to.'

Alice was so astonished that she could not speak for a minute: it quite seemed to take her breath away. At length, as the Tiger-lily only went on waving about, she spoke again, in a timid voice—almost in a whisper. 'And can ALL the flowers talk?'

'As well as YOU can,' said the Tiger-lily. 'And a great deal louder.'

—Lewis Carrol, *Through the Looking Glass*

Poetry

Bent double, like old beggars under sacks,
Knock-kneed, coughing like hags, we cursed through sludge,
Till on the haunting flares we turned our backs,

And towards our distant rest began to trudge.
Men marched asleep. Many had lost their boots,
But limped on, blood-shod. All went lame, all blind;
Drunk with fatigue; deaf even to the hoots
Of gas-shells dropping softly behind.

—Wilfred Owen, "Dulce et Decorum est"

Once in a saintly passion
    I cried with desperate grief,
  "O Lord, my heart is black with guile,
    Of sinners I am chief."

Then stooped my guardian angel
    And whispered from behind,
  "Vanity, my little man,
    You're nothing of the kind."

—James Thomson

Twelve o'clock.
Along the reaches of the street
Held in a lunar synthesis,
Whispering lunar incantations
Dissolve the floors of the memory
And all its clear relations,
Its divisions and precisions,
Every street lamp that I pass
Beats like a fatalistic drum,
And through the spaces of the dark
Midnight shakes the memory
As a madman shakes a dead geranium.

—T. S. Eliot, "Rhapsody on a Windy Night"

"Friends, Romans, and countrymen, lend me your ears!"
(They were all of them fond of quotations:
So they drank to his health, and they gave him three cheers,
While he served out additional rations.)

—Lewis Carroll, "The Hunting of the Snark"

The wayfarer
Perceiving the pathway to truth
Was struck with astonishment,
It was thickly grown with weeds.
"Ha," he said,
"I see that none has passed here
In a long time."
Later he saw that each weed
Was a singular knife.
"Well " he mumbled at last,
"Doubtless there are other roads."

—Stephen Crane

Rough wind, that moanest loud
   Grief too sad for song;
Wild wind, when sullen cloud
   Knells all the night long:

Sad storm, whose tears are vain.
Bare woods, whose branches strain,
Deep caves and dreary main,
   Wail, for the world's wrong!

—Percy Bysshe Shelley

Chapter Five Review

Review the following concepts:

- Terms: loudness, projection, stress
- Amplitude and decibel levels
- Relation of acoustics to voice
- The role of voice support and amplification in projection
- Paralinguistic factors of loudness
- Syllabic stress
- Projection
- Loudness variety

Respond to the following:

1. What factors contribute to your ability to perceive the loudness level of sound?
2. Explain the paralinguistics of loudness changes.
3. What role does syllabic stress play in language?
4. What were Edward Hall's four distances, and how does his theory relate to voice?
5. Explain the concept of voice projection.

APPLICATION

1. Do others often have to ask you to repeat yourself, or do they tend to think of you as angry? Why do you think that is? What can you do to change?

2. When speaking in public how can you adjust your voice so that everyone can hear you?

3. Does your voice tend to tire easily? *Tip:* Reevaluate breath support. (See Chapter 2.)

4. Are you using current and proper syllabic stress? How do you know? *Tip:* Begin listening to network newscasters for current trends in pronunciation.

FOCUS MESSAGE

1. *ESL:* Each culture mandates loudness variations related to spatial dimensions. You may have to override cultural habits in order to increase loudness lev-

els. Remember, too, that syllabic stress is a primary factor in your being understood. Study the delivery of skilled network newscasters in order to habituate yourself to the pronunciation of words.

2. *Acting:* Performers must learn to adjust volume to a variety of spaces, conditions, and emotions. Experiment with as many different venues as possible. As you deliver lines within each space, first focus on specific spots and deliver lines to those near you, to the middle of the space, then to the greatest distance from you. Then, try to fill the entire area with sound. Focus on vowel sounds because these will carry your sound. Above all, work to develop strong breath support to sustain performance.

3. *Broadcasting:* Within the broadcasting studio, volume is seldom a problem for the broadcaster. A conversational level is best. Outside the studio, the broadcaster might have to project above environmental noise. In any case, the announcer should be aware of surrounding sounds and his or her own distance from the microphone. Certain sounds, particularly plosives [p, b, t, d, k, g], when produced too close to the mike will create a "popping" sound. Certain fricative sounds [s, z, ʃ, ʒ] can create excessive sibilance, which a microphone seems to exaggerate. A mike will even pick up quick intakes of air, so your breathing must be relaxed and controlled.

EVALUATION

SEE PAGES 269–270, where you'll find an evaluation form for this chapter. Follow your instructor's directions.

NOTES

1. A. W. Siegman, S. Feldstein, eds., *Nonverbal Behavior and Communication* (Hillsdale, NJ: Lawrence Erlbaum, 1978), p. 217.

2. Edward T. Hall, *The Hidden Dimension* (New York: Anchor Books-Doubleday and Co., Inc., 1969), pp. 116–125.

6 Rate/Duration

. . . he did not sound like a preacher. He did not fall into the singsong chant you hear so often. No, Daddy had a deep ringing voice and spoke real slow, so that every word registered . . .

—Lee Smith

TERMS

Duration [dʊˈreɪʃən]   The time spent producing both the sounds and silences of a language.

Rate [reɪt]   The number of words per minute one speaks.

Pause [pɔz]   A break in speech characterized by no sound.

Speech phrasing [ˈspitʃ ˈfreɪzɪŋ]   Forming a group of spoken words that constitutes a meaningful unit and is surrounded by pauses.

Syllabic stress [sɪˈlæbɪk ˈstrɛs]   The emphasis on a given syllable.

A recent Guinness world record for rapid speech was set by a London salesman who was clocked at over 600 words per minute. Can listeners actually understand what a speaker is saying at that rate? Of course not. How do judges ascertain the word count? The record holder, Steve Woodmore, read a passage from a novel. The reading was recorded, and then it was played back at a slower speed to obtain the word count. No doubt you have frequently wished that you could play back at a slower speed some message someone has communicated to you. Conversely, there may be times when you wish you could speed up a message.

Rate is the speed with which we speak words combined with the *duration* of time we spend producing the sounds and silences of a language. Speaking rapidly or slowly, trippingly or hesitantly can characterize you as intelligent, powerful, and attractive or as the reverse. Your rate of speaking may pinpoint your geographic residence, mood, and profession. Listeners tend to associate slow, hesitant rates of speaking with a lack of intelligence or competence.[1] For example, imagine going to a seminar on financial planning. The seminar features several speakers, all of whom are seemingly qualified to speak on the subject. An accountant, a specialist in taxes, begins the series of presentations. He shuffles through his papers, looks up and down again, moves slowly from side to side and begins speaking with, "Ummm, well, uh, I thought I would say a few words about, uh, how, um, you could reduce your, uh, tax liability." His delivery is slow, ponderous, and peppered with hesitancies. At the close of his presentation, you might come away with some valuable insights about taxes, if you stayed awake and listened very carefully. However, you might also feel that the speaker was not sure of his information. The chances are that his weak delivery caused you to "turn off" your listening switch early in the presentation.

Another speaker, one who sells tax sheltered annuities, begins his speech dynamically with, "You need not be a slave to the system! You can protect your present and your future." He looks directly at the audience and delivers the presentation at a fairly rapid clip. Most of us would be more impressed with this second speaker, though we might deduce that this speaker was merely trying to sell his company's annuity plan. Consider how we generally react to the disparity between these delivery styles.

Admittedly, there are several nonverbal variables operating in this situation. If we isolate only the rate of speech in each case and consider its effect upon listeners, we find that the second speaker will have a greater impact on the audience. That speaker will be considered more dynamic and competent than the accountant whose vocal hesitancies and slow rate will tag him as less sure and less in control of his information, even though that may not be the case. In less formal situations or in distinct interpersonal conversational situations, rate is also important. Think of two radio personalities who may be broadcasting from different booths with little or no eye contact. Timing becomes vital to keeping the broadcast lively. In verbal repartee the timing must be finely tuned in order to produce whatever effect may be intended with puns, jokes, teases, or one-upmanship. In such interpersonal situations, vocal hedges such as "uh" or "um" tend to reduce the power of the speaker.

The acoustic dimension plays a role in one's rate of speech. If the room or space in which you are speaking is large, your audience may not understand you if you speak too rapidly. This happens because of what is called *masking*, which means that sound is reverberating. This is why good speakers slow down, pause, and vary their tempo. We also know that rhythms of speech, like any rhythms, can affect listeners in both a physical and psychological manner. Thus, a good speaker coordinates rate of speech with intended meaning.

The dynamics of vocal delivery are such that we *perceive* a speaker to be competent if he or she can control and quickly deliver large quantities of information. For some reason we ignore that a speaker may be regionally or culturally influenced to speak more slowly as might someone from some southern regions (unless, of course, you are *in* that region); that a speaker is examining several linguistic options; that someone is new to speaking English; or that a speaker is nervous.

We have learned that when a person from another linguistic community is trying to master English, rate is an important factor. Vowels produced more slowly in the learning sequence are produced more accurately.[2] The import of this information lies in the quality of drill that a student undertakes. Begin slowly and work up to a more normal rate of sound production as you master the sounds of a new language.

Silence is another variable and is used differently within and between cultures. In Japanese, for instance, the silence is just as important as the conversation. The rates and rhythms of speech are intricately tied into intonational patterns, and these are unique to each language.

To improve your own rate of speech, pay attention to (1) actual speaking or oral reading rates, (2) use of silence or the pause, (3) integration of these into speech phrasing, and (4) rate variety.

Speaking/Reading Rate

"The average southerner has speech patterns of someone slipping in and out of consciousness. I can change my shoes and socks faster than most people in Mississippi can speak a sentence," notes writer Bill Bryson in his book *The Lost Continent, Travels in Small Town America*. Rates of speaking and reading will vary from region to region and person to person. Your rate of speaking will differ from your rate of reading depending on your oral reading skills. Most people often read more slowly than they speak. Further, the methods for assessing those two rates differ slightly. Your goal should be to align those rates within a given range.

Generally we measure rate at *words per minute (wpm)* because words are what listeners perceive. Understand that measurement will incorporate silence as well as sound. In fact, several variables will alter delivery rates. Some speeches or reading material are more difficult linguistically or semantically. That is to say that there may exist in the material bigger and more difficult words, or the grammatical structure or word arrangement may be harder to say. Additionally, the intended message might alter rate of delivery. Emotional material requires a less regular rate of delivery than unemotional material.

Given those considerations and realizing that variances exist, we can draw some general word per minute guidelines for unemotional material.

> 110 to 130 wpm = Too slow
> 140 to 175 wpm = Excellent rate
> 180 to 220 wpm = Too fast

Pause

Equally important as the number of words per minute that we speak is the amount of silence we place between those words. In spoken English we pause at points that correspond to the punctuation marks of its grammar. The pause is a vocal indicator of meaning or speaking style and, as mentioned earlier, is related to situations, individuals, and cultures. The *degree* of silence given to those punctuation marks is related to the *kind* of mark used. For example, if a period within a paragraph is assigned a beat of silence, as in music, then a comma equals a half beat, and so on. Where that punctuation mark falls may affect the length of the silence given it. If the period marks the conclusion of a paragraph, you might take two beats. In addition, there are in messages certain points at which, though there are no punctuation marks, you are briefly silent because of meaning. Consider this earlier sentence as an example:

> In spoken English, [½ beat] we pause [¼ beat] at points which correspond [¼ beat] to meaning [¼ beat] or to the punctuation marks of its grammar. [2 beats]

Essayist Pico Iyer writes, "Punctuation, in short gives us the human voice, and all the meanings that lie between the words. 'You aren't young, are you?' loses its innocence when it loses the question mark. Every child knows the menace of a dropped apostrophe (the parent's 'Don't do that' shifting into the more slowly enunciated 'Do not do that'), and every believer, the ignominy of having his faith reduced to 'faith.' Add an exclamation point to 'To be or not to be . . .' and the gloomy Dane has all the resolve he needs. . . ."[3] The amount of silence or emphasis we assign to the punctuation of our language is important. Silence or pauses that are not filled by vocalization can be a most effective means of suggesting confidence and authority. You can use silences like these in situations where you will not be interrupted, such as in public speeches or performances. On the other hand, too long a pause might indicate signs of antagonism or lack of respect.[4]

On a more personal level, there may be times when you wish to indicate to a listener that you are not yet finished with your idea or that you wish to maintain control of the conversation. At those times you can judiciously employ the vocalized pause. Usually depicted in writing as "uh," the vocal pause is simply an extended schwa sound frequently used in casual conversation. When engaging in more formalized forms of communication, be cautious. Using too many vocal pauses can make you seem unsure of your ideas. Vocalized pauses (*um*) are often used in conversational turn-taking, but they should never be used in formal speaking situations, such as speeches, report presentations, or business interviews. The following is an example of the vocalized pause.

> **JOHN:** "I was thinking the other day about buying a new car." [downward inflection and silence]
>
> **MARY:** "Oh? What kind of car?" [downward inflection and silence]
>
> **JOHN:** "That new Mercedes is pretty nice, uh, but of course, uh, it's, uh, pretty expensive, uh. . . ."

If Mary were to say something at this point, she would be interrupting John's control of the discussion. If John is silent for several beats after the last "uh," he has given Mary permission to speak. In conversation, when a speaker fails to give a listener these clues, he or she risks interruption. Keep in mind that rate, including pauses and interruptions, is culturebound. That is to say that other cultures utilize rate factors in different ways. Other nonverbal behaviors that operate as indicators of conversational turn-taking are facial expression, eye contact, posture, and pitch variations.

You might try assessing your own verbal and nonverbal interactions and turn-taking abilities the next time you speak with one or more persons. Better yet, try judging your behavior the next time you speak on the telephone. Do you interrupt the other person or do you listen for downward inflection and a pause? While speaking on the phone, you have no access to physical clues and must rely solely on vocal clues for your chance to enter the conversation.

Speech Phrasing

Speech phrasing is a concept that includes speaking some syllables or words faster and some slower and pausing for varying lengths of time. There is an old joke that illustrates in part the idea. John says, "Ask me the secret of telling a good joke." Just as Bill begins, "Wha . . ." John returns with, "Timing."

Speech phrasing involves the rhythms of a language and the amount of time, or duration, spent on certain sounds in the language. This is determined by the structure of the language, the sounds of the language, the intended meaning, and the emotional state of the speaker.

Language is composed of a series of sounds and silences to which we attach meaning. As noted in previous chapters, we manipulate that meaning with pitch and loudness changes. We also manipulate the rates and rhythms of oral language or speech. Sometimes we do this consciously, and sometimes we do it without paying attention to what we are saying or how it might be perceived. For example, rapidly say, "I'd read that." Would you be perceived to be saying the words you see on this page or "I dread that." If you intended to say the latter, you need to use a split second break between "I" and the "d" of "dread." On a television program, the host asked a professional football player if he was surprised that his team was not going to play in the Super Bowl. The football player replied "Yeah, 'cause we was speakin' at the time." What he intended to say, of course, was that the team was in peak form. However, by using improper grammar ("was" for "were") and without a brief pause before "peakin'," the message came out differently.

In casual conversation, none of us takes the time to plan a formally constructed set of rhythms. In fact, we have learned the rhythms of our language in the first few years of our lives. A new field of study is emerging, however, called conversational analysis, that examines every detail of conversations including pauses, length of utterances, simultaneous utterances, and other nuances. There are apparent applications and implications of these types of analysis. It might be applied to business situations, human interaction with computers, politics, or interviews, to name a few situations wherein the analysis of the rhythms of speech might be useful.

The most formal level of rhythmic speech is found in poetry. Poetry often has what we call *meter.* Meter is a particular arrangement of rhythms in a line of poetry. One example is the classic *iambic pentameter.* This simply means five units of a soft beat combined with a harder beat, as in this line from Shakespeare:

My mistress' eyes are nothing like the sun

In reading such a line of poetry, you should be cautioned against hitting heavily on this series of soft and hard stresses since the rhythm here serves only as an undergirding for the meaning of the line. Certainly a Shakespearean actor needs to study the rhythms of the poetic line, what is called prosody. However, that is not our concern here. Furthermore, no one speaks in these formalized rhythms; yet the English language has a rhythm by virtue of the emphasis on certain sounds and words and units of speech.

The *duration,* or rate of delivery, with which you deliver these certain sounds, syllables, words, or phrases affects a listener's perception of your rate of speech. Since English is composed of a series of stressed and unstressed sounds and syllables, less *time* is assigned to unstressed sounds than is given a stressed sound or syllable, as in "a **'book**" or "**'sum** mary." When we wish to emphasize a word or idea we may lengthen the sounds of it. For example, "it is *not* that he can't *do* the job; it's that he *won't.*" Of course, at the same time we are also using a loudness and pitch change.

Four major factors determine the duration we assign to sound: (1) grammatical structure, (2) physical process of articulation, (3) meaning of the message, and (4) mood or emotional state of speaker or message.

1. The *grammatical structure* of English is such that there are certain words or phrases that are considered "helpers." For example, articles *a, an,* and *the* are simple grammatical referents. The first part of prepositional phrases are "directional" in nature. For example, *in the, around the, toward the* tell you where to go. Certain clauses act in much the same way, e.g., *When he was on his way. . . .* These aids of grammar are usually spoken at a more rapid pace than are the nouns and verbs of a sentence or phrase because the nouns and verbs carry the major import of the message.

2. The *physical process* involved in articulating certain sounds of the English language enables you to elongate those sounds or inhibits you from doing so. For instance, some sounds like [m] in *hum,* [n] in *run,* [ŋ] in *sing,* [i] in *see,* [e] in *say,* [ɑ] in *calm,* and many others are easily extended. Certain other sounds such as [t], [k] [f], [b], [ɪ] [g] cannot be elongated without making you sound very awkward.

3. Communicating *meaning* is the objective of speech. Depending on our social or public speaking situations and our intended messages, we may wish to emphasize one word over another. For example, "Mine is the *blue* car"; or "I had such a *good* time"; or "Learning the *stroke* is most important for a swimmer." We therefore extend some of the sounds of those words in order to stress meaning.

4. Sometimes our own *emotional state* or the *emotional messages* in material are conveyed by the rate of delivery. Sad, depressing, or gloomy material is usually delivered at a slower rate than happy, light, or uplifting material. If we are tired or depressed, we may tend toward slower vocal delivery, whereas our delivery picks up with heightened emotional states. In speaking, our own less energetic moods often leak through into our intended messages. This can distort the intent of the message. Imagine the president of the United States delivering the State of the Union Address in an extremely slow and halting manner!

Variety

Whether you are elongating sounds, quickening your pace, or pausing, the general rhythm of your speech needs to flow in such a way as to make you a vital speaker. It is important to remember that all vocal factors interrelate and work together to produce the perceived effect. As with pitch and loudness, a good speaker should incorporate rate *variety* into his or her speech. To speak at a regular rate with little or no variation is to risk being characterized as boring. You can work to speed up or slow down your rate consistent with the ideas you present.

Read the following paragraph in a slow and ponderous manner and discover how you have changed it.

> "Not so fast! You're driving too fast!" said Mrs. Mitty. "What are you driving so fast for? . . . You were up to fifty-five. . . . You know I don't like to go more than forty. You were up to fifty-five. . . . You're tensed up again. . . . It's one of your days. I wish you'd let Dr. Renshaw look you over."
> —James Thurber, "The Secret Life of Walter Mitty"

Now try the opposite. Read the passage below in a rapid-fire manner and note how you have altered it.

> And the mist of snow, as he had foreseen, was still on it—a ghost of snow failing in the bright sunlight, softly and steadily floating and turning and pausing, soundlessly meeting the snow that covered, as with a transparent mirage, the bare bright cobbles. He loved it—he stood still and loved it. Its beauty was paralyzing—beyond all words, all experience, all dreams.
> —Conrad Aiken, "Silent Snow, Secret Snow"

There are two steps you can take, which have been discussed in this chapter, to slow yourself down if you find you are speaking too fast.

- Learn to elongate appropriate sounds.
- Utilize appropriately placed pauses.

The situation in which you find yourself or the context will dictate the rate of speech you should use, but in speeding up your rate, you should be careful to maintain control over your articulation (see Chapter Eight). It is easy when speaking rapidly to slur over sounds or omit some sound entirely. The exercises that follow can be used to improve your rate of speech.

Rate Assessments

Given that there exist numerous variables in delivery—physical differences, sentence structure, word understanding, semantics—you may wish to engage in a couple of exercises to assess your own speaking and reading rates.

1. To assess your rate of conversational speaking, you might place a tape recorder next to your telephone in order to record yourself as you speak to a friend or colleague for at least a minute or more. Do this on several occasions; transcribe your recording, count the number of words, divide by the appropriate minutes spoken. This should give you a rough *conversational wpm.*

2. To assess your public presentational wpm, select a topic of current public interest—world affairs, politics, etc. Prepare a two-minute "speech" on that topic. Again, using a tape recorder, perform the exercise cited above. This will give you your *public speaking wpm.* Compare that figure with your conversational wpm.

3. To assess your reading rate, choose one of the following passages. Each passage contains just over 220 words, and they become progressively more difficult. There is a number listed within the text of the material for every group of words beyond 100. This number should not be read aloud. Note the number of wpm you are able to read aloud for one minute. You might try reading faster or slower. Try adjusting your rate to only 100 wpm (if it is not that already). Then attempt reading at 220 wpm (if you do not already do so). Record yourself so that you can play back your efforts. Note what changes took place in both the actual delivery and your perception of yourself as you played back your recording. Ask yourself if in reading at 100 wpm, did you sound awkward or hesitant? When you read at 220 wpm, did you slur over words or even omit some words?

> ■ Be sure to read the directions and follow precautions before assembling or using your vacuum cleaner. You should not use the cleaner out of doors or on wet surfaces, and you should keep small children away from the vacuum cleaner to prevent injury from moving parts. Remember to turn off cleaner before unplugging, and always unplug the cleaner when it is not in use. A few other precautions are these: Keep hands, feet, and hair away from suction end of hose; change the dust bag frequently; do not vacuum flammables; and keep sharp objects away from the cleaner.
>
> For the [100] best cleaning results, keep the hoses clean and the airflow passage open. As you operate the appliance, push the vacuum [120] cleaner straight away from you and pull straight back toward you. Try to continue across the carpet with smooth and [140] slow motions. There are four other

attachments that may be used for dusting furniture, drapes, and walls. These attachments are [160] the dusting brush, crevice device, fabric brush, and floor brush.

When you need to change the dust bag, first unplug [180] the cord from the electrical outlet, then lift the cannister lid. Carefully pull the bag out of the cannister and [200] throw it away. Unfold a new cannister bag and slide into holder slot. To clean the vacuum cleaner brushes, wash [220] in warm soapy water. Be sure to allow the brushes to dry completely before reinstalling carpet brushes or using the brushes.

■ In the event of an earthquake, you should understand several procedures. If you are at home, go to the safest place in your house. Stay away from heavy furniture, appliances, fireplaces, or windows. Get under a desk or table or stand in a doorway. If you are outside, stay away from buildings and power lines. If you are driving your car, stop your car and stay inside. Do not stop under bridges, trees, signs, or posts. Try to get out of the traffic. After the quake, stay alert for aftershocks. Check [100] for immediate hazards such as fire and broken utility lines. Check chimneys, [120] closets, and cupboards. Examine your food and water supply. Avoid using the telephone. Turn on a portable radio in order [140] to obtain information. Most importantly, do not go sightseeing. Stay where you are until an "all-clear" signal is given. [160] You should take precautions before an earthquake occurs. Keep an adequate food and water supply available. Keep wrenches near gas [180] lines in order to turn off the gas supply. Maintain a fresh supply of batteries. Arrange with family members to [200] meet in a specific place after the quake. Rehearse procedures with your family. Above all, stay calm should you experience [220] an earthquake.

■ What I must do is all that concerns me, not what the people think. This rule, equally arduous in actual and in intellectual life, may serve for the whole distinction between greatness and meanness. It is the harder because you will always find those who think they know what is your duty better than you know it. It is easy in the world to live after the world's opinion; it is easy in solitude to live after our own; but the great man is he who in the midst of the crowd keeps with perfect sweetness the independence of solitude. [100] The objection to conforming to usages that have become dead to you is that it scatters your force. It loses [120] your time and blurs the impression of your character. If you maintain a dead church, contribute to a dead Bible [140] society, vote with a great party either for the government or against it, spread your table like base housekeepers—under [160] all these screens I have difficulty to detect the precise man you are: and of course so much force is [180] withdrawn from your proper life. But do your work, and I shall know you. Do your work, and you shall [200] reinforce yourself. A man must consider what a blindman's-bluff is this game of conformity. If I know your sect, [220] I anticipate your argument.

—Ralph Waldo Emerson, "Self-Reliance"

Exercises: Rate

Exercise 1   With the following passages slow your rate by extending sounds for the underlined words and pause at punctuation marks.
—Simple sentences. Read slowly:

1. <u>You</u> can prevent <u>forest fires</u>.
2. Press the <u>red</u> button.
3. You should <u>walk slowly</u>.
4. Take your <u>time</u> to <u>say</u> these <u>words</u>.
5. He <u>sank back</u> against the <u>pillows</u>.
6. The camera <u>panned</u> the <u>room</u>.
7. Dust <u>gathered</u> in the <u>corners</u>.
8. <u>Clouds float</u> in the <u>sky</u>.
9. <u>Shadows grew</u> along the <u>walls</u>.
10. <u>Stroke</u> the <u>cat</u> softly.

—Simple sentences containing articles, prepositions, and clauses that speed up
delivery. Stress underlined words:

1. She would use the <u>money</u> to <u>pay</u> her bills.
2. The <u>plan</u>, which would mean additional <u>taxes</u>, requires approval by <u>two-
thirds</u> of the <u>voters</u>.
3. A <u>speeding</u> car <u>stopped</u> when it hit a dirt <u>embankment</u>.
4. The <u>rabbit</u> ducked into the <u>hole</u> and out of the path of the <u>fox</u>.
5. The ship's <u>booster</u> rockets were <u>launched</u> after lift-off.
6. The Senate <u>delayed</u> funding that would <u>aid</u> the <u>states</u>.
7. Once I get the hang of it, I will be able to <u>ride</u> this <u>bike</u>.
8. If you will look over the <u>report</u>, we will be able to <u>speak</u> to the <u>issue</u>.
9. <u>Alfredo's,</u> a good place to eat, has the <u>best pasta</u>.
10. When you have passed out the <u>exam</u>, everyone can <u>begin</u>.

—More complex sentences:

1. I <u>earn</u> that I <u>eat</u>, <u>get</u> that I <u>wear</u>, <u>owe</u> no one <u>hate</u>, <u>envy</u> no one's <u>happiness;</u>
<u>glad</u> of other's <u>good</u>, <u>content</u> with my <u>harm</u>.

2. <u>Time</u> is precious, but <u>truth</u> is more precious than <u>time</u>.

3. As the Spanish proverb <u>says</u>, "He who would bring home the <u>wealth</u> of the
<u>Indies</u> must <u>carry</u> the wealth of the Indies with him." So it is in traveling: a man
must carry <u>knowledge</u> with him, if he would bring <u>home</u> knowledge.

4. For <u>precept</u> must be upon <u>precept</u>, precept upon precept; <u>line</u> upon <u>line</u>, line
upon line; <u>here</u> a little, and <u>there</u> a little.

5. We hold these <u>truths</u> to be self-evident,—that <u>all</u> men are created <u>equal;</u> that they are <u>endowed</u> by their Creator with certain <u>unalienable</u> rights; that among these are <u>life</u>, <u>liberty</u>, and the pursuit of <u>happiness</u>.

6. <u>Man</u> passes away; his <u>name</u> perishes from record and recollection; his <u>history</u> is as a <u>tale</u> told, and his very <u>monument</u> becomes a <u>ruin</u>.

7. I do not <u>know</u> what I may <u>appear</u> to the <u>world</u>; but to myself I seem to have been <u>only</u> like a <u>boy</u> playing on the <u>seashore</u>, and diverting myself in now and then finding a <u>smoother pebble</u> or a <u>prettier shell</u> than ordinary, while the great <u>ocean</u> of <u>truth</u> lay all <u>undiscovered</u> before me.

8. <u>Marriage</u>, to <u>women</u> as to <u>men</u>, must be a <u>luxury</u>, not a necessity; an incident of life, not <u>all</u> of it.

9. It is <u>not</u> necessary to finish your sentences in a <u>crowd</u>, but by a sort of mumble, omitting sibilants and dentals.

10. Some women are said to be <u>handsome</u> with<u>out</u> adornment.

11. If we mean to have <u>heroes</u>, <u>statesmen</u>, and <u>philosophers</u>, we should have <u>learned women</u>.

12. Appearances to the <u>mind</u> are of <u>four</u> kinds. Things either <u>are</u> what they appear to be; or they <u>neither</u> are, nor appear to be; or they <u>are</u>, and do not appear to be; or they are <u>not</u>, and yet appear to be.

13. <u>Hatred</u> comes from the <u>heart</u>; <u>contempt</u> from the <u>head</u>; and neither feeling is quite within our <u>control</u>.

14. If a woman be educated for <u>dependence;</u> that is, to act according to the will of another <u>fallible being</u>, and submit, right or <u>wrong</u>, to <u>power</u>, where are we to stop?

15. When you fall into a man's <u>conversation</u>, the first <u>thing</u> you should consider is whether he has a greater inclination to hear <u>you</u> or that <u>you</u> should hear him.

Exercise 2   The following passages have no underlining and no punctuation marks printed. First read through each passage silently in order to determine meaning, then try reading aloud using appropriate rate for emphasis and pauses for timing.
—Simple sentences:

1. He who laughs last laughs hardest

2. I brought a book pencil pen and paper to class

3. When I saw your face I remembered you

4. He has a safe deposit box at the bank in which he keeps his money his jewels and papers

5. In response to the speech the audience clapped

6. Press the button start the pedaling stop if you are tired

7. When in Saginaw Michigan try to keep warm

8. *Eleanor in Her Own Words* is a movie about Eleanor Roosevelt one of the most popular first ladies in history

9. They called him Rags though he was a rich man and they looked up to him

10. She auditioned for the part of Helen of Troy but the role went to another actress

11. The new taxes include a one cent on the dollar sales tax increase on alcohol and sales taxes on such previously untaxed items as snacks candy newspapers and bottled water

12. Rides games prizes and attractions will be provided by ABC Amusements at the county fair next week

13. This is what Ronald Reagan called volunteerism what George Bush called one thousand points of light and what Mother Teresa called light one candle

14. He had an aquiline nose his eyes were light in color his complexion was ruddy his hair was blond but when he turned thirty his hair turned white

15. Teens who overeat refuse to eat or hide what they eat are endangering their health

16. The price at the resort includes 18 holes of golf a golf cart bucket of range balls tennis breakfast and a double king room

17. An estimated two million to four million Americans have Alzheimer's which causes its elderly victims to become progressively more forgetful undergo personality changes and eventually lose control of their bodies

18. A baby girl was born to Jane Doe 30 at 10 am Monday at Central District Hospital said hospital spokesman Bill Smith

19. Even though the pickings are slim what is left may be more interesting than you previously thought

20. Dams such as Glen Canyon Dam in Arizona may be the subject of disputes in the current crisis

—More complex sentences:

1. A tool is but the extension of a man's hand and a machine is but a complex tool and he that invents a machine augments the power of a man and the well-being of humankind

2. I am a Jew hath not a Jew eyes hath not a Jew hands organs dimensions senses affections passions fed with the same food hurt with the same weapons subject to the same diseases healed by the same means warmed and cooled by the same winter and summer as a Christian is

3. When you know a thing to hold that you know it and when you do not know a thing to allow that you do not know it this is knowledge

4. Then I began to think it it is very true which is commonly said that one-half of the world knows not how the other half lives

5. Language is not an abstract construction of the learned or of dictionary makers but is something arising out of the work needs ties joys affections tastes of long generations of humanity and has its bases broad and low close to the ground

6. A girl should not expect special privileges because of her sex but neither should she adjust to prejudice and discrimination she must learn to compete not as a woman but as a human being

7. There is but one law for all namely that law which governs all law the law of our Creator the law of humanity justice equity the law of nature and of nations

8. Liberalism is trust of the people tempered by prudence conservatism distrust of the people tempered by fear

9. Give me the liberty to know to think to believe and to utter freely according to conscience above all other liberties

10. I never did or countenanced in public life a single act inconsistent with the strictest good faith having never believed there was one code of morality for a public and another for a private man

11. To improve the golden moment of opportunity and catch the good that is within our reach is the great art of life

12. It must be a peace the very principle of which is equality and a common participation in a common benefit

13. There is a homely old adage that runs speak softly and carry a big stick you will go far if the American nation will speak softly and yet build and keep at a pitch of the highest training a thoroughly efficient navy the Monroe Doctrine will go far

14. Give us the strength to encounter that which is to come that we may be brave in peril constant in tribulation temperate in wrath and in all changes of fortune and down to the gates of death loyal and loving one another

15. Freedom of conscience of education of speech of assembly are among the very fundamentals of democracy and all of them would be nullified should freedom of the press ever be successfully challenged

Exercise 3   The following passage is excerpted from Abraham Lincoln's second inaugural address. These are the first and last paragraphs with *no* punctuation. (A punctuated version can be found at the end of this chapter.) Try reading the passage, giving it the appropriate vocal punctuation.

Fellow countrymen at this second appearing to take the oath of the presidential office there is less occasion for an extended address than there was at the first then a statement somewhat in detail of a course to be pursued seemed fitting and proper now at the expiration of four years during which public declarations have been constantly called forth on every point and phase of the great contest which still absorbs the attention and engrosses the energies of the nation little that is new could be presented the progress of our arms upon which all else chiefly depends is as well known to the public as to myself and it is I trust reasonably satisfactory and encouraging to all with high hope for the future no prediction in regard to it is ventured

With malice toward none with charity for all with firmness in the right as God gives us to see the right let us strive on to finish the work we are in to bind up the nation's wounds to care for him who shall have borne the battle and for his widow and his orphan to do all which may achieve and cherish a just and lasting peace among ourselves and with all nations.[5]

Exercise 4   The following excerpts are structurally difficult, but they do contain punctuation marks. Try using appropriately placed pauses to convey meaning.

1. So my travels begin. (My travels—not yours. Yours would be written, I think, in a different language—something more razor-edged, aggressive, ignited into full blaze. Mine will be written in gray ink on the cheap paper of a school tablet, an Indian chief on the brickred cover: more tedious and tortured, left-handed, a school boy's broken wrist, the second-grade teacher scolding, "For heaven's sake, Charlie, hurry up—get it said—everyone else has finished—," while I'm struggling to overcome misshapen, almost illegible words; a wretched prose style; a limited vocabulary.) And Margaret, my sister, has spent her S&H Green Stamps to purchase this red-plaid canvas luggage for me. My brother-in-law has given me a five-dollar bill to speed me on the way.

      —Winston Weathers, "Now, Voyager"

2. His father, it appeared, had come down on him for having, after so long, nothing to show, and hoped that on his next return this deficiency would be repaired. The thing, the Master complacently set forth was—for any artist, however inferior to himself—at least to "do" something. "What can you do? That's all I ask!" *He* had certainly done enough, and there was no mistake about what he had to show.

      —Henry James, "The Tree of Knowledge"

3. "What should we drink?" the girl asked. She had taken off her hat and put it on the table.

      "It's pretty hot:" the man said.

      "Dos cervezas," the man said into the curtain.

      "Big ones?" a woman asked from the doorway.

      "Yes. Two big ones."

      The woman brought two glasses of beer and two felt pads. She put the felt pads and the beer glasses on the table and looked at the man and the girl. The girl was looking off at the line of hills. They were white in the sun and the country was brown and dry.

"They look like white elephants," she said.

"I've never seen one," the man drank his beer.

"No, you wouldn't have."

"I might have," the man said. "Just because you say I wouldn't have doesn't prove anything."

—Ernest Hemingway, "Hills like White Elephants"

4. When you walk up Third Avenue toward the IRT, do it quickly. You will have a full bag. People will seem to know what you have done, where you are going. They will have his eyes, the same pair, passed along on the street from face to face, like secrets, like glasses at the opera.

This is what you are.

Rushing downstairs into the steamy burn of the subway.

Unable to look a panhandler in the pan.

—Lorrie Moore, *Self-Help*

5. From time to time the telephone rings in the Professor's study, and the big folk run across, knowing it is their affair. Many people had to give up their telephones the last time the price rose, but so far the Corneliuses have been able to keep theirs, just as they have kept their villa, which was built before the war, by dint of the salary Cornelius draws as a professor of history—a mission marks, and more or less adequate to the chances and changes of post-war life. The house is comfortable, even elegant, though sadly in need of repairs that cannot be made for lack of materials, and at present disfigured by iron stoves with long pipes.

—Thomas Mann, "Disorder and Early Sorrow"

6. Drusilla . . . and I would walk in the garden in the summer twilight while we waited for Father to ride in from the railroad. I was twenty then: that summer before I entered the University to take the law degree which Father decided I should have and four years after the one, the day, the evening when Father and Drusilla had kept old Cash Benbow from becoming United States Marshal and returned home still unmarried and Mrs. Habersham herded them into her carriage and drove them back to town and dug her husband out of his little dim hole in the new bank and made him sign Father's peace bond for killing the two carpet baggers, and took Father and Drusilla to the minister herself and saw that they were married.

—William Faulkner, "An Odor of Verbena"

7. Mrs. d'Amboise, who like all women of quality chewed her gum with her front teeth and rarely popped it within earshot of people with known academic degrees or season subscription boxes to the Opera, was a sculptress who had seen me play a lounge lizard in a high school dramatic production and decided, from some of the supine postures I affected on parlor sofas throughout the course of the action, that I was ideally suited to pose for a major work on which she was about to embark: a piece depicting the drowned Shelley as found washed up on the shore of the Gulf of Spezia.

—Peter DeVries, *Consenting Adults or The Duchess Will Be Furious*

Exercise 5   Read aloud the following material. Read for meaning. Try using rate variety to make the material more vibrant.

1. I will be telling you more about a club I belong to than about me when I say that, as a lawyer, I'm apt to be looked down on by the other members. Artist members of the club are particularly skeptical of giving us lawyers the run of the place, but they're by no means alone in their prejudice—even the architects appear to consider themselves better than we are, though it beats me how a follower of that dog-eat-dog profession could possibly stick up his nose at anyone outside it. Such distinction as we lawyers may have acquired in the world is beside the point in the Parnassus; there we are simply people who are not "creative," whatever that anomalous word may mean, and our supposed uncreativeness makes us the butt of innumerable not very witty jokes.

—Brendan Gill, "Something You Just Don't Do in a Club"

2. Thomas withdrew to the side of the window and with his head between the wall and the curtain he looked down on the driveway where the car had stopped. His mother and the little slut were getting out of it. His mother emerged slowly, stolid and awkward, and then the little slut's long slightly bowed legs slid out, the dress pulled above the knees. With a shriek of laughter she ran to meet the dog, who bounded, overjoyed, shaking with pleasure, to welcome her. Rage gathered throughout Thomas's large frame with a silent ominous intensity, like a mob assembling.

—Flannery O'Connor, "The Comforts of Home"

3. Sir, you have published a review of my story, *The Picture of Dorian Gray.* As this review is grossly unjust to me as an artist, I ask you to allow me to exercise in your columns my right of reply.

Your reviewer, sir, while admitting that the story in question is "plainly the work of a man of letters," the work of one who has "brains, and art, and style," yet suggests, and apparently in all seriousness, that I have written it in order that it should be read by the most depraved members of the criminal and illiterate classes. Now, sir, I do not suppose that the criminal and illiterate classes ever read anything except newspapers. They are certainly not likely to be able to understand anything of mine.

—Oscar Wilde (letter)

4. If she answered, he could not hear it, and he certainly couldn't see her, so he went. First he crawled the rocks one by one, one by one, till his hands touched shore and the nursing sound of the sea was behind him. He felt around, crawled off and then stood up. Breathing heavily with his mouth open he took a few tentative steps. The pebbles made him stumble and so did the roots of trees. He threw out his hands to guide and steady his going. By and by he walked steadier, now steadier. The mist lifted and the trees stepped back a bit as if to make the way easier for a certain kind of man. Then he ran. Lickety-split. Lickety-split. Looking neither to the left nor to the right. Lickety-split. Lickety-split. Lickety-lickety-lickety split.

—Toni Morrison, *Tar Baby*

5. Nobody had answered its cry, in all the world nobody had been moved. The mountains yet remained immobile, even the little earthslides seemed to be reabsorbed; the sky was clear, and without the slightest trace of a cloud; the sun was westering. Nothing, neither brute nor spirit, had hastened to avenge the slaughter. It had been man who wiped out that last, residual stain on the earth; it had been man, the astute and powerful, who everywhere establishes wise laws to maintain order, man the blameless who exhausts himself for progress, and may not concede the survival of any dragon.

—Dino Buzzati, "The Killing of the Dragon"

6. My Father seemed always on horseback, I know this was not So. And yet, how many evenings did we wait at the lower gate, in our pinafores, little hearts thumping wildly, to see him coming in the distance, up the long hill? First a speck we saw, and then the rising dust, and then at length, his gallant Form. When he saw us there, his girls, he would set spur to flank and gallop wildly that last stretch between the glowering pines; "Hi, Jennie!" he'd cry to his spotted horse; he knew we loved it So.

—Lee Smith, *Family Linen*

7. There was silence, broken only by the slow scratching of Novak's pen. Stais thought of the thin, dark mountain faces of the men he had last seen, fading away, waving, standing in the scrub and short silver grass of the hill pasture near the Aegean Sea. They had been cheerful and anxious to please, and there was a look on their faces that made you feel they expected to die.

—Irwin Shaw, "Gunner's Passage"

8. An old lady, in a high drawing-room, had had her chair moved close to the fire, where she sat knitting and warming her knees. She was dressed in deep mourning; her face had a faded nobleness, tempered, however, by the somewhat iliberal compression assumed by her lips in obedience to something that was passing in her mind. She was far from the lamp, but though her eyes were fixed upon her active needles she was not looking at them.... The old lady sat motionless save for the regularity of her clicking needles, which seemed as personal to her and as expressive as prolonged fingers. If she was thinking something out, she was thinking it thoroughly.

—Henry James, *The Chaperon*

9. It is a sin to write this. It is a sin to think words no others think and to put them down upon a paper no others are to see. It is base and evil. It is as if we were speaking alone to no ears but our own. And we know well that there is no transgression blacker than to do or think alone. We have broken the laws. The laws say that men may not write unless the Council of Vocations bid them so. May we be forgiven!

—Ayn Rand, *Anthem*

10. During that burning day when we were crossing Iowa, our talk kept returning to a central figure, a Bohemian girl whom we had known long ago and whom both of us admired.

More than any other person we remembered, this girl seemed to mean to us the country, the conditions, the whole adventure of our childhood. To speak her name was to call up pictures of people and places, to set a quiet drama going in one's brain. I had lost sight of her altogether, but Jim had found her again after long years, had renewed a friendship that meant a great deal to him, and out of his busy life had set apart time enough to enjoy that friendship. His mind was full of her that day. He made me see her again, feel her presence, revived all my old affection for her.

—Willa Cather, *My Antonia*

Chapter Six Review

Review the following concepts:

- Terms: rate, duration, pause, syllabic stress, speech phrasing
- Speaking and reading rates
- Rate assessment exercise
- Uses of the pause
- Speech phrasing and its relation to grammar, physicality, meaning, and emotions

Respond to the following:

1. Explain how rate of speech can pinpoint your geographic residence or your mood.
2. What is the role of the vocal pause in interpersonal situations?
3. How can you assess your own rate of speech?
4. Explain how you can slow your rate of speech in a public speaking situation.

APPLICATION

1. How does your rate of speech indicate your mood or attitude?

2. How is your own speech rate or duration indicative of your regional origins?

3. How do you use the *ums*? In personal conversations? In public?

4. Do you speak too rapidly? *Tip:* Extend vowel sounds, and insert longer pauses where appropriate.

5. Using this sentence as an example, vocally indicate which words you would stress or "set off" with pauses or sound elongation and which you would gather into shorter quicker phrases.

FOCUS MESSAGE

1. *ESL:* For you, the more important concept to keep in mind is that of speech rhythms. Concentrate on drawing out nouns and verbs. However, make sure to include articles *a, an, the;* just say these more quickly. Also concentrate on pausing in ways appropriate to English, instead of the rhythms of your primary language.

2. *Acting:* Speech rhythms can be a challenge to the actor for they can both define character and genre. The rates and rhythms of delivery can suggest the personality of a character. Shakespearean or poetic rhythms (what are called *metrical rhythms*) can be tricky. You should learn the process of scansion or reading the poetic line for its rhythmical patterns. You can better define your character's dialect by using the rhythms of that character's primary language. For example, Spanish speakers have a regular rhythm. East Indian is more stilted.

3. *Broadcasting:* Different broadcasting styles and mediums demand varying rates of delivery. Increased rates for urgent or upbeat messages will require clear articulation. Studying "on air" models, such as popular broadcasters or broadcasting styles, can be helpful, but often you must judge appropriate rates of delivery yourself. Further, time limits may be a factor for you when you are up against the clock. Always remember that variety can be your best tool.

EVALUATION

SEE PAGES 271–272, where you'll an evaluation form for this chapter. Follow your instructor's directions.

NOTES

1. Klaus R. Scherer and Howard Giles, *Social Markers in Speech* (Cambridge, Eng.: Cambridge University Press, 1979), pp. 145–152.
2. Murray J. Munro and Tracey M. Derwing, "The Effects of Speaking Rate on Listener Evaluations of Native and Foreign-accented Speech." *Language Learning,* (June 1998), pp. 159–182.
3. Pico Iyer, "In Praise of the Humble Comma." *Time,* (June 13), 1988, p. 80.
4. Carole Douglas, "The Beat Goes On." *Psychology Today* (November, 1987), p. 39.
5. The following is the punctuated version of Lincoln's speech:

> Fellow Countrymen: At this second appearing to take the oath of the presidential office, there is less occasion for an extended address than there was at the first. Then a statement, somewhat in detail, of a course to be pursued, seemed fitting and proper. Now, at the expiration of four years, during which public declarations have been constantly called forth on every point and phase of the great contest which still absorbs the attention and engrosses the energies of the nation, little that is new could be presented. The progress of our arms, upon which all else chiefly depends, is as well known to the public as to myself; and it is, I trust, reasonably satisfactory and encouraging to all. With high hope for the future, no prediction in regard to it is ventured.
>
> With malice toward none; with charity for all; with firmness in the right, as God gives us to see the right, let us strive on to finish the work we are in; to bind up the nation's wounds; to care for him who shall have borne the battle, and for his widow and his orphan—to do all which may achieve and cherish a just and lasting peace among ourselves, and with all nations.

CHAPTER

7 Quality

He had a super voice. Have you ever noticed how important a person's voice is?
—Marilyn Duckworth

TERMS

Quality/timbre ['kwɑlətɪ 'tæmbɚ] That characteristic of vocal sound determined by resonance. Several vocal qualities will be discussed and defined in this chapter, including: **nasality** [neɪ'zælətɪ], **denasality** [dineɪ'zælətɪ], **breathiness** ['brɛθɪnəs], **gutturality** [gətə'rælətɪ], **stridency** ['strɑɪdənsɪ], **thinness** ['θɪnəs], **hoarseness** ['hɔrsnəs], **harshness** ['hɑrʃnəs], and **raspiness** ['ræspɪnəs].

Shakespeare's Sonnet 130 gently chides a lover for the sound of her voice in saying "music hath a far more pleasing sound." Consider the sound of your own voice. You are known by and you know others by distinguishing vocal characteristics known as *quality*. There may be times when you cannot see a speaker but are nevertheless able to identify the voice. *Quality* is the distinctive timbre or sound of a voice produced by resonance. We may be drawn to certain types of vocal qualities and repelled by others. Some voices we may find intriguing or attractive because of a particular quality; other voices we may endure because the personality behind it is attractive. Self-image and personality are entwined with the sound of one's voice.

Think for a minute about the vocal qualities of your relatives and friends. When one of them calls you on the phone, you know who it is even without a name. That is because of the distinctive quality of each individual's voice. Now think of the vocal qualities of other public personalities you have heard. Listen to the voices around you this minute. Each voice is unique. A sound spectrograph can identify the individuality of voice characteristics, measuring frequency and duration, but its social uses over the last couple of decades have produced controversy.

The quality of your voice is determined by *anatomy, enculturation,* and general vocal *usage.* For instance, the size and shape of your vocal mechanism will in part determine its timbre or quality. Long, thick vocal folds will produce a lower pitch level than short, thin vocal folds. A larger oral cavity can provide highly resonate tones. Adenoids or a deviated septum can produce unpleasantly "stuffy" sounds. Additionally, if you were raised in or live in a dialectically specific area such as New York, Chicago, or Little Rock, your voice may have taken on some of the vocal qualities of nasality or "twang" frequently heard in those locales. Then, if you consistently engage in certain activities, such as excessive shouting, smoking, or drinking, your voice may acquire a hoarse or husky quality.

The three factors addressed in previous chapters—pitch, rate, and loudness contribute to the perceived quality of your voice. For example, if your pitch level is extremely high, your voice may sound strident or strained. If your rate is exceptionally fast, your voice may sound disjointed. If your voice is inadequately supported, you may be perceived as breathy.

Paralinguistics

The quality of voice you use in a given situation can inform listeners beyond the linguistic message you are sending. Its tone can even indicate a particular role in life. Think of the tone or quality of voice used by a news commentator, a teacher, a preacher, a lawyer, a disc jockey, or an auctioneer. A firefighter, in discussing his department's change of dispatchers, commented that the new dispatcher was poor because of the "tone of voice" used. In speaking withing the context of one's role, a person may assume the tone of voice generally thought to be characteristic of that role.

> Try saying the following sentence:
>
> > "Please don't do that again!"
>
> as if you are
>
> - a parent speaking to a three-year-old child.
> - a teacher speaking to a student.
> - a lawyer speaking to a client.
> - a boss speaking to an employee.
>
> Did the tone or timbre of your voice change as you assumed a different role? How would you describe those changes?

Mood or attitude is primarily conveyed by your vocal tone or quality. While subjectively perceived, there are voice attributes that characterize emotional and psychological states. For example, anger is often expressed in harsh tones. Per-

To demonstrate, try this exercise. Deliver the following message:

> On Friday, October 10th, you should travel south on Route 5. Turn left on Park Avenue. Go two blocks. Turn right on First Street. Continue uphill until you reach the entrance to the campus. It will be on your left.

as if you are

- delivering an urgent news broadcast.
- attracting a desirable partner.
- a patient kindergarten teacher explaining danger to a five-year-old child.
- angry with your partner.

ceived sensuality is frequently conveyed in low, breathy qualities. In order to suggest a particular role or mood, you no doubt had to alter the quality of your voice. Conversely in so doing, the listener heard more than the simple message you delivered. That paralinguistic message may have been one of authority and power or kindliness and affection.

Certain qualities of voice are often characteristic of one's geographic location or cultural origins. For example, because of the excessive nasality employed by many persons in some eastern regions of the United States, it is easy to identify the origins of those particular people. Persons who speak with a southern "twang" sound to one another like "good ol' boys," or one of the crowd. But, like it or not, these dialects may also be associated with stereotypes. Whereas a regional identity may be considered a charming and colorful feature of a language as a whole, in the media world or business world a more homogenized dialect is desirable. One would not wear blue jeans and a T-shirt to work on Wall Street. Why not wear your best speech to the business world? It may be desirable to maintain your regional flavor in order to use it where appropriate, but you should have the ability to be "bi-dialectal," that is, to use General American English when in places that might suggest its use. General American English is that sound you most often hear on national television. It is the dialect that most people in the United States use. Its cultivation is particularly important to the student of international business. When foreigners learn English, they generally learn General American English; they don't learn the nuances of regional dialects. Thus, in order to be better understood on the international scene, you should avoid the "laid back" California sound or the "Beverly Hillbilly's" twang.

Extralinguistics

The quality of your voice also conveys to a listener information about your state of health. An excessively *denasal voice* (one lacking appropriate nasality) may indicate a cold or adenoids (an enlarged mass of lymphoid tissue in the upper pharynx). A harsh or husky voice may point toward pharyngeal congestion or inflammation. Vocal nodes or nodules can produce excessive raspiness. Since your voice reveals temporary ill health, any prolonged or unusual characteristic indicates that you should consult a physician.

Exercises: Vocal Qualities

Voice impersonation is a popular form of entertainment. The impersonator utilizes certain vocal factors in order to achieve a sound alike voice. Whereas you may think an impersonator sounds just like the famous personality, the sound will not be an exact duplicate. That is because vocal quality is individual and subjective.

As you work on your own vocal quality, you may have a model in mind, someone after whom you would like to shape your voice. You may never quite reach that goal simply because of anatomical differences. Given your own vocal structure and abilities, however, you can work toward an improved quality of sound—one that is relaxed and open throated, well sustained by adequate breath support, and mid-mouth resonated.

Ironically, good vocal quality may be better understood if we examine several types of generally undesirable vocal qualities. Whereas these may be considered to be undesirable in most situations, in the entertainment world, these qualities may be a performer's trademark. Your instructor should be able to identify current popular personalities whose voices fall into the categories to be described.

Excessive Nasality

In speaking General American English, we nasally resonate only three sounds: [m] as in *come*, [n] as in *run*, and [ŋ] as in *sing*. When many more than these sounds are resonated through the nose, the result is an excessively nasal voice.

As explained in Chapter Two, the velum acts as a "switch" between the oral and nasal cavities. With excessive nasality your velum is not closing off the passage

One way to determine your degree of nasal resonance is to perform the following exercise. Pinch your nostrils together and read aloud this simple passage:

> "Life is too short to waste," said the philosopher. "You should catch the hour, seize the day. Today is the first day of the rest of your life."

This passage contains no nasal sounds. Now read it again without pinching your nostrils. The two versions should sound the same because there are no nasal sounds present in the passage. If in reading it, you sound "stuffed up," you are using too much nasal resonance.

of vibrated sound to the nose. You therefore need to work toward building control. This can be remedied using the following exercise.

Exercise 1   Observe yourself in a mirror as you yawn. Now, force the velum to raise without yawning. Try this several times until you can perform the lift easily. Now repeat the same passage with your nostrils pinched together. As you do so, concentrate on bringing the sound forward in your oral cavity. Once you can recite the passage without a stuffy sound, release your nostrils and recite it again. Using the same process, try the passages that follow until you are able to read without any nasal resonance. These sentences and passages contain no nasal sounds.

1. I thought I could do it.

2. High-school days are over.

3. He that dies pays all debts.

4. Every dog will have his day.

5. Eat to please yourself, but dress to please others.

6. Bread is the staff of life. Faith is the force of life.

7. Of two evils choose the least.

8. It is easy to flatter; it is harder to praise.

9. Look before you leap; see before you go.

10. The safety of the state is the highest law.

11. She is his sister.

12. Take the street to your right.

13. I have a bad headache.

14. Will you look at this?

15. It is a good cause to celebrate.

16. The idea is to choose the best.

17. Years ago the hoola hoop was a fad.

18. Her eyes are blue.

19. He drove the Hollywood Freeway every day.

20. Broadway, the Great White Way, is the place for theater.

21. Crab apples are good with turkey.

22. As far as that goes, I will agree with you.

23. It is a lovely place to eat.

24. Friday or Saturday are good days to play golf.

25. Ask if there is art at that gallery.

26. It is good to see a doctor if you are sick.

27. You should develop a way to teach that step.

28. Is that all there is?

29. Hail Caesar, those who are about to die salute thee.

30. Cast away your fear of failure; strive for positive results as you work toward a clearer voice.

Exercise 2   What follows are several simple little paragraphs that contain no nasal sounds. Try pinching your nostrils together and reading the passages until you can do so without the stuffy sound. Again, you will do better if you work to bring the sound forward in your mouth.

1. Through the woods, beside the river lived a beautiful, youthful girl called Ruby Twoshoes. She was called that because she had acquired two shoes that were colored a scarlet red. At break of day she would rise to go to the village to buy bread, eggs, or cereal for her breakfast. All the villagers liked to see her pass by with her bright red shoes. They would cry out, "Hey, Ruby, click your heels together!" They had thought of *The Wizard of Oz.* The day Ruby actually tried to click her heels together was the day she lost her shoes. There is a precept here: If crowd rule prevails, you could lose your shoes.

2. These are a few outdoor, beach fire safety rules you should follow. Fire pits are provided for your lit fires. Keep lit fires checked. Water should be close by. Be sure to put out fires totally. Cover with lots of dirt. If possible, tell a lifeguard or firefighter that your beach stay is over; the fire is out. You should be happy with your stay at the beach or park, but be respectful of others, cautious of fires.

Denasality

A lack of adequate nasal resonance will make you sound as if your nasal passages are blocked. The cause may be an actual physical ailment such as enlarged adenoids or a deviated septum (a crooked nose bone and cartilage). Both of these ailments block the passage of air through the nose. Instead of saying "come," "run," or "sing," you might say "cub," "rud" or "sig." Following surgery to correct the problem, a speaker may need to retrain for nasal resonance. In many cases this will require the aid of a speech therapist. If you have a degree of denasality not attributable to a physical problem, you can work toward correcting it.

Exercise 1   Being careful to avoid assimilating sounds other than [m], [n], or [ŋ] through the nasal cavities, work with the following passages that contain many nasal sounds.

1. She was made a member of the Women's Hall of Fame.

2. Channel Nine news isn't on anymore.

3. A Senate Committee met in Washington.

4. One more moment and I'll move.

5. Seven months ago I began making plans.

6. If anything goes wrong, let me know.

7. Musical instruments are my business.

8. Don't say I can't, say I can.

9. Mars is not a planet of little green men.

10. Mark danced around the middle of the room.

11. Changing partners is the name of the game.

12. My mother made me eat when I wasn't hungry.

13. Karen's aim might miss the mark.

14. That old gang of mine is coming over tonight.

15. He means that most men enjoy running.

16. Swimming in the ocean can be dangerous.

17. Millicent won ten thousand dollars on a game show.

18. An ignition starts the engine.

19. England, Ireland, and Scotland are different countries.

20. The evening janitor cleans the rooms.

Poems and prose

1. In men whom men condemn as ill
   I find so much of goodness still,
   In men whom men pronounce divine
   I find so much of sin and blot
   I do not dare to draw a line
   Between the two, where God has not.

   —J. Miller

2. More pernicious nonsense was never devised by man than treaties of commerce.
   —Benjamin Disraeli

3. Conceited men often seem a harmless kind of men, who, by an overweening self-respect, relieve others from the duty of respecting them at all.
   —Harriet Beecher Stowe

4. Speech is civilization itself. The word, even the most contradictory word, preserves contact—it is silence which isolates.

—Thomas Mann

5. Reading makes a full man, conference a ready man, and writing an exact man.

—Francis Bacon

Breathiness

As discussed in Chapter Two, breath control is vital to achieving a clear, strong voice. Review the exercises delineating breath support and control in that chapter. Additionally the physical production of some sounds permits the escape of more air than that of other sounds. Plosives and fricatives (see Chapter Ten) are particularly vulnerable. These include [b], [p], [hw], [f], [v], [θ], [ð], [s], [z], [ʃ], and [h]. A few simple exercises to ascertain your degree of air emission follow.

Exercise 1   On a single inhalation count aloud for 30 seconds, one count per second. You should be able to reach 30 without strain. Repeat the process holding a thin sheet or strip of paper within 2 inches of your lips. As you speak try to bend the paper. You will probably not reach a count of 30. Repeat the procedure and reduce air emission. Try to avoid moving the paper at all.

Exercise 2   Once you have achieved the feel of using less air to produce sound, read the following passages, working toward reducing breathiness. These sentences and passages contain many fricatives and plosives which might utilize excess air in production.

1. Be kind to our feathered friends.

2. Thoroughly satisfied with his job, he stopped.

3. Ships pass through the harbor every day.

4. You should first have everyone finish the puzzle.

5. Should you find that I could help, then phone me.

6. Here's to the ladies who lunch!

7. I happen to be more fortunate than he is.

8. The king ordered pepper steak and fish.

9. The particleboard sits against the fence.

10. Gold fell on the stock exchange.

11. The vacation package should encourage travel.

12. He ordered a hamburger and fries.

13. Three soldiers are facing court-martial.

14. The movie was a high-voltage thriller.

15. We give thumbs up to a thousand volunteers.

16. Children and parents alike should be careful while driving.

17. She was talking on the phone for hours.

18. I hope to hand you a check this week.

19. We may soon reach a decision on that plan.

20. The chief of staff found the information leak.

Poems and prose

1. A picket frozen on duty—
   A mother starved for her brood—
   Socrates drinking the hemlock,
     And Jesus on the rood;
   And millions who, humble and nameless,
     The straight, hard pathway trod—
   Some call it consecration,
     And others call it God.

   —W. H. Carruth

2.   See! the mountains kiss high heaven,
     And the waves clasp one another;
       No sister flower would be forgiven
     If it disdained its brother;
     And the sunlight clasps the earth,
     And the moonbeams kiss the sea;—
       What are all these kissings worth,
     If thou kiss not me?

   —Percy Bysshe Shelley

3. When it shall be said in any country in the world "my poor are happy; neither ignorance nor distress is to be found among them; my jails are empty of prisoners, my streets of beggars; the aged are not in want, the taxes are not oppressive . . . —when these things can be said, then may that country boast of its constitution and its government.

   —Thomas Paine

4. The secret of happiness is this: let your interests be as wide as possible, and let your reactions to the things and persons that interest you be as far as possible friendly rather than hostile.

   —Bertrand Russell

5. When in the course of human events, it becomes necessary for one people to dissolve the political bonds which have connected them with another, and to

assume among the powers of the earth the separate and equal station to which the laws of nature and of nature's God entitle them, a decent respect to the opinions of mankind requires that they should declare the causes which impel them to the separation.

—Declaration of Independence

Guttural Quality

A voice that is throaty or guttural is one for which the resonance focal point is far in the rear of the mouth. Though this quality may be characteristic of some spoken languages, such as German, it should be avoided for General American English. As will be explained further in the second half of this book, some English sounds are produced toward the front of the mouth and others toward the rear of the mouth. By exercising with frontally produced sounds you can achieve a better feel for a less guttural voice.

Exercise 1   Try bringing sounds forward with the following passages, which contain many frontally produced sounds.

1. Each and every eatery is exactly the same.
2. Whistle while you while away your time.
3. It dims the senses to see the sense of it.
4. If it will speak, then listen to it.
5. It matters a great deal that we see the light.
6. Be mature and don't display your temper.
7. Make a decision on marriage.
8. It is a bad day for investments.
9. Information is gathered at its point of origin.
10. The jewelry selection is wide at this store.
11. Today is probably Saturday.
12. Touch the baby gently.
13. Put thirty pounds of air in that tire.
14. The leaves on the trees are green in May.
15. Set several places on the table.
16. That is your street address.
17. She has driven less than I have.
18. Tell him I'll be there.

19. We rehearsed the play today.

20. It's sitting on thin ice.

21. We built a fence on the property line.

22. Please sweep the steps.

23. Private eyes are watching you.

24. I believe I've seen him.

25. Life is a beach!

Exercise 2   Once you achieve a more frontally produced sound, try carrying over that feeling with passages that combine sounds.

1. A little more than kin, and less than kind.

—William Shakespeare

2. Give me a kisse, and to that kisse a score;
Then to that twenty, adde a hundred more;
To make that thousand up a million;
Treble that million, and when that is done,
Let's kisse afresh, as when we first begun.

—Robert Herrick

3. Bowed by the weight of centuries he leans
Upon his hoe and gazes on the ground,
The emptiness of ages in his face,
And on his back the burden of the world.

—Edwin Markham

4. There is but one law for all; namely that law which governs all law,—the law of our Creator, the law of humanity, justice, equity; the law of nature and of nations.

—Edmund Burke

5. What a piece of work is a man! How noble in reason! How infinite in faculty! In form and moving how express and admirable! In action how like an angel! In apprehension how like a god! The beauty of the world! The paragon of animals. And, yet, to me, what is this quintessence of dust?

—William Shakespeare

Stridency

A high-pitched, tinny voice is called *strident*. It is characterized by a too-high pitch level and inadequate breath modulation. This type of voice tends to be grating or irritating. To correct this quality, you should review exercises on optimum pitch levels (Chapter Four) and breath control (Chapter Two). Sentences that contain many sounds produced low in the oral cavity should aid you in working toward a lower pitched, fuller sound.

Exercise 1 In drilling with these sentences, be sure that your mouth is open and your lips are rounded.

1. Monica is going to church.
2. Knock on locked doors.
3. It was shocking cargo.
4. Go back to the loft.
5. The urgent news came on the radio.
6. Go home on Monday.
7. Those are close quarters.
8. We shoot at dawn.
9. There was a long pause.
10. Clothes make the man.
11. You know something they don't.
12. It's an ongoing production.
13. You can manage without that.
14. You caught cold.
15. Call at odd hours.
16. Take a ball to the park.
17. Walk away from conflict.
18. Those are contrasting colors.
19. He belongs to the racquet club.
20. Take the law into your own hands.

Thinness

A voice identified as *thin* is one that lacks adequate support and resonation. A thin voice seems to be pitched higher than most voices. It may characterize its user as weak or childlike. A popular actress once said that she was never given serious acting roles because her voice never grew up! Review exercises on breath support and resonance (see Chapter Two, p. 33). Practice with the sentences that follow, which contain rounded sounds.

Exercise 1   As with the previous list, work with an open mouth and rounded lips.

1. Write for more information.
2. That's a good location.
3. Our boys are all over the store.
4. Shoulder the burden for a time.
5. You'll want to watch the race.
6. How much do they cost?
7. You don't know me.
8. They drank coffee and ate rolls.
9. Do you know how to argue?
10. I could have told you so.
11. I've got to keep watching.
12. You're a rogue and a wanderer.
13. Tall ships abound in the harbor.
14. His trousers are in hushed tones.
15. I've clawed my way to the top.
16. More important is the whole report.
17. Fashion can be a compulsion.
18. He wore the uniform.
19. Home is our office.
20. The coat is soaked.

Hoarseness, Harshness, Raspiness

These vocal qualities may indicate a physical ailment such as excessive phlegm or dryness common to illness. One television actress was reported to spend time before each performance screaming as loudly as possible to achieve the raspy quality of voice she had ascribed to the character she played.[1] One might speculate what could eventually happen to this actress's voice. One collegiate basketball coach reportedly felt "useless" with a severe case of laryngitis. This coach is apparently famous for his courtside yelling. It is possible that this man may have to undergo further medical treatment, perhaps even surgery someday. Any person who experiences a chronic condition of this nature should first consult a physician. Barring any physical condition producing these qualities, you may undertake to improve your vocal quality by employing greater breath support and fuller resonance.

Exercise 1   For any of the three previously mentioned qualities, use the following passages in working toward a clearer quality of voice.

Poems and prose

1. Sleep, rest of nature, O sleep, most gentle of the divinities, peace the soul, thou at whose presence care disappears, who soothest hearts wearied with daily employments, and makest them strong again for labour!

—Ovid

2. Out of the night that covers me,
       Black as the pit from pole to pole,
   I thank whatever gods may be
       For my unconquerable soul.

—William Ernest Henley

3. A vessel is known by the sound, whether it be cracked or not; so men are proved, by their speech, whether they be wise or foolish.

—Demosthenes

4. As the Spanish proverb says, "He who would bring home the wealth of the Indies must carry the wealth of the Indies with him." So it is in travelling; a man must carry knowledge with him, if he would bring home knowledge.

—Samuel Johnson

5. In Nature every moment is new; the past is always swallowed and forgotten; the coming only is sacred. Nothing is secure but life, transition, the energizing spirit. No love can be found by oath or covenant to secure it against a higher love. No truth so sublime but it may be trivial tomorrow in the light of new thoughts. People wish to be settled; only as far as they are unsettled is there any hope for them. Life is a series of surprises.

—Ralph Waldo Emerson

Exercise 2   Additional material follows for practice in building a well-supported, well-resonated, and clear sound for your voice.

News releases

1. One official describes it as being like "a horror movie or something." What he is talking about is the annual invasion of east Texas by thousands and thousands of creeping crawfish. They swarm at night, crawl into offices, ruin farmlands, and build clay mounds that can wreck farm machinery and topple tractors. The invasion occurs each spring. So far, efforts to control the crustaceans have failed.

2. Officials in Maryland are taking steps aimed at restoring order at the Old Court Savings and Loan Association. The thrift institution has been strained by a three-day run on its deposits after news reports surfaced of a management shakeup. A spokesman for Maryland Governor Harry Hughes says the day-to-day

operations of Old Court will be managed by a conservator and that withdrawals will be limited to $1000 a month.

3. The House starts work tomorrow on the budget passed by the Senate last week. The White House says as a final vote on the spending package nears, the President will embark on an intense lobbying campaign to see that representatives vote his way on it.

4. The Supreme Court has ruled that, unlike a house, police can search a motor home without a warrant. Writing for the court, Chief Justice Warren Burger said the vehicle's mobility makes it necessary for police to have easier access to search.

5. The phones are finally back on in Middletown, Ohio, after the city's 50,000 residents were without "Ma Bell" for 18 hours. Ohio Bell says leaking rain water caused some equipment to fail. Officials say they used anything they could get their hands on to dry the equipment, including portable hair dryers.

6. More violent weather has followed the rough weekend felt in parts of the plains. Especially hard hit is the city of Hutchinson, Kansas, where baseball-sized hail may have done hundreds of thousands of dollars in damage.

7. Emergency crews cleared more than 2000 pounds of white glue sloshing on the eastbound deck of the San Francisco–Oakland Bay Bridge today. The truck's driver thinks the accident was caused by a nail stuck in a tire. None of the glue ended up in the bay. Officials had feared at first that the glue would end in the bay and endanger marine life. The State Department of Fish and Game waited in a boat below the bridge just in case.

8. The government says wholesale prices went up three-tenths of a percent last month largely because of sharp increases in gasoline and heating oil prices the month before. March energy prices are figured into the April producer price index.

9. U.S. officials say a major earthquake was recorded today in the New Britain area of New Guinea. The quake registered at a preliminary magnitude of 7 on the Richter scale of ground motion and was centered about 400 miles northeast of Port Moresby. A quake of that magnitude is considered capable of widespread heavy damage. A measurement of 8 denotes a "great" quake, capable of tremendous damage.

10. The country's top business leaders say the economy is entering a period of sluggish growth, but they don't see a recession on the horizon. The prediction comes on the heels of the economy's poorest quarterly showing since the end of the recession. Members of the Business Council blame the slowdown on massive budget and trade deficits.

11. Summer will see more Americans on the vacation trail in the U.S. and overseas. A study by the U.S. Travel Data Center projects a 5 percent jump in pleasure trips compared to a 2 percent increase last summer. The study says the boost in the number of vacationers will pour $85 billion into the economies of the United States and foreign countries.

12. If you are looking for a way to fight heart disease, some Dutch researchers say you should eat more fish. They say their findings show the more fish you eat, the less likely you are to die from heart problems.

13. Community colleges say they need $120 million to upgrade vocational programs. According to officials, the 2-year colleges are using equipment that was junked years ago by industries. Overall, they want about $180 million added to their share of the proposed budget.

14. Workers in Lakeport picked up 12 tons of dead carp that washed ashore at Clear Lake in what one worker called "a terrible job." The fish died recently from spawning stress.

15. If you'd guess that the average American farmer had an income of about $24,000 last year, you'd be far off the mark. The actual figure is less than half of that.

Prose literature

1. So bright and moving was the picture of the breeze-swept sea, the blue lagoon, the foam-dashed reef, and the rocking trees that one felt one had surprised some mysterious gala day, some festival of Nature more than ordinarily glad. . . . The lagoon, here deep, here shallow, presented, according to its depth or shallowness, the colours of ultra-marine or sky. The broadest parts were the palest, because the most shallow; and here and there, in the shallows, you might see a faint tracery of coral ribs almost reaching the surface. The island at its broadest might have been three miles across. There was not a sign of house or habitation to be seen, and not a sail on the whole of the wide Pacific.

   —H. DeVere Stacpoole, *The Blue Lagoon*

2. I had seen the Magic Shop from afar several times; I had passed it once or twice, a shop window of alluring little objects, magic balls, magic hens, wonderful cones, ventriloquist dolls, the material of the basket trick, packs of cards that LOOKED all right, and all that sort of thing, but never had I thought of going in until one day, almost without warning, Gip hauled me by my finger right up to the window, and so conducted himself that there was nothing for it but to take him in.

   —H. G. Wells, *The Magic Shop*

3. There was once a velveteen rabbit, and in the beginning he was really splendid. He was fat and bunchy, as a rabbit should be; his coat was spotted brown and white, he had real thread whiskers, and his ears were lined with pink sateen. On Christmas morning, when he sat wedged in the top of the Boy's stocking, with a sprig of holly between his paws, the effect was charming.
   There were other things in the stocking, nuts and oranges and a toy engine, and chocolate almonds and a clockwork mouse, but the Rabbit was quite the best of all. For at least two hours the Boy loved him, and then Aunts and Uncles came to dinner, and there was a great rustling of tissue paper and unwrapping of parcels, and in the excitement of looking at all the new presents the Velveteen Rabbit was forgotten.

   —Margery Williams, *The Velveteen Rabbit*

4. The Mole had been working very hard all the morning, spring-cleaning his little home, first with brooms, then with dusters; then on ladders and steps and chairs, with a brush and a pail of whitewash; till he had dust in his throat and eyes, and splashes of whitewash all over his black fur, and an aching back and weary arms. Spring was moving in the air above and in the earth below and around him, penetrating even his dark and lowly little house with its spirit of divine discontent and longing. It was small wonder, then, that he suddenly flung down his brush on the floor, said 'Bother!'

—Kenneth Grahame, *The Wind in the Willows*

5. It was in the spring of his thirty-fifth year that father married my mother, then a country school teacher, and in the following spring I came wriggling and crying into the world. Something happened to the two people. They became ambitious. The American passion for getting up in the world took possession of them.

—Sherwood Anderson, "The Egg"

6. She lighted the lamp under its broad orange shade, pulled the curtains and drew up the tea table. Two birds sang in the kettle; the fire fluttered. He sat up clasping his knees. It was delightful—this business of having tea—and she always had the delicious things to eat—little sharp sandwiches, short sweet almond fingers, and a dark, rich cake tasting of rum—but it was an interruption. He wanted it over, the table pushed away, their two chairs drawn up to the light, and the moment came when he took out his pipe, filled it, and said, pressing the tobacco tight into the bowl: "I have been thinking over what you said the last time and it seems to me. . . ."

—Katherine Mansfield, "Psychology"

7. Frederick burst into tears in the middle of Regent's Park. His mother, seeing what was about to happen, had cried: "Frederick, you *can't*—in the middle of Regent's Park!"

Really, this was a corner, one of those lively corners just inside a big gate, where two walks meet and a bridge starts across the pretty winding lake. People were passing quickly; the bridge rang with feet. Poplars stood up like delicate green brooms; diaphanous willows whose weeping was not shocking quivered over the lake.

—Elizabeth Bowen, "Tears, Idle Tears"

8. Croquet is a summer game that seems in a curious way, to be composed of images the way that a painter's abstraction of summer or one of its games would be built of them. The delicate wire wickets set in a lawn of smooth emerald that flickers fierily at some points and rests under violet shadow in others, the wooden poles gaudily painted as moments that stand out in a season that was a struggle for something of unspeakable importance to someone passing through it, the clean and hard wooden spheres of different colors and the strong rigid shape of the mallets that drive the balls through the wickets, the formal design of those wickets and poles upon the croquet lawn—all of these are like a painter's abstraction of a summer and a game played in it.

—Tennessee Williams, "Three Players of a Summer Game"

9. Muriel had never, in the long, rich catalogue of her envies, envied the offspring of anyone until she had seen that the trick impressed him: the trick of a child, that child, who need do nothing to be loved, while she, Muriel, studied, thought, refined herself to a thin white slice of moon so that her love for him would be what he most admired: cold, the love of the spirit, knife-sharp, always on the verge of disappearing.

—Mary Gordon, *The Company of Women*

10. I didn't remember her at all. Even in the crowd at that stiff reception, how could I have missed her? She ought to have showed up like a burning lighthouse.

Her talk was as animated as her face. Every fourth word was underlined— she had the habit of feminine emphasis with a vengeance. (Later, when we diverged into different associations and we got letters from her, we discovered that her writing was the same way. You couldn't read it except in her tone of voice.)

—Wallace Stegner, *Crossing to Safety*

Poetry

1. 'Twas brillig, and the slithy toves
　　Did gyre and gimble in the wabe;
All mimsy were the borogoves,
　　And the mome raths outgrabe.

'Beware the Jabberwock, my son!
　　The jaws that bite, the claws that catch!
Beware the Jubjub bird, and shun
　　The frumious Bandersnatch!'

He took his vorpal sword in hand:
　　Long time the manxome foe he sought—
So rested he by the Tumtum tree,
　　And stood awhile in thought.

And as in uffish thought he stood,
　　The Jabberwock, with eyes of flame,
Came whiffling through the tulgey wood,
　　And burbled as it came!

One, two! One, two! And through and through
　　The vorpal blade went snicker-snack!
He left it dead, and with its head
　　He went galumphing back.

'And has thou slain the Jabberwock?
　　Come to my arms, my beamish boy!
O frabjous day! Callooh! Callay!'
　　He chortled in his joy.

'Twas brillig, and the slithy toves
　　Did gyre and gimble in the wabe;
All mimsy were the borogoves,
　　And the mome raths outgrabe.

—Lewis Carroll, "Jabberwocky"

2. I think I will do nothing for a long time but listen,
   And accrue what I hear into myself . . . and let sounds contribute
       toward me.
   I hear the bravuras of birds . . . the bustle of growing wheat . . .
       gossip of flames . . . clack of sticks cooking my meals.
   I heard the sound of the human voice . . . a sound I love,
   I hear all sounds as they are turned to their uses . . . sounds of the city and
       sounds out of the city . . . sounds of the day and night;
   Talkative young ones to those that like them . . . the recitative of fish
       peddlars and fruit-peddlars . . . the loud laugh of working-
       people at their meals,
   The angry base of disjointed friendship . . . the faint tones of the
       sick,
   The judge with hands tight to the desk, his shaky lips pronouncing a
       death-sentence.
                                                              —Walt Whitman

3. Love's a capricious power: I've known it hold
       Out through a fever caused by its own heat,
   But be much puzzled by a cough and cold,
       And find a quinsy very hard to treat;
   Against all noble maladies he's bold,
       But vulgar illnesses don't like to meet,
   Nor that a sneeze should interrupt his sigh,
   Nor inflammations redden his blind eye.
                                                              —Lord Byron

4. I grow old . . . I grow old . . .
   I shall wear the bottoms of my trousers rolled.
   Shall I part my hair behind? Do I dare to eat a peach?
   I shall wear white flannel trousers, and walk upon the beach.
   I have heard the mermaids singing, each to each.
   I do not think that they will sing to me.
   I have seen them riding seaward on the waves
   Combing the white hair of the waves blown back
   When the wind blows the water white and black.
   We have lingered in the chambers of the sea
   By sea-girls wreathed with seaweed red and brown
   Till human voices wake us, and we drown.
                                  —T. S. Eliot, from "The Love Song of J. Alfred Prufrock"

5. So live, that when thy summons comes to join
   The innumerable caravan, which moves
   To that mysterious realm, where each shall take
   His chamber in the silent halls of death,
   Thou go not, like the quarry-slave at night,
   Scourged to his dungeon, but sustained and soothed
   By an unfaltering trust, approach thy grave,
   Like one who wraps the drapery of his couch
   About him, and lies down to pleasant dreams.
                                  —William Cullen Bryant, "Thanatopsis"

Chapter Seven Review

Review the following concepts:

- Terms: quality/timbre, nasality, denasality, breathiness, gutturality, stridency, thinness, hoarseness, harshness, raspiness
- The paralinguistics of quality
- Extralinguistic indicators of health

Respond to the following:

1. Define good vocal quality.
2. What three things primarily determine the quality of your voice?
3. Discuss the role of paralinguistics with regard to vocal quality.
4. Identify one specific negative vocal quality, and discuss how to correct it.

APPLICATION

1. How do you or others characterize the quality of your voice?

2. What are the primary tonal features of your voice?

3. When do you consciously employ different vocal qualities?

4. How can you change any negative qualities? *Tip:* See a doctor if you experience persistent harshness, hoarseness, raspiness, or loss of voice.

FOCUS MESSAGE

1. *ESL:* Certain vocal qualities may be characteristic of some languages. For example, French is a nasal language; German is guttural. Thus the concept of resonance focus is important in creating a more distinct American English quality of sound. Work toward mid-mouth resonance, concentrating on the schwa sound.

2. *Acting:* The performance world will demand of you a repertoire of voices. Before attempting to create new voices, you must have a sound understanding of your own voice, how it works, and its range. Once you have achieved this, avoiding strain, begin to experiment with varied pitches and resonances. As an actor, you probably already have developed the habit of watching others. Now begin to build an auditory file of voices, and work to imitate those which you may be able to use on stage or screen. Vocal play is one of the best ways to develop character voices.

3. *Broadcasting:* Suffice to say that your first job with regard to vocal quality is to rid yourself of any negative, distracting features. Once you have developed a clear, resonant sound, you should begin to develop the ability to adapt the quality of your voice to the variety of materials you will be delivering and the variety of roles you may assume on the air. From the relaxed tone of the classical music announcer to the fevered delivery of the sports announcer, there are numerous variations in

tone. Begin to develop an "ear" for all of the variations on radio and television or the World Wide Web, and work to imitate these vocal qualities. To become proficient as a voice-over artist, you must build a wide range of voice personalities.

EVALUATION

SEE PAGES 273–274, where you'll find an evaluation form for this chapter. Follow your instructor's directions.

NOTES

1. *T.V. Guide,* January 9, 1988, p. 17.

CHAPTER

8 Articulation

You ought to talk like a civilized man and not mumble like a growling Pekingese dog.

—Jack Matthews

TERMS

Articulation [ɑrtɪkjə'leɪʃən] Positioning the articulators to create the sounds of language.

Pronunciation [proʊnənsɪ'eɪʃən] Proper utterance of a word as it is currently being used.

Phoneme ['foʊnim] Individual sound in a language.

Dialect ['daɪəlɛkt] Variation of articulated language characterized by phonemic choices, grammar, vocabulary, syllabic stress, rhythms, inflections.

Speaking is one of the most intricately complex skills that we develop. Oral communication relies on the coordinated functioning of our organs for thinking, breathing, hearing, and speaking. Further, it relies on the cooperation and coordination of numerous muscles, ligaments, and cartilages surrounding those organs.

Articulation is the means by which we, as humans, create intelligent sound. By positioning jaw, lips, tongue, and teeth in a particular way we are able to create the individual sounds of language. Given the possible permutations of over forty sounds in General American English, it is miraculous that we are able to make ourselves understood as well as we do.

Around the country people are working toward reducing distinct regional or foreign accents in order to blend smoothly into the business world or to be more clearly understood. A national periodical reported that "fault by voice communication plays a role in about 80% of all reported aviation incidents."[1] Surely one's life and livelihood are sufficient reasons for working toward a more articulate voice.

This chapter will introduce you to the process of articulation. First, the necessary terminology will be defined. Second, we will discuss the reasons for individual differences in articulation, and third, we will work toward helping you design an individual program for articulation improvement.

Definitions

Articulation/Pronunciation

On a morning talk show, the host held up the Robert Ludlum novel *Icarus.* "I care us," said the cohost. "Is it 'I care us' or 'Ikarus'?" questioned the first. "I don't know," replied the other, "But I'll say 'I care us.' It's a great advertising technique. Pronounce it wrong and people will run out to buy it." Frequently you may hear a word that doesn't sound quite right, or you may be saying a word incorrectly like "ax" for *ask,* or "human bean," for *human being,* or "cat lick," for *catholic.*

This text differentiates between *articulation* and *pronunciation.* Though the two terms seem synonymous, use of the terms suggests that *articulation* deals with the manner in which the individual sounds or phonemes of a language are formed in order to clearly produce a word. *Pronunciation,* on the other hand, incorporates proper utterance of orthographic depictions of sound and syllabic stress. In other words, it refers to the proper way to produce a word. For example (and using mostly orthographic spelling to demonstrate), " 'pro *noun* se ashən" is the *incorrect* pronunciation of that word. "Artikəlashən" is merely a careless manner of articulating that word.

Your *articulators* include your lower jaw, teeth, alveolar ridge (gum ridge), hard palate, soft palate, velum, tongue, and vocal folds. When placed in various positions, you can produce sounds by sending voiced (with vocal fold vibrations) or voiceless air through the configuration created by those positions.

Phonemes

All words are made up of sounds. At the 1930 Prague International Phonological Conference, the *phoneme* was officially defined as an individual sound in any given language. In the International Phonetic Alphabet (IPA), each phoneme is represented by a single symbol, for example, [i], [p], [m], [z], [æ], and so forth. (See Appendix One for IPA Pronunciation Guides, which list phonemes and their symbols.)

The precise utterance of a phoneme may vary depending upon its context in a word. This variance is called an *allophone.* Sounds may change in the environment of other sounds. For example, [p] is a phoneme. When that sound occurs at the beginning of a word, it is articulated with greater energy than when it occurs in the middle or at the end of a word. "Pat," "happy," and "cup"—all these words include the phoneme [p], but each [p] sounds slightly different. When you produce a [t] at the beginning of a word and at the start of a sentence, such as in "Time is on my side," you use greater force than when the [t] occurs in medial positions. For instance, the [t] in *pretty* requires less explosion. If you use the same degree of energy as you would with an initial [t], you will sound artificial. If you reduce the [t] to a [d], "priddy," you sound careless. In final positions, such as in *last,* the [t] requires a gentle *tap* but is too frequently omitted altogether. In some cases, wherein two or more sounds are produced in the same place in the mouth, such as the [t] and [n] in *button,* the [t] may acceptably be omitted in connected, casual speech. In more formal situations, such as onstage, you might be required to slightly tap the [t]. These differences are *allophonic.*

Vowels

The phonemes of a language are primarily distinguished as vowels, diphthongs, and consonants. A *vowel* can be defined by its characteristics and classifications.

Characteristics
1. All vowels are voiced, or have vocal fold vibration.
2. In vowel production there is no interruption of the breath stream.
3. Lip shaping and tongue mass positioning determine the sound.
4. Vowels have a degree of tension or laxity.
5. Vowels have differing lengths.

Classifications
1. Vowels are classified as front, middle, or back according to their production point in the oral cavity.
2. Vowels are classified as high, mid, or low according to the place in the oral cavity of tongue mass placement (see Chapter Nine, Figure 9.1).

Diphthongs

Diphthongs are vowel combinations that result from a continuous glide from one approximate vowel position to another in the same syllable. This glide creates a new sound. An example is [aɪ] as in *ice.*

Consonants

Consonants may be voiced or voiceless; that is, made with or without vocal fold vibration. In several instances in English, two sounds are produced in the same place in the mouth but one is voiced and one is not. These pairs of sounds are called *cognates.* Examples are [p], which is voiceless, and [b] which is voiced, [t] voiceless, and [d] voiced. Consonants are defined by the manner in which they are produced, by the place in the mouth where they are produced, and by the characteristics of voice or voicelessness. Essentially, consonants are formed by setting up an obstruction to the voiced or voiceless breath stream. In the case of the [p], for example, which we define as a bilabial plosive, the lips are closed tightly as air gently builds up and then explodes the lips apart.

International Phonetic Alphabet

The *International Phonetic Alphabet,* or IPA, was devised about 100 years ago as a means for representing all of the phonemes extant in all languages. Each symbol used in IPA is descriptive of a spoken sound. This differs from the orthographic alphabet (A, B, C, D, etc.) used in a dictionary with its accompanying diacritical markings (ēt for "*eat*"). Different dictionaries use different markings for the same sound because there is no international standard. Further, the orthographic symbol may have many soundings. A given letter such as "a" will sound differently when used in various words, such as *laugh, father, place,* or *law.* In order to avoid confusion, we will use the IPA to identify clearly the individual phonemes that we both hear and articulate. However, there is yet another distinction. American linguists use slightly different IPA symbols for American English than do international linguists. This text will feature current American usage.[2] (See Appendix One for IPA Pronunciation Guides.)

Learning IPA can be useful. For example, IPA is used on the Internet to teach foreign languages. In an ever increasing global society wherein a person in business may have to learn a language quickly, this tool could be invaluable. IPA can also serve the broadcaster, actor, singer, or educator in learning difficult words or understanding linguistic differences.

Coarticulation

Because we speak when we are communicating meaning, not simply sound, we do not utter precise individual phonemes. Our sounds overlap and blend into one another. As mentioned earlier, this is called coarticulation, that is, articulation as it occurs in connected speech, which alters primary place of articulation. One sound, in anticipation of creating a sound that follows it, may be produced in a slightly different place in the mouth than what you will find in later chapters to be the described place of production. For example, with the word *seventh,* the [n] ordinarily produced with the tongue touching the alveolar ridge is actually produced at the back of the teeth in anticipation of the [θ]. The lip shape required to produce some vowels will affect the production of adjacent consonants.

Dialects/Individual Differences

The terms *accent* and *dialect* are often used interchangeably, although an accent is generally thought to be that of persons within the same linguistic community, while a dialect is often considered to be that of a person with another primary language. For example, having been raised in the South, you might speak with a southern accent. If your first language was Japanese, you might speak English with a dialect.

Several factors work together to constitute an accent or dialect. Take a look at the following list:

Factors That Constitute a Dialect

Factor	Example
1. Phonemic interchange	"dis" instead of "this"
2. Intonation	"this kind of weather" (Spanish), rather than "weather"
3. Syllabic stress	"bookstore," rather than: "book store" (equal stress)
4. Rhythm	"in the house" might be paced equally, rather than lightly and quickly on "in the"
5. Resonance focus	"low rear mouth" (German)
6. Grammar and syntax	"Put noodles in large bowl," rather than "Put the noodles in a large bowl"

There may be regional differences of spoken language in vocabulary, pronunciation, and grammar. Because of our origins we may articulate or pronounce a word in a particular manner. Depending on where we live we may say [grisɪ] or [grizɪ] for *greasy* or [rum] or [rʊm] for *room*. We may say "ship" for *sheep*, "dis" for *this*, or "sink" for *think*.

Although differences of vocabulary, pronunciation, and grammar appear *within* regions, a recognized standard of articulation usually exists. How your speech compares with that standard depends on where you live in a region, your social status, and your level of education. It is thought that educated people use clear articulation and many are gravitating toward the General American dialect as a standard of articulation because of its similarity to written English. In his book, *Cultural Literacy: What Every American Needs to Know,* E. D. Hirsch, Jr., says, "Although standard written English has no intrinsic superiority to other languages and dialects, its stable written forms have now standardized the oral forms of the language spoken by educated Americans."[3]

In Jerry Van Amerongen's syndicated cartoon series "The Neighborhood," a man is depicted speaking to a couple across a dinner table. The caption reads, "Being new to international travel, Earl enunciates carefully so the Canadian couple might better understand." It is often said that the British and Americans are the same people separated by a common language. There is nothing wrong with having a dialect or with producing a sound differently. In fact, dialects can be part of our individual charm. The important thing is to be clear and to be understood.

British journalists Frank Muir and Denis Norden write, "Until recently the main Class giveaways were speech and dress. If somebody spoke a little too loudly, with a pre–war BBC announcer's accent, keeping the vowels well open, then he or she was an Upper. If all this was attempted and it just failed, then he or she was a Middle. Mumbling mangled vowels, and local colour in the accent indicated Lower. But nowadays, thanks to telly, pop-music, and the media generally, our youth and our trendier middle-aged talk what might be termed Standard Received Disc-Jockey. If you meet a lad in Windsor High Street it is now no longer possible to tell from his speech whether he is Eton or Slough Comprehensive."[4] In fact, a current trend in England is called Estuary English, a cockney variant. But trends are short-lived.

If English is your native language, you need to come to understand your articulatory habits. There seems a trend afoot toward reducing multisyllabic words to fewer syllables. For example, *buying* becomes [baɪn]. Or, as suggested in the first chapter, you might be adding sounds, for example "wouldnent"; or you might be interchanging sounds, such as with "preform." If your first language is not English or if you are influenced by your family members who primarily speak another language, you will need to learn new sounds that will include new phonemes, intonational patterns, and stress patterns. If you have an overbite, underbite, large spaces between your teeth, or any other structural difference, you may need to learn to compensate while improving your articulation. For example, if your teeth are discolored or ill-formed, you may have developed a habit of keeping your lips together; this will affect articulation. If you wear braces, your articulation may be altered. If your hearing acuity has been reduced, sound production may be affected. Your emotions play a part in your efforts to produce clear, crisp articulation. If you are continually lethargic or depressed, you probably lack the energy to produce strong sounds. Emotional distress can cause you to enunciate differently at times. Or, you may habitually produce phonemes in a particular way. But habits can be broken! The most common habits involve too little lip shaping for certain sounds and a lower jaw that does not open enough to produce clear sounds.

In our increasingly media-conscious world and our expanding "global village," it is valuable to achieve sufficient articulatory control to communicate clearly in any situation. As pointed out earlier, you may wish to eliminate a dialect or become "bidialectal," which is to have the ability to use a standard regional dialect or a General American English dialect at will. This is currently called *code switching*, defined as a transactional and contextual process. This means that we switch our manner of speech to suit the context in which we find ourselves.

Program for Improvement

If you are now enrolled in a voice and diction course, you are taking the first step toward change in your articulatory habits. But remember, pressures may bear on you to resist change. Your friends may say to you, "Why are you trying to talk different? You sound so phony. You don't sound like you." In order not to sound phony, you should guard against "artificial speech." Sometimes, in an effort to be more precise, you tend to overarticulate. An extreme manner of articulation involves overproducing some sounds such as the final [t] as in "*get it* off of tha*t*." In many cases those final [t] phonemes are articulated with too much energy. Sometimes, in an effort to sound more articulate, people add sounds. A common error is "dident" for *didn't,* "athalete" for *athlete.*

It is important to monitor yourself, to understand how you sound, and what you do and how you do it when you articulate. Audiotape recording can help you hear how you sound. Videotaping can show you the manner by which you produce sounds. Idiosyncracies in articulation such as too much or too little tongue protrusion for the phonemes [θ] or [ð], tongue placement for [s], and no or little lip movement or lip rounding can readily be distinguished with videotaping. Your improvement can then be tangible and visually charted with, of course, your instructor's guidance.

It is equally important to note that a program for improvement not only involves seeing and hearing positive change, it also involves muscular sense discrimination. If you type, you will understand this concept. Imagine that you are typing a letter, reading from copy to your side when you strike the wrong key on the keyboard. Most of the time you are aware that you made an error. That is because, though simultaneous processes are in operation, you are probably so trained in touch typing that you sensed the error in your fingers. Good articulation requires the same sort of muscular sensing so that should you slip, you are immediately aware of doing so in order to be able to produce improved articulation the next time.

Chapters Nine and Ten explain phonemic production. In these chapters study the production methods for each phoneme and come to understand proper techniques. Utilize the exercises and drills to improve your own phonemic production. As you drill, try using audio or video equipment to record your exercise and progress.

You might wish to observe the following suggestions:

■ The [ə] is the most important sound for the person whose first language is not English to learn to use and the native English speaker to avoid. Generally, the non-native speaker fails to use [ə] or [ʌ] where these are commonly used, such as in "c<u>o</u>mp<u>a</u>ny," for example. The native speaker generally overuses the schwa.

■ Motivation is your best ally.

■ Use drills to work toward achieving muscular flexibility.

■ Decide whether you prefer to begin with vowels or consonants; turn to that section.

■ Focus on a small group of sounds at a time (i.e., front vowels, back vowels, etc.).

■ Utilize the drills within each chapter that follows.

■ Set aside an hour once a week to drill with a videotape.

- Set aside time for personal evaluation and time for consultation with your instructor.

- Begin integrating proper articulation into your daily speech.

Superior diction is not an inborn talent given only to a few. We are born with the potential to produce clear sounds. The dialectal environment in which we are raised, our own habits, and physical makeup ultimately determine the way we sound. Through commitment to an exercise program that will enable you to achieve flexibility and awareness, you can improve your articulation. In turn, this will have an indirect, positive effect on self-perception and on the manner in which you are perceived by others.

Exercises: Flexibility

Chapter Two lists exercises for relaxation and breath support. You should begin by reviewing and performing those exercise sets.

The following exercises are designed to help you achieve flexibility from the neck up, using specific articulators.

Neck/Jaw

Tension can inhibit good phonemic production, and tension is often centered in the neck area. Some of the following exercises may be the same or similar to those in earlier chapters.

Exercise 1   Sit or stand erectly. Using a full 60 seconds, permit your head to fall forward, roll to the left, to the right, and forward again. As you do so, try to focus only on the sensation of your muscles gently stretching. Do not force a stretch but let the weight of your head pull the muscle. Reverse the direction of the head roll. Spend about 5 minutes relaxing these muscles, then raise your head to an upright position.

Exercise 2   Place two fingers on your chin. Imagine that the weight of your fingers is pulling your lower jaw downward. Your impulse will be to resist the pull. Resist this impulse and let your jaw drop until you feel it open to capacity. Take about thirty to 45 seconds. You should achieve the degree of openness that would enable you to insert two fingers between your teeth. Try this sequence several times until you are easily able to achieve a relaxed jaw.

Exercise 3   By alternating individual sounds you can further exercise your lower jaw. Exaggerate the jaw movements required to produce the following combinations and repeat each at least three times. If you have not yet studied IPA, you may have to refer to the IPA lists (see Appendix One) to identify proper sounds.

Sounds	Sample words
[i]—[æ]	eat—ask
[i]—[oʊ]	eat—oat
[i]—[u]	eat—ooze
[eɪ]—[æ]	ate—ask
[eɪ]—[oʊ]	ate—oat
[eɪ]—[u]	ate—ooze
[æ]—[i]	ask—eat
[æ]—[oʊ]	ask—oat
[æ]—[u]	ask—ooze
[ɔ]—[i]	off—eat
[ɔ]—[æ]	off—ask
[oʊ]—[æ]	oat—ask
[oʊ]—[eɪ]	oat—ate
[oʊ]—[i]	oat—eat
[u]—[æ]	ooze—ask
[u]—[eɪ]	ooze—ate
[u]—[i]	ooze—eat

Lips

Inflexible lips directly affect phonemic production. Try a series of lip "play" exercises for several minutes.

Exercise 1   Permit your lips to rest flaccid. Then, as a horse does, blow air out the lips creating a lax buzzing sound. Repeat.

Exercise 2   Purse your lips as if kissing. Hold tightly while vocalizing [u] as in "coo." Relax, then purse again. Alternate with a teeth-baring smile, vocalizing [i] as in "key." Repeat several times.

Exercise 3   Drill with continually repeated bilabial (two lips) consonants:

b,b,b,b,b,b,b,b,b,b,b,b,b,b,b

p,p,p,p,p,p,p,p,p,p,p,p,p,p,p

Add vowel sounds:

be,be,be,be,be,be,be,be,be,be

po,po,po,po,po,po,po,po,po,po

bu,bu,bu,bu,bu,bu,bu,bu,bu,bu

pa,pa,pa,pa,pa,pa,pa,pa,pa,pa

Exercise 4   Use the following sound combinations for repeated lip drill. Use exaggerated lip movements to work facial muscles. Saying first the sounds, then the words, perform each at least three times.

Vowels	Sample words
[i]—[æ]	eat—at
[i]—[u]	eat—ooze
[eɪ]—[ɑ]	ate—on
[eɪ]—[u]	ate—ooze
[æ]—[u]	at—ooze
[u]—[i]	ooze—eat
[u]—[ɑ]	ooze—on
[u]—[æ]	ooze—at

Consonants/vowels	Sample words
[mi]—[bi]	me—be
[mi]—[beɪ]	me—bay
[mæ]—[bæ]	mat—bat
[mɔ]—[bɔ]	mall—ball
[moʊ]—[boʊ]	moat—boat
[mu]—[bu]	moot—boot

Tongue

Clear articulation is characterized by proper tongue positioning, which often requires rapid movement. When you were a child, you no doubt played with sound by wagging and thrusting your tongue. Try the following to achieve the same flexibility you had as a child.

Exercise 1   Extend your tongue as far as possible between your teeth. Open your mouth widely and begin to flap your tongue up and down. Increase speed. Add in vocalization.

Exercise 2   Extend your tongue again. This time wag it rapidly from side to side. Alternate this movement with up and down flapping. Add in vocalization.

Exercise 3   The following sound sequences represent alternate tongue movement from front to back mouth positions. Begin slowly, then increase rapidity of movement. You should strive for clarity over rapidity.

Sound	Sample words
[θ]—[k]	thin—kin
[ð]—[g]	then—give
[t]—[k]	to—kin
[d]—[g]	dog—give
[n]—[ŋ]	no—ring

(Add in vowel sounds)

[i]—[ki]   eat—keep
[oʊ]—[goʊ]   oat—goat
[tu]—[ku]   too—coop
[dɔ]—[gɔ]   daw—gaw
[ni]—[ɪŋ]   knee—sing

Velum

Excessive nasality may result from an inactive velum. Using a mirror, try the following exercises.

Exercise 1   Yawn. Observe the velum rising upward and backward. Now, produce the same movement without yawning. Perform several of these movements.

Exercise 2   Produce the following sounds in rapid succession to aid you in feeling the action of the velum: [ŋ] [ə], [ŋ] [ə], [ŋ] [ə]

Exercise 3   Pinching your nostrils together, read aloud the following sentences. If you sound "stuffy," your velum was not raised. Try the sentences until all sounds are clear. (More sentences of this type can be found in Chapter Seven on pp. 115–116.)

1. You should get relief if you talk to your doctor.
2. Political advisors are worried about widespread views which are opposite theirs.
3. Check it out for yourself before you purchase.
4. The eclipse showed us that our orb is very big.
5. I ask that you be taught the proper way to better your voice.

Exercise 4   Try the following nasal and oral sounds in combination making sure only [m], [n], and [ŋ] are produced through the nose. Work slowly, separating sounds to clearly identify the place of production. Touch your nose to feel vibration. The words in IPA below are separated by space in order to help you isolate the sounds.

[m ɛ n]   men
[m æ n]   man
[r ʌ n ɪ ŋ]   running
[r ɪ ŋ ɪ ŋ]   ringing
[s ɪ ŋ]   sing
[k ɪ ŋ]   king
[n ɑ n s ɛ n s] nonsense
[s a ʊ n d ɪ ŋ] sounding
[n o ʊ z ɪ ŋ]   nosing
[θ ɪ ŋ k ɪ ŋ]   thinking

Integration

Exercise 1   Sit in front of a mirror. You will be "making faces" in a variety of ways. A few facial postures are listed below, but you should feel free to create your own. Using one facial posture at a time, read the sentences listed below. Note the exaggerated feeling and sounds that are produced.

- Draw your eyebrows tightly together and purse your lips tightly.

- Open your eyes as widely as possible and push your pursed lips as far to the left as possible.

- Narrow your eyes into slits, cover your teeth with your lips, and smile tightly.

- Wrinkle your nose and push your lips out like a fish.

- Open your eyes and your mouth as widely as possible.

1. Sneak previews will be shown Friday night.
2. I wouldn't give you the time of day.
3. Greed comes crawling out of the woodwork.
4. I'll give you a run for your money.
5. Let's roll out the barrel.
6. You may have to pay the piper.
7. It's the luck of the draw.
8. Give me lots of space.
9. Next time, try harder.
10. Anything you can do, I can do better.

Exercise 2   The following sentences incorporate common phrases that are often slurred. Work with these repeatedly to improve your articulation. Start slowly, then repeat as you increase rate of delivery.

1. Aren't you coming to the game?
2. Do you believe them when they say they'll do it?
3. Do you want me to stay here or go away?
4. Get it off of here.
5. Give it to them.
6. Give me a little time.
7. Go on outside and play.
8. He must have gone away.
9. He is one of the best.
10. How about you?
11. How are you doing today?
12. It is good as far as I can tell.
13. I just don't know about that.

14. I don't know what to say.
15. I had to do it.
16. I am going away next week.
17. It's been so long since I last saw you.
18. It's half past six o'clock in the evening.
19. It's not so hot today as it was yesterday.
20. I wish I could go there.
21. It wouldn't have happened, not if I'd have had it.
22. Let me see if I can do it.
23. Let's go over the agenda once again.
24. Now more than ever, we should pay attention.
25. One of them played for the other team.
26. See if you can make it to the party Saturday.
27. That's just the way it goes sometimes.
28. They can go anywhere they want to go.
29. They could have believed him when he said he would do it.
30. Think about this one and then think about that one.
31. See if anybody is coming.
32. What do you think you are doing?
33. What did he say about that?
34. What did you do that for?
35. What did I tell you?
36. What did you mean when you said she would go with you?
37. What do you know about all of those things?
38. Where have you been all this time?
39. Why didn't you go with them?
40. You should find your own.

Chapter Eight Review

Review the following concepts:

- Terms: articulation, pronunciation, phoneme, allophone, vowels, diphthongs, consonants, International Phonetic Alphabet, dialect
- The difference between articulation of phonemes and the pronunciation of words
- The definition of a phoneme and allophone
- Vowels, diphthongs, and consonants defined by virtue of characteristics and classifications

Respond to the following:

1. Explain the difference between articulation and pronunciation.
2. How are vowels classified?
3. How are consonants classified?
4. Why do we study the International Phonetic Alphabet?
5. Why is articulator flexibility important to clear diction?

APPLICATION

1. What individual sounds of English do you find challenging?

2. What are some of your own common pronunciation errors or confusions?

3. How might you be able to incorporate IPA into your current or future profession?

4. What are some ways that you can work to achieve greater flexibility in articulation?

FOCUS MESSAGE

1. *ESL:* As you come to understand the definitions of terms, and as you embark on a study of the individual vowel and consonant sounds of English, begin to make a detailed assessment of the differences between the dialect you currently speak and the more commonly acceptable manner of articulation for sounds. For example, if you say *ship,* does it sound more like *sheep?* Do you consistently use that substitution? Once you know your target phonemes, you can zero in on drill exercises.

2. *Acting:* Understanding the overall concepts of articulation and accepting the challenge of learning IPA can be valuable tools for you in achieving clear stage diction and in learning dialects. *Tip:* Begin working with the pronunciation lists in Appendix Two in order to (a) produce each correctly, (b) produce each as an illiterate character might do, and (c) produce each word with a preselected dialect.

3. *Broadcasting:* Like the actor, your job is to clearly articulate messages. Thus, understanding concepts and acquiring a working knowledge of IPA will aid you in pronouncing difficult or challenging words and names. *Tip:* If you haven't already begun to study the pronunciation lists in Appendix Two, start now. Be sure to look up the meanings of any words you don't know. This will affect contextual use.

EVALUATION

SEE PAGES 275–276, where you'll find an evaluation form for this chapter. Follow your instructor's directions.

NOTES

1. *Insight,* December 1988, p. 32.
2. Geoffrey K. Pullum and William A. Ladusaw, *Phonetic Symbol Guide* (Chicago: Univ. of Chicago Press: 1986), p. xxii.
3. E. D. Hirsch, Jr., *Cultural Literacy: What Every American Needs to Know* (Boston: Houghton Mifflin Co., 1987), p. 3.
4. Frank Muir and Denis Norden, *My Word Stories* (New York: Stein and Day Publishers, 1977), p. 151.

9 Vowels

Q: What is a "diphthong"?

A: The Merriam-Webster Dictionary defines "diphthong" as a "word that is used to form a good name for a rock band, e.g. "Earl Piedmont and the Diphthongs."

—Dave Barry

TERMS

Diphthong [ˈdɪfθɔŋ]   A vowel combination resulting from a continuous glide from one approximate vowel position to another.

Schwa [ʃwɑ]   Symbolized by [ə], it is the most common sound in American English.

Vowel [vaʊəl]   Phonemes produced with continuous vocalization.

This chapter will focus on the individual sounds or phonemes we identify as *vowels,* and the next chapter will deal with *consonants.* Since there are over 40 sounds and only 26 letters of the alphabet, we will be using the International Phonetic Alphabet to represent these sounds. In this system, many symbols look just like the English alphabetical symbol for the sound. In some cases, however, an unfamiliar symbol will represent a sound. As you consult various dictionaries, you may note the disparity among symbols and markings used in them. With IPA the symbols never change. Furthermore, there is an added benefit to learning IPA. It can be utilized in other professions and situations. For example, singers often use IPA in order to learn the words to a foreign language song. Theater directors and actors use IPA to learn how to pronounce words accurately.

Because sound changes in spoken contexts, each sound will be shown in the several positions in which it appears in both words and sentences. Discussion and drill on certain sounds that present difficulty for some people are also presented.

In order to better illustrate lip shape and tongue position, photographs are provided for front and back vowels and for those mid vowels that can be depicted by a photo. However, there is little mouth shape change for some consonants, such as [l], [t], [d], [n], [k], [g], or [s]. Photographs, then, are included only for those consonants for which mouth shape is important. Further, realize that it is impossible to show in photographs or charts the degree of tension or exact jaw position for each sound.

> **Remember:**
> **IPA Symbol**
> **= Sound**
> **not spelling**

Today, General American English may be considered the "industry standard" since it is spoken on national television and radio. Explanations, therefore, will be limited to General American English and will make no attempt to comprehensively explain all American dialects, though some may be mentioned.

Approach to Vowel Study

When we think of sound, we may say that vowels carry the music of the language, and consonants carry the meaning. Thus, we will begin study with vowel sounds. You or your class may skip this chapter and begin with consonants, if that is your preference, then come back to vowels later.

Remember that language changes constantly. With respect to change, a study conducted by William Labov has revealed what is termed *phonemic mergers.* This means that sounds that used to be differentiated in production have become alike. Labov indicates that half of speakers of English in the United States now produce two sounds as one. Those are [ɑ], as in Don, and [ɔ], as in Dawn.[1] It is important to remember that sounds will continue to shift as long as people speak the language, and no two persons will say sounds exactly the same way.

In the previous chapter you learned the characteristics and classifications of vowels. As a reminder these are:

Characteristics:
1. All vowels are voiced, or have vocal fold vibration.
2. In vowel production there is no interruption of the breath stream.
3. Lip shaping and tongue mass determine the sound.
4. Vowels have a degree of tension or laxity.
5. Vowels have varying lengths.

Classifications:
1. Vowels are classified as front, middle, or back.
2. Vowels are classified as high, mid, or low.

We will begin with explanation of front vowels, move to back vowels, mid vowels, and end with diphthongs. For each vowel sound there will appear an IPA symbol, sample words that demonstrate how the sound appears in front, middle, and end positions, other sample words that demonstrate how the sound is variously spelled, a sound classification, description of how the phoneme is produced, drill words and sentences, and, in some instances, comparison drills among phonemes. Figure 9.1 places the vowels in the approximate positions in the oral cavity at which they are made. The IPA Vowel Pronunciation Guide (Table 9.1) is included for easy reference to symbols.

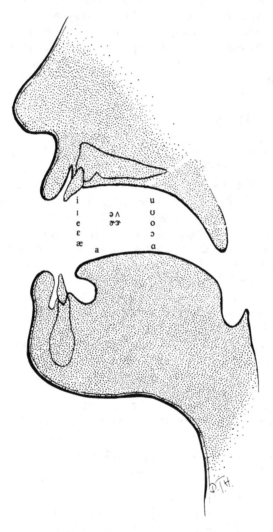

FIGURE 9.1 **Approximate positions of vowels within oral cavity. Though it is impossible to represent the exact tongue and lip positions and degree of tension or laxity for each vowel, this figure represents the approximate place in the oral cavity where each vowel is produced.**

TABLE 9.1   IPA Vowel Pronunciation Guide

Sample word	IPA
eat	i
it	ɪ
ate	eɪ*
pet	ɛ
pat	æ
pat	a†
about	ə
cut	ʌ
rather	ɚ
bird	ɝ
father	ɑ
law	ɔ
oat	oʊ*
look	ʊ
school	u
ice	aɪ
out	aʊ
oil	ɔɪ
Tuesday	ɪu
Tuesday	ju

*These diphthongs are more commonly used and recognized than the short versions, [e] and [o], respectively.

†[a] Most linguists and phoneticians consider this phoneme to be a vowel used primarily in New England as a substitute for [æ]. It is also used as the initial phoneme in some diphthongs.

Front Vowels

eat, neat, key

Other sample words for various spellings:

she, see, each, receive, believe, machine, people

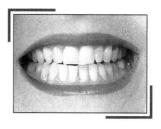

Classification   High, front, tense vowel

- Used in the initial, medial, and end positions in words
- Usually found in stressed syllables in words

Description
- Lips are in a tight, open smile
- Back sides of tongue are against upper molars

- Tip of tongue aims toward upper gum ridge but does not touch
- Vocal folds vibrate

Drill Words

Initial	*Medial*	*End*
each	believe	be
eel	clean	he
ease	dream	key
easy	feet	knee
east	heat	me
eat	least	sea
ego	mean	she
equal	piece	ski
even	receive	tree
evil	zeal	we

Drill Sentences

1. We ordered tea for three.
2. At least he can clean his jet ski.
3. Please eat that piece of meat.
4. Go to the sea to flee the heat.
5. You should believe in your dreams.
6. Beat your feet on the sea sand.
7. She tried her key in the east door.
8. He put the sealer on the tree limb.
9. Even she can be mean.
10. I drink my coffee sugar free.
11. She put her receipts for the green machine in a neat pile.
12. If you need relief from the heat, you can leave the city and go to the beach.
13. The green beans and peas are in a sealed jar in the freezer.
14. We can't foresee next week's deals.
15. The movie reel revealed the queen's history.
16. On our knees, we planted the seeds for the trees.
17. Please return my keys immediately.
18. There is a heap of green peach leaves by the tea cup.
19. The previous chief of police was in a different league.
20. We will need to piece together the keys to the mystery.

it, did, city

Other sample words for various spellings:

exam, business, abyss, women

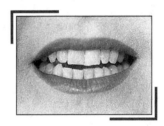

Classification   High, front, lax vowel

- Used in the initial, medial, and end positions in words
- Found in both stressed and unstressed syllables

Description
- Lips are relaxed from producing the [i], slightly less than a smile
- Back sides of tongue are against upper molars
- Tongue is aimed toward the point at which teeth meet upper gums
- Vocal folds vibrate

Drill Words

Initial	*Medial*	*End**
if	did	army
ill	drink	beauty
in	dinner	city
is	listen	every
issue	minute	only
it	quick	party
instead	since	probably
include	thin	really
important	visit	story
itch	win	windy

Drill Sentences

1. Beauty is only skin deep.
2. Give me a minute to fix dinner.
3. Every fifth or sixth kid wins.
4. Which business is having a sale?
5. This is an important issue.
6. Did you notice if there was milk?
7. My single sister lives alone.
8. History will ring true.
9. It's a big bill with six figures.
10. It isn't really my business.
11. This was a typical quick fix.
12. Realistically, his ability fits the prerequisites of the job.
13. Phyllis and six other women visited the windy city.
14. Tim's physician convinced him to have a physical.
15. It was a dismal fifty-minute video.
16. Kit could knit mittens for the women's group.
17. Physics is a pretty difficult course of study.
18. It is important to be issued a permit to build a room addition.
19. The instructor installed a television in the cubicle.
20. It isn't very pretty what a town without pity can do.

*Because this sound is used in unstressed syllables, it is the sound to which we reduce the [i] when that sound seems to appear at the ends of words and especially in connected speech; that is, in sentences. (See pages 152–153 for further information.)

Contrast Drill The phoneme [ɪ] produces little difficulty for most persons who are native speakers of English. However, non-native speakers, those whose primary language is Spanish, Italian, French, or an Asian language, may interchange [i] and [ɪ] which can result in confusion. There is a meaningful difference and a phonemic difference between *sheep* and *ship*. To exchange the two sounds results in a meaning change. It may be helpful for the speaker of English as a second language to utilize the contrast drill lists that follow to drill with words and phrases.

Contrast Drill Words

[i]	[ɪ]
beat	bit
deed	did
deal	dill
feet	fit
feel	fill
heat	hit
heal	hill
keel	kill
meet	mitt
meal	mill
kneel	nil
neat	knit
peat	pit
peel	pill
queens	quince
reel	rill
seat	sit
seal	sill
teal	till
wean	win

Contrast Drill Phrases

[i] [ɪ]	[ɪ] [i]
eat it	drill team
she is	drink tea
beat it	win three
we miss	which week
knee skin	in free
we did	it's east
feel thin	with me
each bit	fit feet
tease it	miss me
free trip	quick speech

Another feature to remember regarding the [ɪ] is that it will appear in words in sentences where you might not expect. For example, when you say the word *busy* in isolation, it would seem that you would say [bɪzi], that is stressing the [i] at the end. However, when words connect in spoken language, sounds change. The end sound, usually written with a *y*, is produced with laxity and becomes the [ɪ] phoneme. For example, try the following combinations.

pity   you
easy   street
funny   girl
any   person
leaky   faucet
city   planners
pretty picture
busy   bee
every   chance
only   one

or

ate, bait, pay

Other sample words for various spellings:

claim, weight, great, day, filet

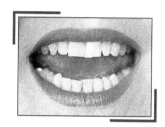

Classification   Mid, front, tense vowel

- Used in initial, medial, and end positions in words. Formerly written as [e], context may even shorten this sound.
- Usually found in stressed syllables

Description

- Lips are more "squared" and tensed
- Tongue tip is aimed toward the top edge of lower teeth
- Back of tongue is against back molars, but with less "push" than with previous phonemes
- Vocal folds vibrate

Drill Words	*Initial*	*Medial*	*End*
	able	afraid	bay
	ace	bait	day
	acre	brave	gray
	age	game	lay
	agent	great	pay
	aim	made	may
	ale	place	play
	amiable	state	stay
	ape	trade	they
	eight	simplification	way

Drill Sentences

1. They are able to make change.
2. May I trade you aces for eights?
3. That's the name of the game.
4. Stay in an amiable place.
5. At the age of eight you play every day.
6. You deserve a break today.
7. The agent made a claim for pay.
8. Your weight will show your age.
9. She was able to make a name change.
10. Friday let's change places.
11. The travel agent okayed the delay of my vacation.
12. They may have to face immigration agents to weigh the crates.
13. Jay looked out at the gray day thinking it was a shame it wasn't going to be a great day.
14. Kay made the arrangements for the remains to be buried in the grave.
15. A good grade of suede won't fade in color.
16. James bought a Great Dane and raised it to obey him.
17. Wait until it's safe to trade in pork bellies and grain.
18. Jason bought several acres in the great state of Maine.
19. They arranged to stay in the same place day after day.
20. I explained that Asian studies is offered later.

[ɛ]

end, get

Other sample words for various spellings:

weather, friend, said, care, square

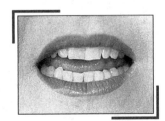

Classification   Mid, front, lax vowel

- Used in the initial and medial positions of words; not found at ends

- Used in stressed syllables in words

Description

- Lips are in "squared" shape without tension

- Tip of tongue is aimed toward lower teeth; back of tongue lightly touches back molars

- Vocal folds vibrate

Drill Words

Initial	*Medial*
air	bed
any	dead
effort	direct
edge	head
egg	get
else	met
end	object
enter	strength
evident	yes
expect	when

Drill Sentences

1. Make any effort to be direct.
2. Expect to get a head start.
3. Wear a sweater in cool weather.
4. Have you ever felt better?
5. It ended up in the dead letter bin.
6. The friends met together.
7. Spend what is necessary for the present.
8. Take a guess whether or not I'll remember.
9. She said it made sense to share.
10. The redhead wore a size ten dress.
11. When Ed ran out of strength, he made an extra effort to exercise.
12. A friend recommends that you eat eggs for breakfast.
13. Evidently, Freda spent her inheritance on art objects.
14. He banged his head against the edge of the ledge.
15. There wasn't any question about the evident debt.
16. Pin the hem of the dress when you expect to wear it.
17. We made a bet that direct mail was better.
18. The president signed the testament with ten pens.
19. I wanted to get seven presents for your birthday.
20. I said that we get paid on the tenth and the twentieth.

Contrast Drill   Although the phoneme [ɛ] causes few people difficulty, some speakers may substitute the sound [ɪ] for the [ɛ]. This frequently occurs in regional dialects, particularly southern dialects, but these sounds seem to be merging in other areas of the country. Speakers whose primary language is one of the Native American languages or Vietnamese may also experience confusion between these two sounds. Below are contrast drill words and phrases for practice to differentiate between these two sounds.

Contrast Drill Words

[ɪ]	[ɛ]
bit	bet
did	dead
fill	fell
mitt	met
knit	net
pit	pet
quill	quell
sill	sell
till	tell
will	well

Contrast Drill Phrases

[ɪ] [ɛ]	[ɛ] [ɪ]
in bed	get in
is every	any drink
miss them	end it
fit extra	red hill
first question	said it
his strength	ten wins
did end	neck itch
will set	every trick
it's best	very pretty
big present	head wind

at, cat

Other sample words for various spellings:

aunt, plaid, or daiquiri

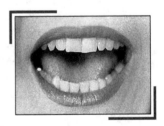

Classification Low, front, tense vowel

- Used in the initial and medial positions of words
- Used in stressed syllables of words

Description

- Lower jaw drops slightly from position for [ɛ]
- Tongue is almost touching lower teeth
- Tongue has slight degree of tension
- Vocal folds vibrate

Drill Words	*Initial*	*Medial*
	accent	bad
	act	can
	action	fat
	add	man
	answer	pass
	animal	placid
	am	perhaps
	ask	shall
	attribute	thank
	after	value

Drill Sentences

1. Practice your character until you are a master.
2. Plan to plant the grass near the path.
3. There is a chance to travel first class.
4. I can't accept "no" for an answer.
5. I am trying to add up half of the samples.
6. Shall I act my age?
7. Thank you for the chance to dance.
8. It's a fact that a family tree branches out.
9. Can you fathom why they went to battle?
10. The captain commanded the troops to set up camp.
11. Daniel saluted as the flag passed by.
12. For dinner we had lamb, salmon, and candied bananas.
13. Sam came from Manhattan, Kansas.
14. The camera caught Nancy dancing in front of the band stand.
15. Aunt Janet ransacked the room looking for her hat.
16. It was a crass and dastardly act to laugh at the practical joke.
17. Fran managed to look attractive in her fancy pants.
18. Magic and fantasy go hand in hand.
19. Make it a habit to ask without an accent.
20. An angry cat attacked the dapper man.

Some speakers, especially those with some Eastern and Midwestern dialects, have a tendency to nasalize the phoneme [æ]. If you relax the degree of tongue tension and pull the tongue back very slightly, you can achieve a softer sound. First be sure your velum is raised as you attempt to produce a softer or less flat sound. You might try pinching your nostrils together as you drill with the following list of words. These words contain no nasal sounds.

Drill Words			
act	add	apt	ax
back	baffle	bag	bat
cab	cat	crab	crass
dab	dad	dapper	dastardly
fad	fascist	fat	flag

habit	hack	had	hat
lab	bad	lap	laugh
pack	pad	pal	pass
rack	raffle	rag	rat
sack	sad	sag	sassafras

Now try using the list that follows. This list includes words with the [æ] followed by a nasal sound. Raise your velum and release your nostrils for this list.

Drill Words

bamboo	banana	band	bandit
camera	can	candor	Kansas
dam	dance	dandy	Daniel
famish	fan	fancy	fantasy
ham	hand	hangar	hanging
lamb	lance	land	language
mammal	man	manage	Manhattan
pamper	pan	panic	pants
ramp	ran	rank	ransom
Sam	sand	sanguine	sanitary

Front Vowel Contrast Drill

Now that you have learned the front vowel sounds of General American English, you may wish to review those sounds. The following lists may help you to distinguish individual front vowels as you review. As you go through the lists, take care to produce each vowel precisely.

[i]	[ɪ]	[eɪ]	[ɛ]	[æ]
beet	bit	bait	bet	bat
creep	crypt	crepe	crept	crack
deed	did	Dade	dead	dad
eat	it	ate	etcetera	at
feet	fit	fate	felt	fat
greet	grit	great	Greta	gratitude
heat	hit	hate	heterosexual	hat
leak	lick	lake	lecture	lack
meat	mitt	mate	met	mat
neat	knit	Nate	net	gnat
peat	pit	pate	pet	pat
reek	Rick	rake	wreck	rack
seat	sit	sate	set	sat
teal	till	tale	tell	tally
weep	whip	wait	wept	wrap

Back Vowels

alms, father

Other sample words for various spellings:

college, hearten, guard

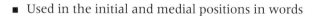

Classification   Low, back, lax vowel

- Used in the initial and medial positions in words
- Usually found in stressed syllables

Description
- Lower jaw is as low as possible for speech
- Tongue is very flat in the bottom of the mouth, but relaxed
- Vocal folds vibrate

Drill Words

Initial	*Medial*
alms	follow
arch	god
are	hock
arm	knowledge
art	modern
article	probable
on	rock
obvious	stock
option	upon
argue	want

Drill Sentences
1. It is obvious the guard had honor.
2. Follow your hunch on the stock option.
3. The article on modern design expanded my knowledge.
4. The college art gallery is locked.
5. Stay calm when the alarm is on.
6. It is probable she will be honest about what she wants.
7. Father believed that God was his rock.
8. The doctor acted properly at the party.
9. One dollar will buy a box of large tops.
10. He has a job at a body parts shop.
11. Economics are based in part on farm crops.
12. March is often spring break for college students.
13. Tom took an option to buy modern art for fewer dollars.
14. Rock and roll was played at the sock hop.
15. It is probable that Mom will have to hock her rocks and gems.

16. Father's rod and reel was not at the dock.
17. The cop defused the bomb planted by the mob.
18. Bonnie is studying psychology, botany, political science, and art.
19. Don's hobby is building model cars.
20. It is probable that a little knowledge can be a big problem.

awful, caught, law

Other sample words for various spellings:

gone, taught, brought

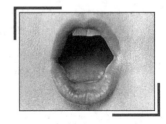

Classification   Mid, back, lax vowel

- Used in the initial, medial, and end positions in words
- Used in stressed syllables in words

Description
- Lips are slightly rounded and pushed slightly out
- Back of tongue is raised slightly
- Vocal folds vibrate

Drill Words

Initial	Medial	End
all	brought	claw
almost	caught	draw
already	gone	gnaw
also	lawn	jaw
although	morning	law
auction	song	paw
off	talk	raw
office	taught	saw
often	wall	slaw
order	wrong	straw

Drill Sentences
1. Already the lawn is gone.
2. I taught her to draw at the office.
3. He often gnaws with his jaw.
4. There is song and`talk across the hall.
5. It is wrong according to the law.
6. We thought it was a lost cause.
7. My daughter lost a small dog.
8. We took a short walk in the morning.
9. She caught the call near the wall.
10. I often order my food raw.
11. Paul's lawyer tried to stall the opposing office.

12. The auction was called off this morning.
13. Salt rubbed in raw meat can make it last longer.
14. Dawn thought we had gone to the morgue.
15. The tall ships are almost off shore.
16. The medicine was wrong for such a strong cough.
17. Take the chalk and draw broad strokes on the wall.
18. Give me a call when you have almost thought of it all.
19. We will take a straw vote to see if we ought to take a walk.
20. "Law and Order" is an authored television show.

Contrast Drill   Many speakers do not clearly distinguish between [ɑ] and [ɔ]. Certain U.S. Eastern variations may substitute [ɑ] as in *gone.* It is important to note that there are some subtle variations among [a], [ɑ], and [ɔ] that require careful listening and production. Should you substitute [ɑ] for [ɔ] in some words, such as *ball,* no meaning change occurs. However, a meaning change does occur in some other words, for example, *cot* [ɑ] and *caught* [ɔ] or names *Don* [ɑ] and *Dawn* [ɔ]. Many non-native speakers have difficulty distinguishing between these two sounds. Speakers of Asian languages, Spanish, German, and Middle Eastern languages might benefit by concentrated drill on these phonemes. Here is a list of words wherein a meaning change occurs when one sound is substituted for another.

Contrast Drill Words

[ɑ]	[ɔ]
Otto	auto
bot	bought
cot	caught
Don	dawn
fond	fawned
god	gaud
hock	hawk
la	law
moll	maul
ma	maw
Mom	Maugham
nod	gnawed
not	naught
pod	pawed
Ra	raw
tock	talk
tot	taught
wok	walk
yon	yawn

A few words may sound the same but may mean and be spelled differently. We call these homophonous words, or homophones. Here are examples of these using the phoneme [ɔ].

all   awl
ball   bawl
call   caul
hall   haul
mall   maul

or

open, almost, ago

Other sample words for various spellings:

show, soul, coal, foe, sew

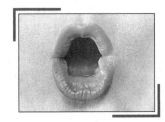

Classification Mid, back, tense vowel

- Used in initial, medial, and end positions in words
- Used in stressed syllables in words

Description
- Lips form an "o" shape, slightly tensed
- Tongue aims toward lower teeth; back of tongue is raised
- Vocal folds vibrate

This is more often a diphthong in use, but for some speakers may be produced as a "pure vowel," one for which the mouth does not change shape during production. Moving from one position to another during vocalization creates the diphthong [oʊ].

Drill Words	*Initial*	*Medial*	*End*
	oak	almost	ago
	oat	broken	dough
	ocean	code	ego
	odor	gold	follow
	old	lower	grow
	omit	moment	know
	only	notice	low
	open	post	so
	over	rode	though
	own	story	zero

Drill Sentences

1. The old oak no longer grows.
2. I'm the only one who knows the story.
3. Follow the report of lowered prices on gold.
4. I don't suppose you mind if I come home.
5. Most people control clothes buying.
6. Both shoulders of my coat are tight.
7. The horse won't be broken.
8. I'll phone the moment the post office posts the notice.
9. Those ocean odors offend my nose.
10. I suppose I told you long ago that I did that.
11. Joe was the local host and set our goals.
12. He broke the code of the Wyoming four.
13. There was a notice in the post office about the gold.
14. Home can be a boat on the open ocean.
15. Although her hair is shoulder length at the moment, she almost cut it only this morning.
16. I groaned at the cold as I trudged through the snow covered hills.
17. Joan knows that the secret code can be broken.
18. The bolt was so low you could almost open it with your big toe.
19. Nobody likes to go on Mr. Toad's Wild Ride better than Moe.
20. My only goal is to tell a joke as well as Cole.

cook

Other sample words for various spellings:

foot, should, sure, woman

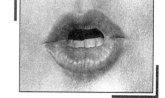

Classification High, back, lax vowel

- Used only in medial positions in words
- Used in stressed and unstressed syllables in words

Description
- Lips are rounded and pushed slightly out
- Tongue tip touches back of lower teeth; back of tongue is raised
- Vocal folds vibrate

Drill Words

Medial

book	put
butcher	stood
foot	sugar
full	would
good	your

Drill Sentences

1. The butcher hung the wooden spoon on a hook.
2. You should avoid cooking with sugar.
3. That woman wrote a good book.
4. You could take a good look at your foot.
5. The bully couldn't push me around.
6. I couldn't get the tank full.
7. Be sure to put the bush in the yard.
8. One cookie couldn't hurt.
9. Don't pull the wool over your eyes.
10. You should tell me which cookbook you use.
11. The bullet was put into the chamber crooked.
12. He would eat until he was full of cookies.
13. The wolf was hiding in the bushes in the woods.
14. The new cushions looked good on the couch.
15. Robin Hood pulled an arrow out a foot away from where he stood.
16. The butcher told us how to cook the pullet.
17. Mr. Good pulled a wool hood over his head.
18. I took a full cup of coffee to the kitchen nook.
19. Take a good look at the crooked wooden path through the woods.
20. You should show off your good looks.

oops, moon, woo

Other sample words for various spellings.

into, brew, fruit, group, true, rule, shoe, soon, two

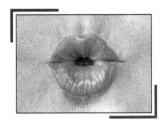

Classification   High, back, tense vowel

- Usually used in medial and end positions in words, although a few words begin with this phoneme

- Used in stressed syllables in words

Description
- Lips are pursed and tense

- Tongue tip touches back of lower front teeth; back of tongue arches high in rear of mouth

- Vocal folds vibrate

Drill Words

Initial	Medial	End
oodles	group	blue
oops	include	due
ooze	lose	goo

oozy	move	moo
uzi	pool	shoe
	prove	sue
	rule	through
	school	true
	whom	who
	youth	woo

Drill Sentences
1. Be true-blue to your school.
2. Pay your dues to cool off in the pool.
3. Who stepped on my blue suede shoes?
4. "Moon, June, tune, and spoon" are words to a song.
5. He blew on the spoonful of hot soup.
6. The coupons were stuck with glue.
7. Our school group insurance includes family.
8. That is the exception to prove the rule.
9. Who trekked through the ooze?
10. Please don't lose my ruler.
11. The news was that Sue was accused of lewd conduct.
12. Luke chewed noodles and fruit and ate until he was full.
13. Stuart flew to New York to buy a new suit.
14. The group had to prove they could include the youth.
15. For dinner Shubert had soup that looked like gruel.
16. You could lose your proof of school attendance.
17. Gould was not in the mood for such a rude awakening.
18. The brute was a nuisance for everyone at the dude ranch.
19. The bluebird cooed throughout the cool evening.
20. My bills came due too soon.

Contrast Drill   Non-native speakers may confuse [ʊ] and [u], especially speakers of Spanish, Chinese, Vietnamese, Italian, French, Indonesian, and some Middle Eastern languages. The following lists may help in practicing to distinguish between the two phonemes. The first list includes words in which spellings differ. In the second list, many vowels are spelled the same way in both words. For that reason it is important to distinguish between [ʊ] and [u].

Contrast Drill Words

[ʊ]	[u]
could	cooed
look	Luke
full	fool
good	ghoul
nook	nuke
pull	pool
put	poor

rook	rule
soot	suit
would	wooed

[ʊ]	[u]
book	boot
cook	cool
foot	fool
hood	hoot
look	loot
stood	stool
took	tool

Back Vowel Contrast Drill

Now that you have learned the back vowels of General American English, you may wish to review them. The following lists will help you to distinguish among these back vowels. As you go through the lists, be careful to produce each vowel with care.

[ɑ]	[ɔ]	[oʊ]	[ʊ]	[u]
bot	bought	boat	butcher	boot
cot	caught	coat	could	cool
fond	fawned	foal	full	fool
god	gaud	goad	good	Gould
hock	hawk	hole	hook	who
la	law	low	look	loot
moll	maul	mole	moor	move
nod	gnawed	note	nook	nuke
pod	pawed	pole	pull	pool
Ra	raw	row	rook	rude
tot	talk	tote	took	toot
wok	walk	woke	wood	woo
yon	yawn	yoke	your	youth

Mid Vowels

The four mid-vowel sounds we will examine in this section are highly characteristic of General American English. The vowels in *un*stressed syllables, and sometimes stressed syllables, are reduced to a mid-mouth "grunt" called the *schwa*. Sometimes this phoneme is combined with an [ɚ] or [ɝ] sound, as in *father* or *earth*. Non-native speakers have a particularly difficult time identifying which phonemes (seen as letters in a word) should become the schwa sound. In Spanish, for example, each letter clearly and consistently represents a sound. You have already learned that this just is not true of English. Almost all non-native speakers have trouble distinguishing the schwa [ə] from some other English vowels. The difficulty may not matter much in some words, for example, if for *agree* you say [agri] as opposed to [əgri]. The difference, however, is important in distinguishing between the sounds in these words, for example: *tuck* and *talk, gull* and *goal, jug* and *jog, luck* and *look.*

The schwa is produced primarily mid-mouth, and it is found in different contextual situations. For example, it may occur in a monosyllabic, unstressed word, "*the* book"; an unstressed syllable in a polysyllabic word, *happening;* or in a monosyllabic stressed word, "It was *mud."*

American linguists use two symbols to describe the basic schwa sound. The [ə] represents unstressed schwa sounds and the [ʌ] represents stressed schwa sounds. We can draw the same comparison between the "er" sounds. These are vowel-like "r" phonemes. The symbol [ɚ] represents only unstressed sound, and [ɝ] symbolizes stressed sound. What follow are individual descriptions and drills for each of these mid-mouth sounds.

about, happen, the

Other sample words for various spellings:

a̲bout, fam̲ou̲s, c̲omplete, milli̲on, beautifu̲l, childre̲n, preside̲nt, oce̲an, speci̲al

Classification   Mid, central, lax vowel (called the *schwa* [ʃwa] or [ʃva])

- Used in the initial, medial, and end positions of words
- Used *only* in *unstressed* syllables in multisyllabic words and in *unstressed* monosyllabic *words* in sentences
- Considered the most common sound in American English

Description
- Lips are slightly apart
- Tongue lies relaxed about mid-mouth
- Vocal folds vibrate

Note: Before beginning drills, you may wish to identify the places in words or the words themselves in which the sound occurs.

Drill Words	*Initial*	*Medial*	*End*
	above	company	America
	across	given	area
	again	happen	camera
	alone	often	gorilla
	among	method	opera
	another	national	orchestra
	around	probably	soda
	away	special	the
	obtain	taken	tuba
	upon	woman	data

Drill Sentences

1. Once upon a time there was another arena for the circus.
2. America is not famous for opera.
3. It so happened the company was given special recognition.
4. You can probably have the data among other things.
5. That is another possible solution.
6. We called the police again.
7. Are you often alone in the area?
8. Try to obtain a special camera.
9. We agree that the method was aboveboard.
10. The action the department took was brought to my attention.
11. The orchestra probably doesn't use the tuba.
12. A woman rented the Honda for a special reason.
13. The committee has given permission to pool our computer data.
14. The parent company had the idea to hold a general meeting.
15. I was away from my desk when the calendar was taken.
16. Congress is in the dark about the scandal.
17. She suggested that the gorilla be given bananas.
18. Maria was the target of a relatively common hoax.
19. Optional equipment will help your company stay ahead of the competition.
20. Communities along the river embankments need to develop protection.

[ʌ]

up, money

Other sample words for various spellings:

young, blood, love, under

Classification Mid, central, lax vowel

- Used in initial and medial positions in words
- Used *only* in *stressed* syllables in words and in monosyllablic *words* which are *stressed* in sentences

Description
- Lips are slightly open
- Tongue is in relaxed position mid-mouth
- Vocal folds vibrate
- This phoneme is given more emphasis than [ə]

Note: Take a moment to identify the place in words where this sound occurs.

Drill Words

Initial	Medial
onion	club
other	come
oven	blood
ugly	double
ulcer	love
ulterior	mother
umbrella	one
umpire	study
under	touch
utter	young

Drill Sentences

1. Some of the money came in hundred dollar bills.
2. The other company suffered a summer setback.
3. Mother suffered a severe sunburn.
4. Stay out of trouble and study at the club.
5. The judge, a public figure, was above reproach.
6. Put onions in the oven just at two hundred degrees.
7. What has become of love of country?
8. When I am done, you can double-check the results.
9. Nothing will keep her from running for public office.
10. The America's Cup race was much more wonderful than we dreamed.
11. The honeysuckle bud was under the hut.
12. The sunshine was shut out by the shutters.
13. The gull was stunned when it fell with a thud.
14. You can double your money if you study.
15. He made such a good one-putt on the other green.
16. Bud was the umpire for the young Cubs.
17. The suburban club had fun shucking peanuts.
18. The young mother loved to bake buns in the oven.
19. The duck stood under the umbrella studying the rain.
20. I have a gut feeling one of us has an ulcer.

Contrast Drill The following brief list of words and word combinations contrasts between [ə] and [ʌ]. The marks above the sound indicate stressing or unstressing of sound; ə̆ indicates lack of stress and ʌ́ indicates stress.

Contrast Drill Words

ăbóve
úppă̆nce
húntĕ̆d
lúnchĕ̆on
ă̆ssúnder

Contrast Drill Word Combinations

thĕ̆ júdge
ă̆ hút
óf sóme
thĕ̆ búm
ă̆ búddy

Non-native speakers may confuse some back vowels with the mid-mouth [ʌ]. The following contrast drill serves to distinguish among the [ɑ], [ʌ], and [oʊ]. Notice that spelling is not very helpful in learning how to say words!

[ɑ]	[ʌ]	[oʊ]
body	club	both
god	company	four
got	cover	hope
knowledge	done	known
possible	enough	most
shop	from	nosey
watch	public	road
rock	sun	shoulder
watch	touch	spoke
watt	young	told

perhaps, ever

Other sample words for various spellings:

answer, treasure, sugar, forward,
color, soldier

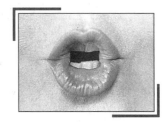

Classification Mid, central, lax vowel with an "r" quality

- Used in medial and end positions in words
- Used *only* in *unstressed* syllables in words

| Description | ■ Lips are slightly open and pushed forward |
| | ■ Blade of tongue is slightly humped; tongue tip curls back slightly |

Drill Words

Medial	*End*
afternoon	after
effort	doctor
exercise	labor
federal	measure
forward	offer
government	other
modern	pleasure
perhaps	power
record	solar
western	sugar

Drill Sentences

1. The farmers are in danger of losing federal funding.
2. Make an effort to exercise every afternoon.
3. Never overestimate the power of the government.
4. The other letter was sent with proper postage.
5. The water from the river was wonderful.
6. Perhaps I should set the record straight so that you will understand.
7. She is a better teacher of modern literature.
8. I would rather leave the matter on record.
9. The service to those persons was rather slow.
10. Was the weather as you remember?
11. Mr. Baker performed the measure with little effort.
12. Father persuaded Curtis to work in the solar plant.
13. Hubert gave the federal government one hundred percent of his income.
14. This weather is the worst record in western history.
15. Remember that exertion will cause you to perspire.
16. Catherine was a modern dancer who twirled on her toes.
17. My brother is a better actor than I ever imagined.
18. Never offer to drive a herd of cows across the desert.
19. Another discoverer came forward.
20. Doctor Roberts was a soldier for the U.S. government.

earth, first, her

Other sample words for various spellings:

irk, urge, word, were, journal

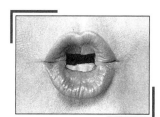

Classification   Mid, central, lax vowel with an "r" quality

- Used in the initial, medial, and end positions in words

- Used *only* in *stressed* syllables

Description
- Lips are slightly open and pushed forward

- Blade of tongue is slightly humped; tongue tip curls back slightly

- Seems to be produced with greater force since it appears in stressed syllables

Drill Words

Initial	Medial	End
early	bird	burr
earth	church	cur
earn	first	fir
ergot	heard	her
err	hurt	lure
irk	learn	per
urban	return	purr
urge	third	sir
urgent	word	stir
urn	worth	whir

Drill Sentences
1. Were you disturbed to be the first to learn of the earth's problems?
2. That person wrote about her in his journal every thirty days.
3. Sir, be sure to put a return address on third-class mail.
4. The girl got up early to feed the bird in the fir tree.
5. Learn that words can lure us or can hurt us.
6. You can further your purpose with certain actions.
7. Learn to take your turn to serve in tennis.
8. The First World Church is on Third Street.
9. Don't be nervous if the news is urgent.
10. Attorneys earn more than they are worth.
11. Bert Churchill was a former army colonel.
12. The nurse purchased the perfect purse to go with her pearls.
13. Curse words are not worth being heard.
14. Myrtle was determined to reserve a space at the terminal.
15. The urban university was an early choice.
16. The expert took his turn in the quality circle.
17. The girl was personally hurt when she heard the news.
18. We heard the search continued for the murderer.
19. She burned the preserves she was serving.
20. Perfume stained the shirt Dirk had purchased.

Contrast Drill The following words and word combinations distinguish between the sounds of [ɚ] and [ɝ]. The markings above vowels represent the stress or lack of stress on those vowels. The [ɚ] represents lack of stress, shown by the mark ˘, and [ɝ] represents stress, shown by the mark ´. These two phonemes always appear as a vowel-like r.

Contrast Drill Words

éarnĕr
fúrthĕr
fúrriĕr
sérvĕr

Contrast Drill Word Combinations

retúrn offĕr
húrt hĕr
othĕr pérson
measŭre fírst
propĕr wórd

Diphthongs

A diphthong is a combination of two vowels wherein the articulators begin in one approximate vowel position and glide to another approximate vowel position on a single vocalization. In General American English there are three major diphthongs, one minor diphthong, two extended pure vowels that may be considered diphthongs, and some dialectal diphthongs. These occur when one vowel of the diphthong combination is omitted or another vowel is substituted for one generally used. We will not be considering those diphthongs which are used in dialectal communities.

Understand that in these vowel combinations, the second vowel is produced with less tension and thus becomes [ɪ] instead of [i] or [ʊ] rather than [u].

eye, beside, by

Other sample words for various spellings:

kind, try, tie, high, buy, height, guide, island, aisle

Classification
- Diphthong that starts at approximately the [a] (see p. 148) and glides to an approximate [ɪ]

- Used in stressed and unstressed syllables in words and stressed words in sentences

Description   ■ Tongue starts in a position slightly pulled back from [æ], low, just back from front, and glides to a position near [ɪ] high front

■ Vocal folds vibrate continuously through the glide

Drill Words

Initial	Medial	End
aisle	arrive	buy
eye	child	cry
ice	exercise	die
icon	desire	fly
identical	might	high
idea	smile	lie
idle	surprise	my
ire	require	try
iron	white	sky
island	wide	why

Drill Sentences

1. My reply tonight is silence.
2. You might try to arrive at the height of the season.
3. The sign outside was a sight for sore eyes.
4. The child tried to smile at the bright idea.
5. My wife can drive a five-speed car.
6. I like the light to the right of my writing desk.
7. Try to find out the price for the white tights.
8. The five and dime sells identical sizes.
9. The idea is to require a guide.
10. Wear a bright, wide tie for nighttime.
11. The right side of your face is not identical to the left side.
12. It surprised me that the choir sang a song without rhyme.
13. Diane admired Mike's biceps and sighed.
14. My choice of a diet would include ice cream.
15. What style of china are you eyeing?
16. The idea of a loiterer outside is annoying.
17. The tiny island exported quite a lot of iron.
18. Click on an icon to change the style and height of the type.
19. Kindly smile and show me your white teeth.
20. *Blythe Spirit* is a play to enjoy from an aisle seat.

out, house, now

Other sample words for various spellings:

hour, brown, bough

Classification	■ Diphthong that starts at an approximate [a] and glides to an approximate [ʊ]
	■ Used in initial, medial, and end positions in words
	■ Used in stressed syllables in words

Description	■ Tongue starts in a position slightly pulled back from [æ], low, just back from the front and glides to a high back position
	■ Vocal folds vibrate continuously through glide

Drill Words

Initial	Medial	End
hour	about	allow
hourly	amount	bough
ouch	cloud	cow
ounce	doubt	how
our	found	now
oust	ground	plow
out	house	pow
outer	mountain	row
outlet	pound	sow
outside	town	wow

Drill Sentences

1. I found the total amount at the outlet to be less.
2. There was quite a row in our house over the accounts.
3. Now the crowd began to shout.
4. A cloud floated south of the mountain.
5. The ground in our town is hard to dig out.
6. We left downtown about an hour ago.
7. The brown cow stood in the plowed field.
8. Sixteen ounces equals a pound.
9. I doubt that the sound came from outside.
10. You should allow about an hour for the powder to dry.
11. Howard could eat a pound of clam chowder at the Round House.
12. Try to change the sounds coming out of your mouth.
13. Pronounce aloud a fair amount of proper nouns.
14. This county has many fowl such as grouse and owls.
15. Once doubt clouded my mind but now I have found the light.
16. The housekeeper was outraged that her hourly pay was in doubt.
17. The bough of the tree in the south court touched the ground.
18. There was no doubt that the coward would stay away from the house.
19. The scouts hired a clown for the roundup.
20. The founder of the devout has vowed to build a town.

oil, boil, boy

Other sample words for various spellings:

voice, destroy

Classification   Diphthong that glides from a low back vowel position to a high, front vowel position

- Used in the initial, medial, and end positions of words
- Used in stressed syllables in words

Description

- Tongue begins in low back position approximating [ɔ] and glides to a high front position approximating [ɪ]
- Vocal folds vibrate continuously though glide

Drill Words

Initial	Medial	End
oil	appoint	annoy
oilcan	boil	boy
oiler	boycott	convoy
oily	coin	coy
ointment	join	destroy
oyster	loin	employ
	poignant	enjoy
	point	joy
	soil	soy
	voice	toy

Drill Sentences

1. The sign pointed the convoy in the right direction.
2. The oil company employed oilers.
3. Her voice had a plaintive and poignant sound.
4. The boy played with his toys.
5. Boil the oysters in oil.
6. Sing a joyful noise.
7. Jingling coins annoy me.
8. I hope you enjoy the soy sauce.
9. The smell of ointment can be annoying.
10. The top soil was destroyed in the flood.
11. A strong boycott can destroy the oyster industry.
12. I try to avoid overly boisterous boys.
13. There will be a joint employment meeting in Boise.
14. Her appointment to royalty limited her choices.
15. It is better to broil the sirloin than to boil it.

16. You should avoid loitering on the streets of Detroit.
17. What's the point of destroying the oil fields?
18. Sigmund Freud was poised on the brink of a choice discovery.
19. Her coyness annoyed me, so I avoided her.
20. Royden enjoyed buying toys for his baby boy.

Special Diphthong

The following sound combinations become a diphthong when used in particular ways. There are optional manners of articulation. For example, some words may be pronounced with [ɪʊ], [ɪu], [ju], or [u]. To demonstrate the differences for yourself, use the word *neutral* and speak it in the following ways: [nɪʊtrəl], [nɪutrəl], [njutrəl], [nutrəl]. Each instance produces a slight variation. An optional manner of articulating this sound combination is to use the consonant [j] (see Chapter Ten) and the vowel [u]. This combination, [ju], produces a slightly different resulting sound than [ɪu]. Though the sound [ɪu] is infrequently used and may even be dropping out of American speech, if you are studying for broadcasting or the theater, you might want to cultivate use of [ɪu] or [ju] as used in *Tuesday* or *news.*

[ɪu] *

unit, beauty, hue

Other sample words for various spellings:

utility, few, neutral

Classification: Diphthong that starts in the high front of the mouth and glides to a high back position in the mouth

- Used in initial, medial, and end positions in words

- Used in stressed positions in words

Description:
- Tongue begins in a position approximating [ɪ], high front of mouth and glides directly to a high back position in the mouth, approximating [u]

- Vocal folds vibrate continuously throughout glide

*[ju], an approximate diphthong (see p. 235).

Drill Words	*Initial*	*Medial*	*End*
	unicorn	beauty	avenue
	uniform	duke	few
	universal	duty	imbue
	united	neutral	hue
	unison	museum	new
	usurp	music	mew
	utility	pure	renew
	use	tune	residue
	usual	Tuesday	view

Drill Sentences

1. The Duke of Earl is coming on Tuesday.
2. Use a pure substance to neutralize the water.
3. A few of us can sing the new tune.
4. To honor the United States is your duty.
5. Hers is a universal beauty.
6. It is a rather unusual museum on Fifth Avenue.
7. On Tuesday be sure to renew your utilities.
8. Don't let me usurp your view of the duke.
9. The uniform was in a neutral hue.
10. You can keep the residue for a new use.

Additional Drill

Poetry utilizes the repetition of vowel sounds in order to create rhyme. The next several poems may be used for drill with a variety of vowel sounds.

1. A wind sways the pines,
     And below
   Not a breath of wild air;
   Still as the mosses that glow
   On the flooring and over the lines
   Of the roots here and there.
   The pine tree drops its dead;
   They are quiet, as under the sea.
   Overhead, overhead
   Rushes life in a race.
   As the clouds the clouds chase;
       And we go,
   And we drop like the fruits of the tree,
       Even we,
       Even so.

—George Meredith

2. Here it is night: I stop at the Summit Temple.
Here I can touch the stars with my hand.
I dare not speak aloud in the silence
For fear of disturbing the dwellers of Heaven.

—Li Po

3. Does the road wind uphill all the way?
    Yes, to the very end.
Will the day's journey take the whole long day?
    From morn to night, my friend.

But is there for the night a resting place?
    A roof for when the slow dark hours begin.
May not the darkness hide it from my face?
    You cannot miss that inn.

Shall I meet other wayfarers at night?
    Those who have gone before.
Then must I knock, or call when just in sight?
    They will not keep you standing at that door.

Shall I find comfort, travel-sore and weak?
    Of labor you shall find the sum.
Will there be beds for me and all who seek?
    Yea, beds for all who come.

—Christina Rossetti

4. Having met my love,
    Afterwards my passion was,
When I measured it
    With the feeling of the past,
    As, if then, I had not loved.

—Atsutada

5. This is the ship of pearl, which, poets feign,
    Sails the unshadowed main—
    The venturous bark that flings
On the sweet summer wind its purpled wings

In gulfs enchanted, where the Siren sings,
    And coral reefs lie bare,
Where the cold sea maids rise to sun their streaming hair.

—Oliver Wendell Holmes

6. "Faith" is a fine invention
When Gentlemen can *see*—
But *Microscopes* are prudent
In an Emergency.

—Emily Dickinson

7. Was it something said,
    Something done,
Vexed him? was it touch of hand,
    Turn of head?
Strange! that very way
    Love begun:
I as little understand Love's decay.

—Robert Browning

Chapter Nine Checklist

VOWELS/DIPHTHONGS

Directions: The following passage includes words that contain front vowels, back vowels, mid vowels, and diphthongs in the sequence in which they appeared in this chapter. There are at least three or four words containing each phoneme. An IPA symbol above letters and underlining will aid you in identifying sounds. To the left of the passage is a checklist column for vowel/diphthong phonemes. Use an audio or video recorder or a partner to assist you in your evaluation. Make a checkmark beside any phoneme for which you require additional practice.

(See page 277 for a tear-out version of this form.)

i _____
    i I II i I i I I I I
    Each of us thinks it is easy enough to believe in important issues. In

I _____
    I I i i I I
    the city even dreams exist. So that begins the story.

e _____
    eI eI $ɛ$ $ɛ$ $ɛ$
    The name of the game is to get what you can, a friend had said. I was

ɛ _____
    eI $ɛ$ $ɛ$ eI eI
    afraid that wasn't ethical, and I cared to stay in the trade business. Is

æ _____
    $æ$ $æ$ $æ$ $ɛ$ $æ$ $æ$ $æ$
    that so bad? Perhaps! Still there was a chance to challenge my values.

ɑ _____
    $æ$ $ɔ$ $ɑ$ $ɔ$ $ɑ$
    After all, my father called it honor.

ɔ _____
    $ɑ$ $ɔ$ $æ$ $ɑ$ $ɔ$ $ɑ$
    "Be honest," he always said. That was his argument, his talk, what he

o _____
    $ɔ$
    taught me.

ʊ _____
    $ɔ$ $oʊ$ $oʊ$ $oʊ$ $oʊ$
    That was long ago when I was open and willing to grow. Though he

u _____   st<u>oo</u>d for g<u>oo</u>d, the sch<u>oo</u>l of hard knocks pr<u>o</u>ved many exceptions to

ə_____   the r<u>u</u>le, told me that no matter where y<u>ou</u> st<u>oo</u>d on issues y<u>ou</u> c<u>ou</u>ld

ʌ _____   l<u>o</u>se.

ɚ _____   <u>A</u>b<u>o</u>ve th<u>e</u> advice and <u>amo</u>ng any <u>u</u>lterior motives, I have c<u>o</u>me to

ɝ _____   treas<u>u</u>re his rath<u>er</u> t<u>er</u>se w<u>or</u>ds. I have r<u>u</u>n for p<u>u</u>blic office and have

aɪ_____   bec<u>o</u>me a sold<u>ier</u>, p<u>er</u>haps, for th<u>e</u> gov<u>er</u>nm<u>e</u>nt. N<u>ow</u>, <u>I</u> real<u>i</u>ze h<u>ow</u>

aʊ _____   p<u>ow</u>er b<u>uy</u>s t<u>i</u>me in cities and t<u>ow</u>ns. So, the b<u>oy</u> becomes the man

ɔɪ _____   and j<u>oi</u>ns the v<u>oi</u>ces which went before him. There is j<u>oy</u> and some

ɪu_____   b<u>eau</u>ty in that. There is a n<u>ew</u> sense of <u>u</u>niversal d<u>u</u>ty.

Chapter Nine Review

Review the following concepts:

- Vowels: characteristics/classifications
- Front vowels
- Back vowels
- Mid vowels
- Diphthongs

Respond to the following:

1. Why do vowels carry the "music" of language?
2. Which vowels may more easily be extended in sounding?
3. Which vowels are said to be produced with tension?
4. Which is the highest front vowel?
5. Which is the lowest back vowel?
6. Which are the three most commonly heard diphthongs?
7. What is the most common phoneme in the English language?
8. Of what use are diacritical markings in dictionaries?
9. Explain the difference between the pure vowels [e] and [o] and the diphthongs [eɪ] and [oʊ].

A P P L I C A T I O N

1. Which vowels are most problematic for you?

2. Are there any vowels that you tend to nasalize?

3. Are you rounding back vowels?

4. How are you using the schwa?

F O C U S   M E S S A G E

1. *ESL:* There will be several factors that influence you to use one vowel sound over another. Those are: the influence of your primary language, an inability to hear the new or different vowel sound, or the discrepancy between the visual impression of the sound and the actual sound predominantly used by speakers of English. *Tip:* The sounds [i] and [ɪ] may prove to be a challenge. Master the difference between these two sounds. Remember that the letters "a" and "o" as in *banana* or *convention* are produced with the [ə].

2. *Acting:* In order to project dialogue in a large theater or to communicate the intent of a dramatic message, vowels will carry the sound. A flexible actor will learn to produce each vowel clearly and should learn which vowel sound can serve as a substitute for another in order to create dialects for characterization.

3. *Broadcasting:* In order to create a fulsome on-air sound, work toward rounded back vowel sounds, avoid nasalization of [æ], and avoid overuse of [ə].

N O T E S

1. William Labov, "The Organization of Dialect Diversity in North America" (paper), ICSLP4, October 6, 1996.

10 Consonants

I eee oai o ooa a e ooi eee o oe.
Ths sntnc cntns n vwls nd th prcdng
sntnc n cnsnnts.

—Douglas R. Hofstadter[1]

TERMS

Affricates ['æfrɪkəts]   Combinations of two approximate consonant sounds that result in a new sound.

Alveolar ridge [æl'viələ-'rɪdʒ]   Upper gum ridge.

Bilabials [baɪ'leɪbɪəlz]   Consonants produced with the lips.

Blends [blɛndz]   A combination of two sounds; in this chapter, two consonants.

Cognates ['kɑgneɪts]   Two consonants produced in the same place in the mouth, one is voiced and one is voiceless.

Consonant ['kɑnsənənt]   Phonemes produced by setting up an obstruction to the vocalized or unvocalized breath stream.

Continuant [kən'tɪnjʊənt]   A consonant produced in one spot and given duration.

Dental ['dɛntəl]   Pertaining to the teeth.

Fricatives ['frɪkətɪvz]   Consonants produced with friction.

Glides [glaɪdz]   Consonants for which articulators begin in one position and move to another.

Glottal ['glɑtəl]   Voiceless consonant produced by sending air through the glottis.

Labio ['leɪbɪoʊ]   Lips.

Laterals ['lætə-əlz]   Consonants produced around the sides of the tongue.

Lingua ['lɪŋgwə]   Tongue.

Nasal ['neɪzəl]   Nose.

Palatal ['pælətəl]   Hard palate.

Plosives ['ploʊsɪvz]   Consonants that are exploded by momentarily stopping the air stream and then releasing it.

Velar ['vilə-]   Soft palate or velum.

Voiced ['vɔɪst]   Consonants produced with vocal fold vibration.

Voiceless ['vɔɪsləs]   Consonants produced without vocal fold vibration.

The lines quoted above clearly demonstrate the functions of vowels and consonants in words and sentences. Douglas R. Hofstadter, former columnist for *Scientific American,* calls these "self-referential" sentences, ones that speak of themselves. However, you would be hard pressed to determine just *what* it was the first "sentence" was saying. The second sentence, on the other hand, unfolds its meaning as you begin to insert the missing vowels. As we can see, consonants carry the meaning of language. There are 24 consonants in English. Some languages have fewer numbers of consonants, but some languages contain two or three times the number.

This chapter will denote and describe the individual consonant sounds of General American English. Though consonants carry the meaning of language, often the consonants cause problems. We frequently omit end sounds, particularly "ng" [ŋ] or "t" [t]; fail to explode sounds with adequate force; eliminate consonants in the middle of words, such as in *February*; or distort sounds, such as "s." We will examine some of these errors in articulation as we discuss each consonant. Remember that, with a few exceptions, consonants appear in initial, medial, and end positions in words, which causes an allophonic difference among phonemes (that is, a variance of sound depending on its context in a word). In addition, adjacent sounds will slightly alter the sound of each consonant, although it may take a trained ear to note such differences.

In Chapter Eight you learned the characteristics and classifications of consonants. As a reminder these are:

1. Consonants may be voiced or voiceless. Those consonants that are made in the same place in the mouth, one voiced and one not voiced, are called *cognates*.
2. Consonants are classified according to the place in the mouth where they are made and the manner in which they are made.

Figure 10.1 places consonants in the approximate places in the oral cavity at which they are produced.

Approach to Consonant Study

As noted, consonants are classified according to manner produced and place of production. This means that some are produced with a great deal of "friction" or "explosion," and some are produced only by sending the sound through the nose. Some consonants are produced in combination with other consonants thereby creating new consonant sounds. "Place" means that the consonant is produced in the front of the mouth with your two lips if it is bilabial, or that it is produced in the rear of the mouth with the back of your tongue up against the soft palate area if it is called lingua-velar.

There are several ways to approach the examination of consonants. We will begin with those phonemes produced in the front of the mouth (bilabial) and progress to those produced in the rear of the mouth (velar). In most "place" categories, as you can see from Table 10.1 (see "Terms" at

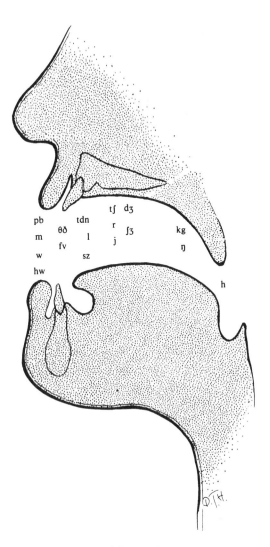

FIGURE 10.1 Positions of consonants in oral cavity. Though it is impossible to represent the exact tongue and lip positions, voice or voicelessness, and manner of production, this figure represents the approximate place of production for consonants.

beginning of chapter for definitions), there are several phonemes produced in the same area of the mouth; in fact, many of these are cognates. The difference among them, then, is the manner in which these sounds are produced. Since there are only three consonant phonemes that are

TABLE 10.1   Consonants of General American English

Manner	Bilabial	Labio-dental	Lingua-dental	Alveolar	Palatal	Velar	Glottal
Plosives	pb			td		kg	
Fricatives		fv	θð	sz	ʃʒ(šž)*		h
Nasals	m			n		[ŋ]	
Laterals				l			
Glides	hw w				r**j		
Affricates					tʃ ʤ (tš dž)*		

*These symbols represent IPA approved alternatives. These are the symbols more widely used by linguists and in books written especially for students of English as a second language.

**The current acceptable symbol for this phoneme is [ɹ]. But this text will use the upright [r] for ease in reading.

TABLE 10.2   IPA Consonant Pronunciation Guide

Sample Word	IPA
pay	p
been	b
met	m
whether	hw
weather	w
feather	f
voice	v
think	θ
the	ð
ten	t
den	d
see	s
zebra	z
no	n
lip	l
shoe	ʃ or š
persuasion	ʒ or ž
check	tʃ or tš
jar	ʤ or dž
read	r or ɹ
yes	j
keep	k
get	g
sing	ŋ
help	h

emitted nasally, all descriptions of consonant production, except for those three nasals, will assume closure to the nasal passages.

With all consonants you will be given an IPA symbol, sample words that demonstrate how the sound appears in front, middle, and end positions, other sample words that demonstrate how the sound is variously spelled, a sound classification, description of how the phoneme is produced, drill words and sentences, and in some instances, comparison drills among phonemes. Photographs are included for those consonants for which mouth shape is important.

The IPA Consonant Pronunciation Guide (Table 10.2) is provided for easy reference to symbols.

Bilabial Consonants

pay, hoping, soup

Other sample words for various spellings:

happy, appoint

Classification	Bilabial, plosive, voiceless consonant

- Used in the initial, medial, and end positions in words
- Used in stressed and unstressed syllables
- Cognate to [b]

Description	

- Lips are pressed together
- Teeth are slightly apart
- Air builds up behind lips, then explodes lips apart—the degree of explosion will depend upon where in a word the sound occurs
- No vocal fold vibration

Drill Words

Initial	*Medial*	*End*
pace	bespoke	cup
pad	captain	dip
page	deport	flop
pail	flippant	gap
pair	hepatitis	hip
palm	lipstick	lip
panda	maple	map
parade	nuptial	nap
park	repent	quip
pass	tepid	rip

Degree of Explosion or Aspiration of Air   Many non-native speakers, especially speakers of Asian languages and Spanish, have trouble with the degree of aspiration required to produce this phoneme. The degree of explosion or aspiration of air connected with the production of [p] varies depending on its place in a word, whether it is in a stressed or unstressed syllable, and whether or not it is followed by other consonants. Though the degree of aspiration is reduced when [p] occurs in the final positions in words, careful articulation requires that the [p] receive a slight degree of explosion when in the final position. The strongest [p] occurs in initial positions in words wherein it is followed by a vowel. The following are instances in which the degree of explosion is lessened.

Unstressed Syllables

apple	grasping
company	multiple
cheaper	rapid
empathy	reparation
flippant	superintendent

Blends Because [p] is found in combination with other consonants (l, r, t, s), that blend may reduce the explosion of the sound. Because there is little aspirate quality to the [p] when it is followed by another plosive, it may sound omitted in connected speech, such as in the following sentence: *Read this excer**pt** from the newspaper about the esca**ped** criminal.* With the following blends, be sure to produce a clear [p] in all positions.

[pl]	**[pr]**	**[pt]**	**[ps]**
applaud	approximate	accept	cups
apply	approve	capped	dips
complete	deprive	chopped	flops
deploy	disprove	concept	grips
display	oppress	excerpt	hips
explain	press	hopped	lips
place	prospect	kept	maps
plan	protect	optic	perhaps
please	prune	trapped	taps
stapler	repress	wrapped	wraps

Drill Sentences

1. It was plain that the captain was pleased he won the cup.
2. I apologize if the price of the maple syrup is not on the wrapper.
3. Put the powder in a cup of tepid water.
4. We passed the time making a quip or two about the nuptials.
5. She rapidly paced back and forth across the path.
6. The inspector led the parade in the park.
7. I suppose a nap would help.
8. He repaid every penny upon his departure.
9. Point to the place on the map where we will pitch the tent.
10. She inspected the rip in her slip.
11. We hoped the applause would show approval.
12. Perhaps you could explain the concept of the prospectus.
13. She kept her cups in place with clips.
14. Please complete the approval form for your optical exam.
15. The maps were displayed appropriately next to the plans.
16. You can protect your lips if you apply lipstick.
17. He planned to disprove the theory with one excerpt from his book.
18. We praised your acceptance speech.
19. It was a pleasure to make an exception that proved the rule.
20. He hopped over the wall and escaped repression.

[b]

been, table, cube

Other sample words for various spellings:

rub, rubber

Classification Bilabial, plosive, voiced consonant

- Used in the initial, medial, and end positions in words
- Used in stressed and unstressed syllables
- Cognate to [p]

Description
- Lips are pressed together
- Teeth are slightly apart
- Air builds up behind lips, then explodes lips apart but with less explosion than with [p] and depending on the place in a word the sound occurs
- Vocal folds vibrate

Drill Words

Initial	Medial	End
baby	about	cube
back	carbolic	club
balance	debate	drab
bare	embarrass	fib
beat	fabulous	grab
best	liberty	herb
bind	nobility	knob
board	obstinate	lab
bone	robust	mob
bug	trombone	tab

Degree of Explosion or Aspiration of Air As with the [p], the degree of explosion associated with the [b] is related to its position in a word. Since this phoneme is voiced, it is never aspirated or exploded as strongly as its cognate [p]. Its strongest aspiration comes in the initial positions in words and stressed syllables. In the following list the [b] is used in unstressed syllables.

Unstressed Syllables

arbitrator	labor
cabin	mobilize
fable	robot
habit	tuber
ibis	vibrate

Blends The [b] requires a definite release of sound when it is used in combination with other consonants [l, r, d, z]. Try producing a crisp [b] with the following blends.

[bl]	[br]	[bd]	[bz]
black	brand	cubed	bibs
bland	break	described	cribs
blame	breathe	disturbed	curbs
bleed	broom	grabbed	dabs
blend	February	mobbed	knobs
blur	Hebrew	probed	mobs
giblets	inbreed	robed	ribs
oblivion	library	rubbed	robs
problem	librarian	stabbed	scrubs
public	sobriety	webbed	sobs

Drill Sentences

1. The best seats are in the back of the club.
2. Try to keep a balance in the debate instead of being obstinate.
3. A bare-faced lie is not an embarrassing fib.
4. We kept the bone on a board in the lab.
5. Liberty and nobility bind together the nation's brave.
6. Bugs and sunburn ruined the day at the beach.
7. He played a borrowed trombone in a brass band.
8. The batter robustly hit the baseball.
9. Barbara fumbled at the doorknob.
10. Bob grabbed the best of the lumber.
11. Beth described it as a black, ribboned banner.
12. February is a blend of drab and sobering weather.
13. Bill is a librarian for the public library.
14. The public mobs a well-built building.
15. Bruised ribs can be a problem.
16. Brown blooms are a blight in any garden.
17. She blinked, breathed, and sobbed out the story.
18. Sobriety is the best habit.
19. Everybody grabbed ribs at the bar-be-que.
20. The police nabbed the robber for disturbing the peace.

Contrast Drill Students speaking English as a second language, whose primary language is Thai, Vietnamese, Chinese, Korean, or Spanish, may tend to voice the [p], which reduces aspiration and makes it sound more like, but not quite, a [b]. It is important that a speaker clearly distinguish between [p] and [b]. The following list demonstrates a few cases for which this distinction is called, because interchanging the two phonemes can create new words.

Contrast Drill Words

[p]	[b]
pack	back
pall	ball
pane	bane
pass	bass
peak	beak
peat	beet
peck	beck
picker	bicker
plink	blink
putt	but
cap	cab
lop	lob
lip	lab
loop	lube
mop	mob
pole	bowl
rip	rib
rope	robe
slop	slob
tap	tab

met, emit, team

Other sample words for various spellings:

summer, limb, column

Classification Bilabial, nasal, voiced continuant

- Used in initial, medial, and end positions in words
- Used in stressed and unstressed syllables in words

Description

- Lips remain compressed throughout production
- Velum should be relaxed and down
- Vocal folds begin to vibrate sending sound through nasal passages

Drill Words

Initial	*Medial*	*End*
machine	almost	aim
made	among	come
magic	cement	fame
mail	demand	him

mayor	emissary	home
meal	human	name
middle	remain	room
might	remove	some
mother	semester	them
mountain	tomorrow	time

Unstressed Positions

almond
column
important
problem
salmon

Blends   In some instances the [m] is found in combinations with other phonemes that may require special attention. Here are some examples:

- *chasm, schism, bottom*—insert [ə] between the [s] and [m]

- *column, autumn, hymn*—the [n] is silent. Whereas the [n] is silent in final positions when preceded by [m], it is added back in when the word becomes an adjective such as "columnar," "autumnal," or "hymnal."

- *attempt* or *camp*—some people gently explode the lips following the production of the [m] in order to produce a light [p]

- *diaphragm*—the [g] is silent

- *thumb* and *plumber*—the [b] is silent

- *salmon, calm, almond, palm*—the [l] is silent. Speakers frequently sound the [l] erroneously.

Drill Sentences

1. Time and man make demands on machines.
2. Make a tag for your name and homeroom number.
3. Right in the middle of our home-cooked meal, the mailman arrived.
4. Some of them remained after the performance.
5. I attempted to remove the bad memory.
6. Math problems are performed in columns.
7. Tomorrow the semester begins for them.
8. We ordered salmon almondine at the famous restaurant.
9. Mountain climbing might take a major effort.
10. Mother made an important move.
11. The emissary had a problem remembering names.
12. Mary may use the same comb as Mike.
13. The groom almost missed the ceremony.
14. The plumber might be able to make the chrome glimmer.

15. The room was warm, but at the same time all was calm.
16. A poem sometimes will rhyme, but then it might not.
17. Some bum gave Martha a dime to phone home.
18. An autumn moon casts magic on summer love.
19. For whom did the team buy the game mitt?
20. Mark has a special room in his home for his computer.

whether, awhile

Always spelled "wh"

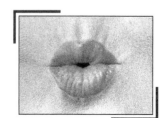

> *Note:* In practice, most speakers no longer use this sound but substitute the phoneme [w]. Whereas this is acceptable diction for conversational speech, you may wish to cultivate this phoneme for optional use.

Classification Bilabial, voiceless glide

- Used in initial and medial positions in words

- Used in stressed and unstressed syllables

- Cognate to [w]

Description
- Lips are pursed

- Air is sent through lips as they shift to position for vowel that follows

- No vocal fold vibration

Drill Words

Initial	Medial
what	anywhere
whale	bobwhite
wheel	elsewhere
when	everywhere
where	flywheel
whether	meanwhile
which	nowhere
while	pinwheel
whiskey	somewhat
why	somewhere

Drill Sentences

1. We saw a whale somewhere near the horizon.
2. When was the last time you had a pinwheel?
3. Anywhere the bobwhite flies, it is sunny.
4. Where did you put the whiskey?

5. "Wheel of Fortune" is a television program which I watched.
6. Meanwhile, he changed the wheels somewhat.
7. The motor whirred when I turned it on.
8. Whistle while you work.
9. She ate wheat and whey.
10. Which way did the whittler go?
11. While I was somewhat concerned, I didn't ask why.
12. Meanwhile, there were white birds flying every which way.
13. Which wheel is making that whining sound?
14. You can whisk me away to anywhere.
15. Why did the whale cross the ocean?
16. The child was whirling in a whimsical manner.
17. The whiskers on the whippet were somewhat stiff.
18. She whirled in a white dress.
19. The whereabouts of the boy were printed elsewhere.
20. I just got a whiff of the skunk and began to wheeze.

weather, away

Other sample words for various spellings:

linguistic, liquid, one, quart

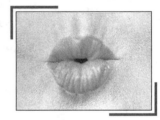

Classification   Bilabial, voiced glide

- Used in initial and medial positions in words

- Used in stressed and unstressed syllables

- Cognate to [hw]

Description   ■ Lips are pursed

- Vocal folds begin to vibrate

- Lips glide toward the vowel that follows as sound passes through

Drill Words

Initial	Medial
wall	always
wail	awake
way	bewilder
well	dwell
were	everyone
wide	forward
with	quiet
woman	quit

wonder   require
would   reward

Drill Sentences   1. Everyone at Weight Watchers weighs in.
2. We were wondering about the reward.
3. The wailing wall is near his dwelling.
4. We will require you to be quiet in this library.
5. It was a bewildering warning written on the sign.
6. I always awaken early and wash up.
7. The width of the window will accommodate a planter.
8. Will you give rewards for scoring high on the midweek quiz?
9. Is it wise to serve wine at the wedding?
10. We went West only to find that we were not welcome.
11. A war is a quarrel gone wrong.
12. Wayne's bewildering request made me aware of the water shortage.
13. The woman was washing and waxing her Volkswagen.
14. The weaving was between a wide sculpture and another work.
15. Wishes are a coward's way of requesting.
16. The twins went to the wedding wearing matching woven shirts.
17. Once a week some wise guy will get an award.
18. One night I was wide awake until toward dawn.
19. The earthquake was worse in the west.
20. Twice on Wednesday you worked on the dwelling.

Sound Substitution   Some non-native speakers, especially those whose primary language is a Middle Eastern language, German, Scandinavian, or some Asian language, may substitute a [v] for [w]. The following lists contrast those two sounds.

[w]	[v]
wail	vail
wane	vane
wary	vary
wet	vet
went	vent
west	vest
wick	Vic
wise	vise
worse	verse
wow	vow

Contrast Drill   Several words would appear to be the same if the voiced cognate [w] were used in place of [hw]. Indeed, as noted earlier, not everyone produces a clearly voiceless [hw]. In some cases, this phoneme may be "half-voiced." Ordinarily, context differentiates between these words. The following list will provide practice contrasting these phonemes.

Contrast Drill Words

[hw]	[w]
whale	wail
what	watt
when	wen
whether	weather
whet	wet
where	wear
which	witch
while	wile
whine	wine
whirred	word

Labiodental Consonants

[f]

fire, sofa, golf

Other sample words for various spellings:

photo, laugh, staff, calf

Classification   Labiodental, voiceless, fricative

- Used in initial, medial, and end positions in words
- Used in stressed and unstressed syllables in words
- Cognate to [v]

Description
- Upper teeth press gently against lower lip
- Tongue is slighty pulled back
- Air passes through space left between teeth and lip
- No vocal fold vibration

Drill Words

Initial	Medial	End
face	affair	belief
faculty	after	cough
father	beautiful	graph
feather	coffee	half
fee	differ	if
few	effect	laugh
fiber	laughter	puff
figure	muffle	rough
follow	therefore	safe
former	waffle	tough

Blends Consonant combinations ([f] with l, r, s, t) can reduce the degree of friction with which this phoneme is produced. Practice producing a clear [f] with the following blends.

[fl]	**[fr]**	**[fs]**	**[ft]**
affluent	afraid	cliffs	after
flag	fraction	coughs	buffed
flatter	frame	fluffs	coughed
flee	free	graphs	hefty
flesh	French	handkerchiefs	laughed
flight	fresh	laughs	left
flip	fright	puffs	raft
float	frozen	reefs	safety
fluid	fruit	safes	soft
fly	refresh	whiffs	waft

Drill Sentences
1. A few of us are going to play golf with father.
2. She has a fresh face and beautiful figure.
3. He is a former faculty member of the French Academy.
4. The muffled laughter followed the comic performance.
5. It was a rough and tough feather pillow fight.
6. Frozen fruit was served on a flat plate.
7. If you value your safety, you won't float on the raft.
8. Use a handkerchief if you have the sniffles.
9. The waffles were followed by free coffee.
10. The affluent have different beliefs regarding money.
11. We framed the flag in a fraction of the time.
12. Whiffs of frost wafted on the air.
13. The fibers began to fray into a fringe.
14. The former chief of staff drew a graph on the wall.
15. You can afford to laugh in the safety of your office.
16. He huffed and puffed and blew the rafters down.
17. I'm afraid that your inflexible position fails to persuade me.
18. She ran frantically from the figure who confronted her.
19. That fraternity was the fourth one to hold a Fall Frolic.
20. He refuted the charge of fraud and asked for freedom.

voice, even, love

Other sample words for various spellings:

of, I've

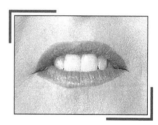

Classification Labiodental, voiced fricative

■ Used in the initial, medial, and end positions in words

■ Used in stressed and unstressed positions in words

■ Cognate to [f]

Description

■ Upper teeth lightly press against lower lip

■ Tongue is slightly pulled back in lower mouth

■ Air passes through opening between lips and teeth

■ Vocal folds vibrate

Drill Words

Initial	*Medial*	*End*
vacant	avoid	above
vain	bevel	brave
valid	devil	five
vary	eleven	gave
vegetable	favor	have
vehicle	gavel	pave
velvet	hover	relative
vend	moving	slave
vice	nervous	twelve
volume	travel	wave

Blends   As with previous phonemes, consonant combinations ([v] with z, d) require practice. The following are plurals and past tense words. For a discussion of these concepts, see the rules pertaining to plurals and past tense (pp. 207, 210, 215, and 217).

[vz]	[vd]
achieves	carved
curves	dived
deceives	gloved
dives	loved
gloves	paved
knives	raved
lives	received
moves	saved
proves	shoved
slaves	waved

Drill Sentences

1. The vending machine gave no vegetables.
2. As a favor, could you leave a key above the door?
3. The driver of the vehicle was cited for a moving violation.
4. My relatives have moved eleven times.

5. He dived through the waves to save the drowning victim.
6. The vegetables are above the stove.
7. Thieves will deceive you out of your life savings.
8. She saved her velvet gloves.
9. Vary your travel plans and pay me a visit.
10. Vote for Victor for vice president.
11. Twelve slaves worked to pave the road.
12. He was given to believing that he should shave every evening.
13. *Vogue* magazine advises vital living.
14. We received notice of the vacancy on the vice squad.
15. There were oval shaped, bevelled windows above the pane.
16. He believed the world revolved around his love.
17. Vienna proved to be a valuable vacation.
18. The volume of the television moved the vase on top of it.
19. The village streets were paved with gravel.
20. High achievers strive for improved voices.

Sound Substitution   Non-native speakers may substitute a [b] (Spanish) or a [v] (German) for [w], which results in a different word. The following lists contrast these sounds.

[v]	[b]	[w]
vale	bale	wail
vane	bane	wane
veer	beer	weir
vend	bend	wend
vent	bent	went
vest	best	west
vet	bet	wet
vile	bile	wile
vine	bine	wine
vow	bow	wow

Contrast Drill   Remember that it is important to clearly distinguish between these cognates since interchanging them can result in different words. The following list provides practice for [f] and [v].

Contrast Drill Words

[f]	[v]
fat	vat
fast	vast
feel	veal
few	view
file	vile
fine	vine
half	have

leaf   leave
proof   prove
safe   save

Lingua-dental Consonants

think, nothing, truth

Always spelled "th" as in *theme*

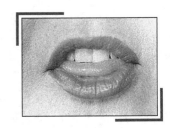

Classification   Lingua-dental, voiceless fricative

- Used in initial, medial, and end positions in words
- Used in stressed and unstressed syllables in words
- Cognate to [ð]

Description
- Lips are apart
- Teeth are slightly apart
- Tip of tongue is thrust slightly between teeth
- No vocal fold vibration
- Air is sent through space between tongue and upper teeth

Drill Words

Initial	*Medial*	*End*
thank	author	birth
thaw	anything	death
theory	birthday	earth
thermal	everything	mouth
thick	healthy	oath
thigh	method	path
thing	nothing	south
thought	ruthless	truth
thread	something	youth
thrift	wealthy	worth

Blends   The phoneme [θ] preceded by various consonants can prove tricky. Additionally [θ] followed by [s] proves a challenge because many people omit the [θ]. The following lists provide drill with these consonant combinations. If you have difficulty with these combinations, first practice the sounds in isolation.

consonant + [θ]	[θs]
breadth	berths
depth	booths
earth	deaths
fifth	faiths
health	fifths
ninth	hearths
month	lengths
sixth	myths
warmth	sixths
worth	tenths

Drill Sentences

1. The author thinks the thermal theory is well thought out.
2. Ruthless people are not always wealthy, but can be thrifty.
3. The youth swore an oath to truth.
4. The earth is full of healthy things.
5. He would do anything and everything for his faith.
6. Birth usually takes place in the ninth month.
7. The snow began to thaw by the path.
8. I thought you were worth something.
9. Is there anything I can buy you for your birthday?
10. There are many myths in both the North and the South.
11. A theme is a thread that runs through the story.
12. I think I have an unhealthy toothache.
13. Kathy thought she heard a thud by the hearth.
14. Matthew thinks his method makes him a wizard at math.
15. Thursday is the thirteenth of the month.
16. Nothing will threaten my faith.
17. Use cloth, thread, and a thimble for sewing.
18. I thank you from the depth and breadth of my heart.
19. She thought she had thick thighs.
20. Three thousand people celebrated the warmth of summer.

Sound Substitution   A majority of non-native speakers have trouble with this sound and its cognate [ð]. Speakers of French may substitute [s], Spanish speakers may substitute [t] or [θ]. In addition, some persons may substitute [f] for [θ]. The following lists provide drill with these sounds. Note that sound substitution creates either a new word or no word at all (as in the case of parenthetical words in the [f] column).

[s]	[t]	[f]	[θ]
bass	bat	(baff)	bath
face	fate	(faff)	faith
mass	mat	(maff)	math

miss	mit	miff	myth
sank	tank	(fank)	thank
seem	team	(feem)	theme
sick	tick	(fick)	thick
sin	tin	fin	thin
sigh	tie	fie	thigh
sought	taught	fought	thought

the, brother, bathe

[ð]

Always spelled "th" as in *that*

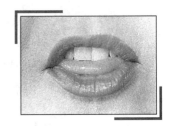

Classification   Lingua-dental, voiced fricative

- Used in initial, medial, and end positions in words
- Used in stressed and unstressed syllables in words
- Cognate to [θ]

Description

- Lips are slightly apart
- Tongue is positioned slightly between teeth
- Vocal folds vibrate
- Sound passes through space left between tongue and teeth

Drill Words

Initial	*Medial*	*End*
that	although	bathe
then	another	breathe
thence	brother	clothe
there	clothing	lathe
these	father	loathe
they	lather	scythe
this	mother	soothe
though	rather	teethe
thus	together	tithe
thy	weather	writhe

Blends   The most difficult combinations are those found in final positions in words that have been pluralized or made past tense. The following lists give you some samples of these. First practice the combinations in isolation in order to get the feel of the sounds.

[ð̪d]	[ð̪z]
breathed	breathes
clothed	clothes
loathed	loathes
seethed	seethes
soothed	soothes

Drill Sentences

1. Although my brother is in another country, I phone him often.
2. Together we will weather this storm.
3. I loathe that style of clothing.
4. You should try to soothe a teething baby.
5. I would rather lather up with liquid soap.
6. Father and Mother are together.
7. That is one way to further the cause.
8. "Thy" and "thee" are found in the Bible.
9. They swathed themselves in leather.
10. Either do the job or don't bother.
11. I loathe bathing in the other tub.
12. The baby breathes easier when it is not teething.
13. My brother is the father of those children.
14. They rode their horses farther than we did.
15. He would rather we were betrothed at this time.
16. We took the used clothing to another leather store.
17. The weather has been either rather warm or wet.
18. The rhythm of the song soothed the writhing listeners.
19. That's another feather in your cap.
20. This is enough, that we are together.

Sound Substitution

Non-native speakers often substitute a [z] (French) or [d] (Spanish and several other languages) for [ð]. The following lists provide drill for contrasting those sounds. As with [θ] note that the substitution often creates a new word. (Note that words in parentheses are not real words, but you may hear these as words spoken by someone who has substituted the [z] for [θ].)

[z]	[d]	[ð]
breeze	breed	breathe
zan	Dan	than
(zare)	dare	their
(zay)	day	they
Zen	den	then
(zoze)	doze	those
(zoe)	dough	though
(lazzer)	ladder	lather
rise	ride	writhe
(uzzer)	udder	other

Contrast Drill   Because these cognates are spelled alike, it is difficult to distinguish them. Following are some general rules:

- the voiceless [θ] is usually used after a consonant, such as *depth*. However, there are exceptions, such as *although*.

- the voiced [ð] is used with words ending with *ther*, such as *brother*, and words ending in *the*, such as *breathe*.

The following provides you with contrast drill.

Contrast Drill Words

[θ]	**[ð]**
bath	bathe
breath	breathe
cloth	clothe
ether	either
mouth	mouth
sheath	sheathe
teeth	teethe
thigh	thy
with	with (optional)
wreath	wreathe

Lingua-alveolar Consonants

ten, entire, fate

Other sample words for various spellings:

faced, light, pretty, ptarmigan

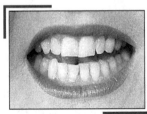

Classification   Lingua-alveolar, voiceless plosive

- Used in the initial, medial, and end positions in words
- Used in stressed and unstressed syllables in words
- Cognate to [d]

Description
- Lips are open
- Teeth are apart
- Tip of tongue is against gum ridge just above upper teeth; sides of tongue are against upper molars
- No vocal fold vibration
- Air builds up, tongue "explodes" away from gum ridge as air is released

Drill Words	*Initial*	*Medial*	*End*
	table	attempt	ate
	tag	between	bet
	take	continue	coat
	teach	entire	eat
	teeth	intend	height
	tide	literate	mat
	time	material	night
	toad	return	ought
	today	satisfy	wrote
	tune	until	yet

Degree of Explosion or Aspiration of Air   As with [p] and [b], and because it is also a plosive, the degree of explosion of air used for the phoneme [t] is related to whether or not it is found in a stressed or unstressed syllable, in combination with other consonants, or in the final position in a word. The degree of aspiration is reduced when [t] occurs in the final positions in words, but remember to give this sound a slight degree of explosion in final positions. The strongest [t] occurs in initial positions in words when it is followed by a vowel. The following list provides practice with the [t] in unstressed syllables.

Note: The word *often* presents the problem of spelling pronunciation. The preferred pronunciation of *often* is currently [ɔfən] with no [t] sounded. However, many people do articulate the [t]. It is probable that this word is undergoing change.

Unstressed Syllables		
	after	matter
	character	party
	daughter	sister
	doctor	water
	fifty	written

Blends   The phoneme [t] is found in combination with many other consonants. Whereas this sound is classified and produced as a plosive, its context often calls for a slightly different manner of production, one that results in a slightly different sound. Here are the most common combinations.

[tθ] example: *might think*—Requires a dentalization of the [t]. The tongue tip, instead of touching the upper gum ridge, touches the inside of the upper teeth then slides to the edge of the upper teeth and slightly through.

Drill Words			
	bright things	cut through	don't think
	fat thigh	get thread	hate threats
	late Thursday	met three	net thousands
	pat theory		

[tð̣] example: *write those*—In addition to dentalization of the [t] with this combination vocal fold vibration begins immediately after it.

Drill Words

at them	bet those	get there
left that	meet then	not this
put these	rate those	seat them
write that		

[tl] example: *battle*—With this combination, the tip of the tongue does not lift away from the upper gum ridge, but the sides of the tongue do break away from the upper molars in order to produce the lateral effect of the [l], which is orally emitted. You may note that dictionaries show a superscript schwa [ə] between the [t] and [l]. However, the schwa is not usually sounded in connected speech.

Drill Words

bottle	cattle	fettle
glottal	kettle	mettle
mottle	rattle	settle
tattle		

[tn] example: *button*—With this combination, the tip of the tongue also remains on the upper gum ridge. However, instead of the sides of the tongue breaking away from the upper molars, the velum lowers and the [n] is sent through the nasal passages. As with the previous combination, dictionaries note [ə] between [t] and [n]. Again, the schwa is not usually sounded in connected speech.

Drill Words

bitten	cotton	fatten
gotten	platen	rotten
satin	smitten	Sutton
written		

[tr] example: *true*—The tongue must clearly lift off the upper gum ridge and cannot slide off.

Drill Words

trap	trash	trot
treat	tree	tribute
trigger	trip	tropic
trust		

[tw] example: *twice*—With this combination, the lips are usually more pursed than with most other sound combinations. Again, clearly lift the tongue from the upper gum ridge as you blend with the [w].

Drill Words

twain	twang	tweeze
twelve	twice	twilight

twill   twin   twinkle
twist

[kt] example: *fact*—Because the [k] is produced in the back of the mouth, the tendency might be to omit the [t]. You will need to concentrate to produce the [t] at the ends of words. Begin the drill by producing the combination in isolation, then go on to drill words.

Drill Words

attacked	attract	blocked
connect	correct	direct
fact	hacked	knocked
select		

[st] example: *pest*—As with the above, the tendency is to omit the final [t]. Be sure to touch the tip of the tongue against the upper gum ridge after the [s].

Drill Words

best	crest	dust
first	gust	haste
list	must	past
rust		

Plurals   Making nouns plural requires adding an [s]. This is particularly troublesome when a word ends with [st]. The following list provides practice with this difficult combination. Try to tap the tongue against the gum ridge between [s] sounds. For example, if you fail to tap the tongue, the word *guests* could become *guess,* changing meaning entirely.

Drill Words

bests	crests	dusts
firsts	gusts	lists
masts	pests	posts
rusts	trusts	wrists

Past Tense   *Rule:* When a word ends in a voiceless phoneme, continue the voicelessness by producing the voiceless [t] even if the word is spelled with "ed." If the word ends with a [t] as in *dust* and is made past tense (*dusted*), you will then sound out the [ə] and, because the word then ends with a voiced phoneme, you will use the [d].

Drill Words

braced	encased	faced
lunched	munched	punched
raced	sipped	trapped
wrapped		

Sound Substitution   In cases wherein the [t] is found in medial positions, as in *pretty,* a speaker may often substitute a [d] because it is easier to continue voicing than it is to stop voicing for a split second. Practice including the [t] in the following list. You need not "punch" the sound. Just lightly tap the tongue against the gum ridge and momentarily cease voicing.

Drill Words

Betty	cutey	duty
fritter	getting	hatter
later	matter	pretty
writer		

Drill Sentences

1. We talked over tea about teaching.
2. The entire trip was intended to be spent in one town.
3. When I return I will try to get new tires.
4. Take a towel with you to the tide pools.
5. The city offers plenty of thrifty opportunities.
6. I hope to continue to treat the right things with these pills.
7. Bright thoughts suited his personality.
8. She was witty, pretty, and fifty-two.
9. I am betting that the cattle haven't eaten.
10. Look at the time; it's later than you noted.
11. Pests had gotten into the plants.
12. When traveling, you ought to notice the costs of seeing the sights.
13. The writer had written literate material.
14. What is your height and weight?
15. He ate at the table with his teeth out.
16. List those tunes on the bestseller list.
17. The show was intended to attract the entire audience.
18. Tom persists in making a pest out of himself.
19. The little kitty was cute.
20. You'll hear this radio station's greatest hits.

den, fading, need

Other sample words for various spellings:

ladder, hide

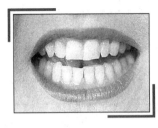

Classification   Lingua-alveolar, voiced plosive

- Used in initial, medial, and end positions in words

- Used in stressed and unstressed syllables in words

- Cognate to [t]

Description
- Lips are apart

- Teeth are slightly apart

- Tip of tongue is against upper gum ridge; sides of tongue are against upper molars

- Vocal folds vibrate

- Sound builds up and explodes tongue tip away from gum ridge

Drill Words

Initial	*Medial*	*End*
daily	building	afraid
date	consider	beside
dear	edict	could
decent	hundred	glad
deed	industry	head
dental	lady	laid
depress	leader	made
dial	modern	paid
dim	window	ride
done	wonder	word

Blends As with its cognate [t], the [d] is often found in combination with other sounds which affect its production and resulting sound. The following are descriptions and sample lists of those combinations.

[dθ] example: *had things*—The tip of the tongue hits the back of the upper teeth rather than the gum ridge. Vocalization ceases and the tongue slips through the teeth slightly to produce the [θ].

Drill Words

bad throat	fed through	heard thunder
crude thought	made think	loud thud
paid three	said thanks	staid theory
tried thrusting		

[dð] example: *had those*—With this combination, the tongue again is against the back of the upper teeth and slides through the teeth. However, this time voicing does not stop.

Drill Words

add those	bed the	dared them
fade that	had those	lead them
made that	nod then	paid them
said they		

[dl] example: *ladle*—The tip of the tongue remains against the upper gum ridge as the sides of the tongue pull away from the upper molars to produce

the [l]. Remember that for improved diction the [ə] found in the dictionary is usually not sounded.

Drill Words

cuddle	diddle	fiddle
huddle	ladle	muddle
puddle	riddle	toddle
waddle		

[dn] example: *laden*—The tip of the tongue remains against the upper gum ridge for the [d]. The sides of the tongue are against the upper molars. The velum opens the passage to the nose, and the [n] is sent through the nasal passages.

Drill Words

didn't	hadn't	hidden
leaden	madden	pardon
sadden	sudden	tendon
widen		

[dr] example: *drew*—The lips purse in anticipation of the [r]. One might have the tendency to slide the [d] away and should concentrate on pulling the tongue clearly away from the upper gum ridge.

Drill Words

drab	drain	draw
dress	drip	drive
drop	drove	drug
drum		

Plurals   Pluralizing nouns that end in the phoneme [d] produces a difficult sound combination. The voicing of the [d] continues with the phoneme [z] even though the word may end in [s]; for example, "adds."

Drill Words

beds	cads	dads
fads	heads	leads
maids	pods	suds
wads		

Past Tense   *Rule:* When a word ends in a voiced consonant, the voicing continues with [d]. In cases when the word ends spelled with an "ed," the "e" does not become a [ə] unless the word ends with a [d]; for example, "sounded."

Drill Words

amazed	cabled	deemed
famed	grazed	hosed
lured	muddled	nabbed
rubbed		

Sound Substitution Though not as common as the substitution of [d] for [t], sometimes in an effort to be very "articulate" a speaker will inadvertently substitute a [t] for a [d] (often producing a humorous result); for example, "The couple were wetted by a minister." Take care to avoid this.

Drill Sentences
1. It is usually damp and cold in December.
2. We stood on the dock at dawn with the dog.
3. He listened to the radio as he danced.
4. Donna raised funds for new roads.
5. Don spoke aloud regarding the indoor odors.
6. He could say that he had heard that before.
7. The width of the door was measured by the draftsman.
8. I doubt that you could abide another dull day.
9. The kid hid the candy under the bed.
10. The drapes draw from the middle.
11. The poodle hadn't had a trim since Monday.
12. I doubt that his adversity will dampen my dream.
13. Each day the crowd had thought the Pope would arrive.
14. It is odd that you should go bald so young.
15. The brides were ready on their wedding day.
16. Rosebuds are pretty with dew on their petals.
17. The clouds were fading as the brood went out to play in the yard.
18. Did you ever wonder if the president has a degree?
19. The department store has a high demand for bold things.
20. I could see the garden from the window.

Contrast Drill Remember to distinguish clearly between the cognates [t] and [d]. Often, a substitution can produce a new word. Try the following list.

Contrast Drill Words

[t]	[d]
bat	bad
bet	bed
bit	bid
boat	bode
cat	cad
coat	code
got	God
hat	had
late	laid
mat	mad
mutt	mud
rot	rod
sat	sad
sot	sod

ten   den
tip   dip
wetting   wedding
written   ridden

see, last, brass

Other sample words for various spellings:

scene, century, sass, psoriasis, fix

Classification   Lingua-alveolar, voiceless fricative

- Used in initial, medial, and end positions in words

- Used in stressed and unstressed syllables in words

- Found in many consonant combinations

- Cognate to [z]

Description
- Lips are open

- Teeth are slightly apart

- Tip of tongue may aim toward either the upper or lower gum ridge

- No vocal fold vibration

- Air is forced through the space created by the configuration of the articulators creating a gentle "hiss"

The phoneme [s] can be particularly troublesome. There seem to be as many variations as there are persons speaking. Because there is not quite a specific point for the tongue to touch or direction in which to aim and because the space between the teeth can vary considerably from person to person, the result is different with each person and sometimes different at various times for one person. There are several problems that can occur. Excessive sibilance occurs when too much air escapes or the [s] is held too long. A whistle can be the result of too tight a space configuration. A lisp results from substituting a [θ] for the [s]. A lateral lisp results from the tongue tip approximating the alveolar ridge too closely forcing air around the sides of the tongue. If you observe a pronounced distortion of this phoneme, you may benefit from special therapeutic work. However, many people can compensate by concentrated drill.

Drill Words	*Initial*	*Medial*	*End*
	sack	also	glass
	safe	answer	house

sea	discover	ice
section	frequency	kiss
side	glassy	mass
sight	lonesome	pass
social	missing	piece
solid	officer	this
soup	peaceful	us
suburb	proceed	voice

Blends There are probably more consonant blends and combinations with the phoneme [s] than with any other. Some of these combinations are found only in the initial positions in words, but some are found in initial, medial, and end positions. What follows is a listing of common combinations. We will deal with plurals following this list.

	Initial	*Medial*	*End*
[sk]			
	scat	asked	ask
	scan	basket	bask
	scoff	casket	disk
	scoop	discount	frisk
	school	landscape	husk
	skate	masquerade	mask
[skr]			
	scrap	discreet	
	scratch	inscrutable	
	scream	indiscretion	
	screw	prescribe	
	scrutiny	unscrupulous	
[skw]			
	squad	squall	
	squander	esquire	
	square		
	squeeze		
	squire		
[sl]			
	slab		
	slap		
	sled		
	slide		
	slow		
[sm]			
	small		
	smell		

smile
smog
smooth

[sn]

snail
snap
sneak
snob
snow

[sp]

space
span
spark
spear
spook

[spl]

splash
splendid
splice
splint
split

[spr]

sprawl
spray
spread
spring
sprint

[st]

stable	blaster	cost
stagger	esteem	dust
stand	frosty	first
steam	gusty	last
stiff	toasted	kissed

[str]

straight	construction
strain	destroy
stream	frustrate
strike	instruct
structure	restrain

[sw]

swallow
sweat

swell
sweep
swelter

[ns]

ensue	bounce
inspire	enhance
institution	fence
insulate	lance
pensive	romance

Plurals

Rule: When a word to be made plural ends in a voiceless phoneme, continue the voicelessness by using the [s]; for example, *cats.* There occur in the English language some tricky combinations of pluralized words such as [sts] combinations; for example, *posts.*

Present Tense

When speaking in the present tense, third person (he, she, it) you add [s]; for example, "She scrapes her knee." Here the above voicing rule applies. If the verb ends with a voiceless phoneme, continue the voicelessness with [s].

Drill Words

Plurals	*Present tense*
apes	beats
bits	conducts
books	dissipates
dips	equates
freaks	gets
lips	greets
meats	hates
plates	lets
rats	meets
sweets	rates

Difficult Combinations

Take special care to pronounce the [t] and [k].

[sts]	**[sks]**
bastes	asks
blasts	basks
casts	casks
dusts	desks
firsts	flasks
masts	masks
rusts	rusks
wrists	risks

Drill Sentences

1. Sandy decided to study medicine.
2. Sutton sent that baseball right over the home base sack.
3. I took a bus to Sunday supper.
4. Once you start the race, be sure to pace yourself.
5. Sue kissed both cheeks, then scurried away.
6. It was a blessing that we sold the house so fast.
7. Many summer nights seem peaceful.
8. What's the price of that cassette?
9. Steve was sweating after he completed his exercise circuit.
10. My stepsister sings quite sweetly.
11. That speech could inspire even an atheist.
12. There is a piece missing out of this whole section.
13. The stranger described his past.
14. My schedule won't permit me to stop to listen to your story.
15. The snow swirled around the landscape.
16. Swallows swarmed and screeched around the roofs.
17. You are the last person I expected to see.
18. Our guests were basking in the sun.
19. The bear asked, "Where is the honey pot?"
20. Sam took his ice axe up the cliffs.

zebra, lazy, please

Other sample words for various spellings:

fuzz, nose, xylophone

Classification   Lingua-alveolar, voiced fricative

- Used in initial, medial, and end positions in words
- Used in stressed and unstressed syllables
- Cognate to [s]

Description
- Lips are apart
- Teeth are slightly apart
- Tip of tongue is aimed toward either the upper or lower gum ridge; the sides of the tongue are against the upper molars
- Vocal folds vibrate
- Sound is emitted through the space created by the articulators

Drill Words

Initial	Medial	End
Xerox	caused	buzz
zeal	desire	chose

zealot	example	exercise
zenith	hazard	news
zero	music	rose
zest	noisy	size
zinc	razor	suppose
zodiac	resign	use
zone	result	was
zoo	Wednesday	waves

Blends   Most blends or consonant combinations result from using a conjugated form of a present tense verb or pluralizing a noun. There are a few exceptions such as [zm] in *chasm* or *spasm*. With this phoneme, most blends occur at the ends of words.

Rule: When a word ends in a voiced phoneme, continue the voicing in order to make it plural or a conjugated form of present tense by using the [z].

Below are lists of examples.

	Plurals	*Present Tense*
[bz]		
	bulbs	bobs
	cribs	dabs
	labs	grabs
	mobs	lobs
	tabs	robs
[dz]		
	beds	bleeds
	duds	fades
	frauds	floods
	grids	hides
	lads	rids
[lz]		
	baubles	boils
	ghouls	hails
	males	mails
	pills	piles
	tolls	tells
[nz]		
	canes	grins
	fines	hones
	lines	loans
	tons	remains
	tunes	turns

[mz]

brooms	calms
crumbs	drums
fumes	frames
limbs	lames
names	tames

[vz]

calves	believes
doves	drives
fives	lives
halves	roves
nerves	serves

Drill Sentences

1. The zebra is not raised in New Zealand.
2. You deserve to browse through the zoo.
3. My cousin was a zealous Zionist.
4. Zach used preservatives in his desserts.
5. It is wise to resign before your boss goads you into it.
6. The noise of the music was making me dizzy.
7. We pulled the weeds from the zinnia beds.
8. Daisy spent her days trying to please her husband.
9. A spasm in my leg caused me to stop the exercise.
10. The buildings and grounds have been set with alarms.
11. Girls and boys with pencils and pens attend their classes.
12. Do you suppose he observes the rules?
13. What size in men's clothes do you wear?
14. Are there rules to zodiacal predictions?
15. Lines were painted as grids in the quiet zone.
16. Did you realize the dishes were broken before you opened the packages?
17. It was a hazard to change the light bulbs.
18. Flies buzzed around the Arizona lizard.
19. The zealot resigned both jobs on Tuesday.
20. Zelda says there are many rules to many games.

Contrast Drill It is important to distinguish between [s] and [z], since interchanging the two phonemes could create a new word. The following list provides contrast words:

Contrast Drill Words

[s]	**[z]**
dose	doze
hiss	his
loose	lose
niece	knees

mace   maze
peace   peas
price   prize
rice   rise
spice   spies
sink   zinc

never, dinner, bean

Other sample words for various spellings:

knee, sign, pneumatic

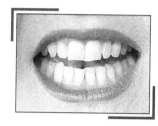

Classification   Lingua-alveolar, voiced, nasal continuant

- Used in initial, medial, and end positions in words

- Used in stressed and unstressed syllables

Description
- Lips are slightly open

- Teeth are apart

- Tip of tongue is against upper gum ridge; sides of tongue are against upper molars

- Velum is lowered

- Vocal folds vibrate

- Sound is emitted nasally

Drill Words

Initial	*Medial*	*End*
knit	anything	bin
knowledge	corner	can
name	evening	fun
near	general	hone
neither	landed	lean
next	minute	mane
none	pander	pain
nothing	tinder	rain
number	vandal	train
pneumonia	wonder	won

Blends   As with the phonemes discussed earlier, when the [n] is found in combination with other sounds, it may require extra care to produce the sound nasally. For example, with words such as "kitten" you need to shift from the orally emitted [t] to the nasally emitted [n]. Try the following combinations:

account	fend	patten
against	grind	pend
button	gotten	rotten
branch	hand	round
cent	land	sent
chance	leaden	sudden
cotton	madden	went
dent	mount	widen
deaden		

Try these for clarity:

din dint	did didn't	dint dent didn't
den dent	din den didn't	

Drill Sentences

1. Neither of us knew that he had pneumonia.
2. The general landed the plane near the dunes.
3. Thunder sounded and lightning shone in the evening sky.
4. I wonder if she went at the last minute.
5. You can have fun if you wear your name tag.
6. Seven bins were filled with green beans.
7. I bent my fender while in the corner lot.
8. The pain from the burn is nothing.
9. I used a mitten to open the oven.
10. Insects have infested the garden.
11. The train is coming around the corner any minute.
12. I was anxiously thinking about vandals nearby.
13. The branch of language is Indo-European.
14. The round tinderbox was against the sink.
15. Oranges need the sunshine and rain to grow.
16. Nancy sent a patent pending notice by train.
17. You need nutrients like vitamins and minerals.
18. Norman Newman was my insurance agent.
19. The dance was held near the lawn.
20. Her once thin knees began to widen with age.

lip, ballad, doll

[l]

Always spelled with "l" or "ll"

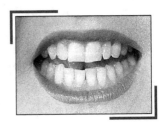

Classification   Lingua-alveolar, voiced lateral consonant

- Used in initial, medial, and end positions in words
- Used in stressed and unstressed syllables

Description

- Lips are apart
- Teeth are apart
- Tip of tongue is against upper gum ridge; sides of tongue do not touch upper molars
- Vocal folds vibrate
- Sound is emitted orally around the sides of the tongue

This phoneme is particularly subject to the influence of those sounds around it insofar as the shape of the mouth and position of the tongue change to accommodate those adjacent sounds. For example, first say *leap;* then say *school.* Did you note the different quality the [l] assumed in each word? We call this quality in the first instance a *clear* or *light* [l] and in the second instance a *dark* [l]. Some speakers may have a tendency to make the [l] too *dark.* Take care to avoid raising the tongue too high in the back of the mouth when you produce this sound. You may note the difference in quality as you go through the list that follows.

Drill Words

Initial	*Medial*	*End*
lap	alleviate	all
last	allow	bell
laugh	believe	eagle
leave	belong	flail
length	crawling	girl
less	early	hall
let	follow	mail
lost	public	pearl
love	reality	smile
lust	silence	while

Blends   In discussing other phonemes, we have covered the [l] in various combinations with [t], [d], and [n]. Because all of these phonemes are lingua-alveolar, you need not remove the tongue from the upper gum ridge in order to produce the [l] that follows them, for example, *battle, cradle, channel.* In addition, as was also previously noted, the [l] is found in combination with several consonants that precede it. The following list provides practice with these combinations.

blast	bless	blossom	bluster
class	clean	cling	cluster

flask	fleas	flesh	fluster
glass	gleam	glint	glutton
plaster	please	plenty	plunder
slave	sleeve	slip	sloop

Sound Substitution   Non-native speakers, particularly those whose primary language is Asian, may substitute the phoneme [r] for [l]. This happens when the tongue pulls back from the gum ridge. In addition, some speakers may substitute the [w] for [l], which results in an infantile sound. Here, the tongue fails to make contact with the upper gum ridge and the lips glide from a pursed shape to the shape required for the vowel that follows. The list below provides contrast drill with these sounds.

[r]	[w]	[l]
racks	wax	lax
raid	wade	laid
rag	wag	lag
rare	wear	lair
Ray	way	lay
reap	weep	leap
reek	weak	leak
rife	wife	life
rink	wink	link

Drill Sentences

1. He who leaves first has the last laugh.
2. Do not believe that love and lust are the same feelings.
3. You will be all right if you smile.
4. The child flailed around in the public pool.
5. Please pick up the mail in Eagle Hall.
6. Already I have lost my pearl necklace.
7. I won't blame Lisa for playing after lunch.
8. The class listened to the lecture until the bell sounded.
9. A criminal plot may land you in jail.
10. At the play we sat near the middle aisle.
11. There is a location where you can eat lobster for eleven dollars.
12. The lady liked to blink her eyelashes.
13. The elevator alarm will ring only if the light is lit.
14. Please sail the ship into the last slip on the left.
15. April was a horrible month for blossoms.
16. If you will please smile, we will see your teeth gleam.
17. The frail girl believed that she was ugly.
18. It's wonderful to get plenty of mail as long as it's not bills.
19. Lucy collected glistening pearls.
20. The public will follow some lousy politicians.

Lingua-Palatal Consonants

shoe, ocean, hush

Other sample words for various spellings:*

anxious, sure, pressure, charlatan, inflection

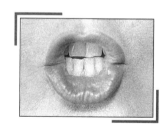

Classification Lingua-palatal, voiceless fricative

- Used in initial, medial, and end positions in words
- Used in stressed and unstressed syllables in words
- Cognate to [ʒ]

Description
- Lips are pursed
- Teeth are slightly apart
- Tip of tongue is closely aimed toward area just above gum ridge; sides of tongue touch upper molars; tongue is generally more rounded
- No vocal fold vibration
- Air is forced through open space

Note: This sound especially requires pursed lips. This is often difficult to perform in conversation because we speak so rapidly. For example, *leashing* requires that your lips move rapidly from a tight, smiling position to a pursed position. Take special care to purse your lips as you drill with this sound.

Drill Words

Initial	Medial	End
shall	anxious	bash
shape	action	crush
share	ashamed	dash
she	caution	fish
ship	delicious	fresh
shock	especially	harsh
shop	fashion	punish

*This sound is also represented by [š]. In order to remain consistent with other texts, this text will use the phonetic symbol [ʃ]. However, it should be noted that students in English as a second language studies will be more familiar with the second IPA symbol. The symbols are interchangeable.

short	issue	rush
should	machine	vanish
show	special	wash

Sound Substitution   Non-native speakers, especially those whose primary language is Spanish, may substitute [tʃ], as in *church,* for [ʃ]. The following list contrasts these two sounds.

[ʃ]	[tʃ]
bash	batch
cash	catch
dish	ditch
flesh	Fletch
hash	hatch
lash	latch
mash	match
share	chair
sheep	cheap
sheet	cheat
ship	chip
shin	chin
shoe	chew
wash	watch

Drill Sentences

1. There will be a special fashion show in Chicago.
2. Take caution to wash well in the shower.
3. The fresh fish and hush puppies are delicious.
4. The insurance company wants cash before they issue the papers.
5. Shawn said he was Irish or Welsh.
6. The machine crushed the crashed cars.
7. Pressure can cause tension, not relaxation.
8. I mentioned that sugar is a temptation.
9. She should share the burden of the mission.
10. She sells seashells down by the seashore.
11. It was my intention to add relaxation to my vacation list.
12. She splashed and washed in the shower.
13. The army issued shields, shoes, and rations.
14. She is conscious of current flashy fashions.
15. They had a bash short sheeting the beds.
16. Shells were washed ashore during the monsoons.
17. The action shaped the special Senate session.
18. Shelly opened a shop to sell plush animals.
19. Surely you can show some passion.
20. That notion should vanish in the rush.

persuasion, garage

Other sample words for various spellings:*

rouge, treasure, seizure

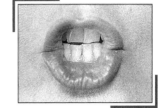

Classification   Lingua-palatal, voiced fricative

- Used in medial and end positions in words
- Used in stressed and unstressed syllables in words
- Cognate to [ʃ]

Description
- Lips are pursed
- Teeth are slightly apart
- Tip of tongue is aimed closely toward area just above upper gum ridge; sides of tongue are against upper molars; tongue is generally more rounded
- Vocal folds vibrate
- Sound is forced through space

Note: As with its cognate, it is important to purse the lips for this sound.

Drill Words

Initial**	Medial	End
gendarme	azure	barrage
genre	confusion	beige
jacquerie	decision	camouflage
jete	explosion	corsage
	fission	dressage
	leisure	entourage
	measure	massage
	pleasure	mirage
	version	prestige
	usual	rouge

Drill Sentences
1. The explosion was the result of nuclear fission.
2. Jacques was measured for a beige leisure suit.
3. One of life's great pleasures is my usual massage.
4. Heat created an illusion on the azure sea.

*The symbol [ž] is more common to those texts for studies of English as a second language. We will be using [ʒ].

**The phoneme [ʒ] occurs in the initial position in words of foreign origin, especially French.

5. She put the horse through the dressage in her usual manner.
6. Your decision about the garage has created much confusion.
7. His entire entourage had a different version of the story.
8. She applied her rouge, then pinned on the corsage.
9. That barrage of gunfire hit the area that was camouflaged.
10. Prestige is not the measure of man.
11. Camouflage, mirage, and illusion are similar concepts.
12. She reached the usual conclusion about how to spend her leisure time.
13. Having vision helps to avoid confusion in decision making.
14. A massage is always a pleasure.
15. Dress casual in a leisure suit.
16. The collision didn't happen in the garage.
17. Before the invasion of Asia, there was a barrage of information.
18. His composure adds to his prestige.
19. We sat in the loge seats during the second version of the film.
20. It is not so unusual to reach this conclusion.

Contrast Drill   Though there is usually not too much confusion between the two cognates, [ʒ] and [ʃ], the following brief lists demonstrate that interchanging the two can create new words.

Contrast Drill Words

[ʒ]	[ʃ]
azure	assure
fission	fishing
illusion	Aleutian
glazier	glacier
liege	leash

read, dream, are

Other sample words for various spellings:

rhyme, berry, wrap

Classification   Lingua-alveolar/palatal, voiced, (retroflexed) fricative/glide (depending on use)

- Used in initial, medial, and end positions in words

- Used in stressed and unstressed syllables in words

- Not to be confused with central vowels [ɚ] or [ɝ] with "r" quality

*[ɹ] was formerly written as [r], which is *now* used for a trilled sound. This text will use the upright [r] for reader ease.

Description   *Note:* There are several variations of this phoneme depending upon dialect and its position in a word. Phoneticians and linguists utilize many symbols and diacritical markings for this phoneme to clearly identify its sound in various contexts. However, we will confine our use to [ɾ] as the symbol for the consonant and consider the following two general descriptions.

1. Initial position in words followed by a vowel; for example, *red.* This is also true of consonant combinations wherein the [ɾ] is followed by a vowel; for example, *true.*

- Lips are pursed open

- Teeth are apart

- Tongue tip is curled upward but not touching area just slightly above the alveolar ridge; sides of tongue are against upper molars

- Vocal folds vibrate

- Sound is orally emitted

Drill Words

rap	afraid
rate	bread
raven	brown
reach	creek
rebel	crime
receive	dream
red	drink
reflect	friend
rise	front
river	grape
road	grunt
robust	pray
rung	price
wrap	trap
wrist	try

2. Usually found in medial positions after a vowel; for example, "error," or final positions after a vowel; for example, "tour."

- Lips open and not as pursed as described above

- Teeth are apart

- Tongue tip is lowered to a more orally central position; sides of tongue are against upper molars

- Vocal folds vibrate

- Sound is emitted orally

Drill Words	*Medial*	*End*
	art	bar
	bared	car
	dark	explore
	fork	deplore
	garden	fair
	harden	for
	lard	gore
	marry	hair
	moral	more
	nearly	pure
	party	quagmire
	quarrel	rare
	tarring	soar
	veering	tear
	wearing	war

Blends   As you might note from the list above and in previous phonemic discussions, the [r] is found in several consonant combinations. The following lists exemplify those blends.

[br]	**[dr]**
brace	drab
braid	dream
brake	drip
brick	drop
broke	droop
[fr]	**[gr]**
frame	grape
freeze	grease
fresh	green
froze	grip
fruit	grope
[kr]	**[pr]**
crab	pray
crack	preen
creep	prince
crib	prick
crumb	prod
[tr]	
trap	
trash	
tread	
trip	
trod	

Sound Substitutions Two substitutions might take the place of the [r]. In the first instance, non-native speakers (Asian) may substitute [l]. In this instance, those speakers are failing to remove the tongue from the upper gum ridge and curl it backward. The second substitution results in an "Elmer Fudd" sound. In this case, the [w] is substituted for [r]. The lists that follow contrast these three separate sounds and demonstrate that different words are created by their use.

[r]	[l]	[w]
rag	lag	wag
rare	lair	wear
rate	late	wait
red	led	wed
reap	leap	weep
reed	lead	weed
reek	leek	week
rest	lest	west
rise	lies	wise
room	loom	womb
row	low	woe
rude	lewd	wooed
wrist	list	wist
writ	lit	wit

Dialectal Variations With each dialect there seems to be a variation of this sound. Spanish speakers roll or trill it. Germans give it a guttural quality. The French nasalize it. Some British variations appear to omit it or "breeze" over it. When it appears within a word or at the end of a word, some American Eastern and Southern dialects omit it, while some hit upon it quite hard, seeming to give it a hardened curl. Many Easterners articulate an intrusive [r]. This sound occurs in contexts wherein one word ends with a vowel and the next word begins with a vowel; for example, "Cuba is a country" becomes "Cuber is a country."

Drill Sentences
1. Read the writings of the preacher and pray.
2. She rode around the room on her broom.
3. The royal family brought about an abrupt change.
4. The crime rate is lower when compared to yesteryear.
5. April is the cruelest month.
6. The green grapes are ripe enough to eat.
7. Fran is attracted to rocks and trees.
8. Dru's address is on the roadside rounder.
9. Frank dreamed about trains and rails.
10. Ralph burned the raffle tickets.
11. The orator said that he came to bury Caesar, not to praise him.

12. The crowd dared to come from near and far.
13. Marion and Marvin were married in March.
14. The North Star will lead the direction of the tour.
15. A millionaire can afford pearls, cars, and trips.
16. I like oranges, raspberries, and grapefruit.
17. The story was about a girl whose hair caught on fire.
18. More than one car was hired to drive the group.
19. At the first sign of a storm, sound the alarm.
20. Take a rest if you are wearing down and feeling tired.

check, beaches, each

Other sample words for various spellings:*

patch, question, cello

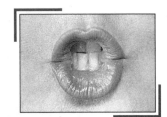

Classification Lingua-palatal, voiceless affricate (a combi-nation of two consonant sounds, a plosive and a fricative)

- Used in the initial, medial, and end positions in words

- Used in stressed and unstressed syllables in words

- Cognate of [ʤ]

Description ■ Lips are in an extended pursed position

- Teeth are apart

- Tip of tongue touches area slightly above gum ridge; sides of tongue touch upper molars

- No vocal fold vibration

- Air builds up against tongue, then only tongue explodes away from gum ridge

Note: This is a sound created by beginning as though you are going to make a [t], then ending with [ʃ]. As you drill with the following words, be sure that your tongue tip first taps the gum ridge before air escapes through the space between your teeth.

*The symbol [tš] represents an alternative usually used by those specifically studying English as a second language.

Drill Words	*Initial*	*Medial*	*End*
	chafe	actual	batch
	chain	bachelor	catch
	chance	century	ditch
	change	coaches	each
	cheap	kitchen	glitch
	check	nature	hatch
	cheese	picture	match
	chess	teacher	pitch
	chime	question	rich
	choice	watched	stitch

Sound Substitution   As indicated earlier, non-native speakers (Spanish) may substitute [ʃ] for this phoneme. Again, here is a list of contrast words to help you drill with this sound.

[tʃ]	[ʃ]
catch	cash
chair	share
chew	shoe
chip	ship
chop	shop
chore	shore
churl	surely
ditch	dish
Fitch	fish
hatch	hash
march	marsh
notch	nosh
watch	wash
witch	wish

Drill Sentences
1. Please check to see if you have any change for the check.
2. The teacher watched the chess game.
3. The coaches cheered at the tennis match.
4. Nachos is a dish of chips and cheese.
5. Chet searched under the couch for the broach.
6. Each choice is checked off the list.
7. Chuck's research was based on a hunch.
8. We churned out a batch of cookies in the kitchen.
9. There were chunks of clams and bunches of chopped potatoes in the chowder.
10. Each of you should have a speech teacher.
11. Each of the ladies wanted to catch the bachelor.
12. The pitcher changed his style and pitched a choice inning.

13. The nature of the question matches my own churlish query.
14. In March, we had a cheap lunch of fish-and-chips.
15. A chain of glitches prevented me from checking with you.
16. In spite of the search, we didn't catch any perch.
17. Each of you will achieve that which you choose.
18. This chapter features a few chosen words.
19. You can use crutches or a wheelchair.
20. If you have an itch, don't scratch.

jar, agent, huge

Other sample words for various spellings:*

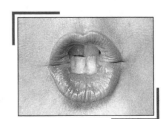

adjunct, stage, sledge, legion, soldier

Classification Lingua-palatal, voiced affricate (combination of two consonant sounds, a plosive and a fricative)

- Used in the initial, medial, and end positions in words

- Used in stressed and unstressed syllables in words

- Cognate to [tʃ]

Description
- Lips are in an extended pursed position

- Teeth are apart

- Tip of tongue is against area just above upper gum ridge; sides of tongue are against upper molars

- Vocal folds vibrate

- Sound builds up behind tongue, then is exploded into a fricative sound

Drill Words	*Initial*	*Medial*	*End*
	gentle	adjust	age
	germ	budget	bridge
	ginger	danger	college
	gym	enjoin	edge
	gyrate	imagine	knowledge
	jade	larger	judge

*The symbol [dž] is an alternative usually used by those studying English as a second language.

jagged	ledger	marriage
jeer	merger	page
joint	subject	surge
juice	register	wedge

Sound Substitution Because this phoneme is frequently spelled with "j" as in *jet,* some non-native speakers (e.g., Swedish) may substitute the phoneme [j], as in *yet,* for the sound [ʤ]. Speakers whose primary language is Spanish may substitute [h] for [ʤ] because that phoneme is often spelled with "j," and a "j" is pronounced with [h] in Spanish. For example, in Spanish the month of July [ʤʊlaɪ] is pronounced [hʊlɪo] and spelled *julio.* It is important to avoid these interchanges since they often create words other than the ones intended. The following lists provide contrast drill for these sounds.

[ʤ]	[j]
Jack	yak
jam	yam
jell	yell
jet	yet
jewel	yule
juice	use
John	yawn
joke	yoke

[ʤ]	[h]
Jack	hack
jag	hag
jail	hail
jay	hay
jazz	has
jeep	heap
jeer	here
jell	hell
Jew	hue
Jim	him
jog	hog
joist	hoist
jolly	holly
jot	hot
jug	hug
jump	hump

Contrast Drill Since the phoneme [ʤ] doesn't exist in many other languages, it may be a difficult one to produce. Use this list to contrast it with its cognate [tʃ].

Contrast Drill Words

[tʃ]	[dʒ]
chain	Jane
chalk	Jock
char	jar
chard	jarred
cheap	jeep
chest	jest
chin	gin
chip	gyp
choice	Joyce
choke	joke
choose	Jews
chug	jug
chunk	junk
perch	purge
rich	ridge

Drill Sentences

1. The judge subjected Jack to twenty years in jail.
2. Be sure to register your jewels in the ledger.
3. John imagined his marriage to be a better merger.
4. Jacqueline enjoined the band to play jazz.
5. The message was that the gym had a juice bar.
6. The garbage barge floated up and down as if on a junket.
7. The jeep sat near a jagged ridge.
8. Jane likes jam and jelly on a wedge of bread.
9. Jock earns small wages working for the legion.
10. At what age do you quit joking around?
11. Jim was jogging near a hedge.
12. A little knowledge can purge the danger of ignorance.
13. Damage was done to the joist.
14. The jet's engine was jammed.
15. The siege was caused primarily by rage.
16. We arranged the college reunion.
17. The blue jay sang a jolly tune.
18. There was a surge of water under the barge.
19. Jerry and Joe both wore badges.
20. The subject was a large one.

yes, human

Other sample words for various spellings:

billiard, eulogy, few, feud, future, fusion, review, unite

Classification   Lingua-palatal, voiced glide

- Used only in initial and medial positions of words
- Used in stressed and unstressed syllables in words

Note: Do not let the phonetic symbol confuse you.

Description
- Lips assume an anticipatory position in advance of the vowel that follows
- Teeth are apart
- Blade of tongue is against the hard palate; sides of tongue are against upper molars
- Vocal folds vibrate
- Sound is continuous as it blends into vowel

Drill Words

Initial	*Medial*
eulogize	amuse
unit	beyond
use	commune
yard	continue
year	few
yellow	human
yeoman	humor
yield	million
yolk	senior
yonder	value

Sound Substitution   The substitution of [ʤ] for [j] was noted in the previous section, p. 233. If you need extra practice, review that section.

Variations   Speakers of some words in which this phoneme is in a medial position can include [j] or omit it; for example, *Tuesday.* Further, some speakers refine articulation further by using the diphthong [ɪu]. The choice is yours. Remember that in speech for broadcasting or for some roles on the stage, you should incorporate these phonetic combinations. Below, words are listed in three columns. In the first column, use the [u], for the second column use the [j], for the third column use [ɪu].

[u]	[j]	[ɪu]
due	due	due
duel	duel	duel
duet	duet	duet

duke	duke	duke
duty	duty	duty
institute	institute	institute
knew	knew	knew
numerous	numerous	numerous
neutral	neutral	neutral
new	new	new
nude	nude	nude
reduce	reduce	reduce
tube	tube	tube
tune	tune	tune
Tuesday	Tuesday	Tuesday

Drill Sentences

1. You knew, didn't you, that Tuesday was the last day to file for senior status?
2. Yesterday, my companion, who was just a youth, was in New York.
3. That unit does a huge volume of business.
4. The beauty of the Grand Canyon is unusual.
5. Daniel reviewed the volume and gave his opinion.
6. Let's try to reduce the abuse of humans.
7. The yellow yacht sailed into view.
8. The mute student sat and yawned as he looked into the yard.
9. The feud between the Yanks and the South has become quite familiar.
10. Your yearly dues are yet to be paid.
11. You can continue another year at Yale.
12. A million dollars doesn't have the value it used to have.
13. The future of California is at stake unless we unite.
14. The institute will continue to search for a cure for cancer.
15. You seemed amused beyond what was due the joke.
16. I don't think they use egg yolks in yellow yogurt.
17. Jack worked as a yeoman in a yacht yard.
18. Numerous senior citizens have visited Europe.
19. We yearned to visit the futuristic commune.
20. The youngster knew he should stay in the yard.

Velar Consonants

keep, become, sick

Other sample words for various spellings:

chemical, comic, fix, liquor, raccoon, stick, quip

Classification   Lingua-velar, voiceless plosive

- Used in initial, medial, and end positions in words
- Used in stressed and unstressed syllables in words
- Cognate to [g]

Description
- Lips are shaped in anticipation of vowel that follows
- Back of tongue is pressed against the soft palate or velum; tip of tongue is lowered
- No vocal fold vibration
- Air builds up and is released as tongue pulls away from velum

Drill Words

Initial	*Medial*	*End*
came	action	back
care	became	duck
coat	doctor	hock
could	exercise	like
count	market	music
keep	practice	plaque
key	success	rack
kiss	require	sick
kite	taken	took
kiwi	welcome	work

Blends   Two consonant combinations, [kl] and [kr], can be tricky since the [k] is a plosive and not a fricative. It is therefore important to produce a cleanly exploded sound before moving to the next sound. Practice with these combinations:

[kl]	**[kr]**
clam	cram
clash	crash
class	crass
claw	craw
clean	cream
clipped	crypt
clock	crock
clout	kraut
clown	crown
clue	crew

Special Considerations   Some written combinations can cause consternation when a native, not to mention a non-native, speaker attempts to pronounce them; for example "cc" as in *accidental* and "xc" as in *excavate*. The pronunciation of "x" will be covered in the next section (see p. 240). The following lists should be helpful.

	[k]	[ks]
acc		
	acclaim	accede
	acclimate	accelerate
	accommodate	accent
	accompany	accept
	accomplish	access
	accord	accessory
	account	accident
	accurate	accidental
occ		
	occasional	occidental
	occlude	occipital
	occult	
	occupant	
	occur	

Drill Sentences

1. We could go back to Cape Cod this summer.
2. Kerry's backhand knocks your socks off.
3. The crowd at the club sat around talking about the clergy.
4. Ken walked like a common duck.
5. German chocolate cake has coconut as a key ingredient.
6. Clouds were blackening over the lake.
7. Kansas has had strict liquor laws.
8. Lucky you got off work so quickly.
9. Keep calm when traffic slows to a crawl.
10. You can clean the cushions with a chemical and cloth.
11. Keith Newmark is a kind man with an odd accent.
12. In the old days we could say we made hand-cranked phone calls as well as crank calls.
13. Did you recognize the character in the raccoon coat?
14. The accessories were taken from the crypt.
15. The occupant is a practicing doctor.
16. Prerequisites to the class are the keys to success.
17. It was our luck that the Coast Guard came when we called.
18. A person with clout will have access to the crown.
19. It was no accident that Kate came to like your music.
20. You can fix up your accent with exercise and practice.

get, began, frog

Other sample words for various spellings:

examine, ghost, leggings, vogue

Classification Lingua-velar, voiced, plosive

- Used in initial, medial, and end positions in words
- Used in stressed and unstressed syllables in words
- Cognate to [k]

Description
- Lips are shaped in anticipation of the vowel that follows
- Teeth are apart
- Back of tongue is against soft palate or velum; tip of tongue is lowered
- Vocal folds vibrate
- Sound builds up and is quickly released as the tongue breaks away from the velum

Drill Words

Initial	*Medial*	*End*
gain	again	big
galley	example	dog
gamble	finger	egg
gang	forget	hog
get	giggle	lag
ghostly	haggard	mug
gimmick	regard	pig
give	sugar	rag
goal	suggest	vague
guttural	together	wag

Blends The [g] requires a clear explosion when found in combinations with other consonants. The following list will provide drill practice.

[gl]	**[gr]**
glad	grad
glade	grade
glaive	grave
glance	grants
glass	grass
glaze	graze
glean	green

gleed	greed
gleet	greet
gloom	groom

Special Considerations

As noted in the previous discussion of [k], words spelled with "x" often create problems for speakers. In some cases you use the phonemes [ks] and in other instances [gz]. With words beginning with "ex" a general rule to follow is to use [gz] when the "ex" is followed by a stressed vowel. The following lists should be helpful.

[ks]	[gz]
excavate	exact
exceed	exaggerate
excel	exam
exception	example
excerpt	executive
excess	exemplify
exchange	exhaust
excise	exhibit
excite	exhort
exclude	exhume
excuse	exist
execute	exorbitant
exercise	exotic
exhale	exuberant
explode	exude
expose	exult
express	
extend	
extreme	

Contrast Drill

Though context will usually give listeners clues to intended meanings, it is important to differentiate between cognates. The cognates [k] and [g] are used in numerous words that, should you interchange the two, you would be using a different word than you wanted to use; for example, "I sat in the glass (class)." The list below gives you some of these contrasting words.

Contrast Drill Words

[k]	[g]
calf	gaff
call	gall
came	game
cane	gain
cap	gap
cash	gash
cause	gauze

cave	gave
clad	glad
class	glass
clue	glue
coat	goat
coast	ghost
code	goad
cool	ghoul
craft	graft
curd	gird
kale	gale
kilt	guilt
hack	hag
pick	pig
rack	rag
sack	sag
tack	tag

Drill Sentences

1. The guest forgot to give a hostess gift.
2. Executive fatigue can begin to exhaust you early in the day.
3. Greta got some grade A eggs, sugar, and garlic.
4. Gypsy sang, "You gotta have a gimmick."
5. I suggest that you get some more examples.
6. Put a green string around your finger so that you don't forget.
7. I am glad that I got a grant that would enlarge the exhibit.
8. Together we can grow toward our goal.
9. The guard began digging around the grave.
10. A green light is a signal to go.
11. We were exhausted, hungry, and eager to come to an agreement.
12. Her colleagues in the legal profession agreed.
13. Good executives will set goals to be gained.
14. Gay set her mug on the glass table and gazed out the window.
15. From this angle, your dog looks a little haggard.
16. The movie that garnered high ratings was called gleefully ghoulish.
17. We will navigate this gale with grit and grace.
18. Garish and gaudy decor can be ugly.
19. We were giggling at the pig wagging its tail.
20. I am glad that you got exactly what you wanted in a gift.

[ŋ]

single, sing

Other sample words for various spellings:

sink, angle, incubate, larynx

Classification	Lingua-velar, voiced nasal continuant

- Used in the medial and end positions in words
- Used in stressed and unstressed syllables in words

Description
- Lips are apart
- Teeth are apart
- Back of tongue is against soft palate or velum; tip of tongue is lowered
- Vocal folds vibrate
- Sound is emitted through the nose

Drill Words

Medial	Final
angle	among
banker	bring
England	evening
finger	going
hunger	hang
language	long
single	morning
sprinkler	thing
thinking	young
uncle	wrong

Sound Addition Some speakers with a "New York" accent may add a slight [g] sound following the [ŋ]; for example, *wrong* becomes [rɔŋg] or *singing* becomes [sɪŋgɪŋg]. The following lists can give you practice avoiding this addition.

bang	banging
bring	bringing
clang	clanging
gang	ganging
hang	hanging
long	longing
ping	pinging
ring	ringing
sing	singing
wrong	wronging

Drill Sentences
1. My uncle was asking about visiting England.
2. The king was thinking about going to Rangoon.
3. The congress used the English language in questioning at the bankruptcy hearings.
4. The young think they can never be wrong.

5. I'll be calling you either in the morning or evening.
6. He was singing the "Star Spangled Banner" and banging on a pan.
7. She was doing everything she could to write a better ending to the song.
8. To see a boy pretending to be flying is not so amazing.
9. The flying machine was in the hangar on the landing strip.
10. While speaking, use your larynx, pharynx, and tongue.
11. As the gong was sounding, I rang a bell.
12. A bee sting is nothing to ignore for long.
13. The English language is ever expanding.
14. Officials were thinking about banning zinc from our water supplies.
15. Everything is happening to cause me anxiety.
16. A single banker was among the evening's guests.
17. My younger uncle had sunk money into stocks.
18. "Going, going, gone," is the song of the auctioneer.
19. Long ago there were more jungles.
20. "Morning on Long Island" would be a good song title.

Glottal Consonant

help, ahold

Other sample words for various spellings:

whole, who, hale

Classification   Voiceless glottal

- Used in initial and medial positions in words
- Used in stressed and unstressed syllables in words

Description
- Lips are shaped in anticipation of the vowel that follows
- Teeth are apart
- Tongue positioned in anticipation of the vowel that follows
- No vocal fold vibration
- Air is emitted through open mouth

Drill Words

Initial	*Medial*
habit	ahead
half	behave
hammock	behind
handicap	dehydrate

happen	inhale
heart	enhance
hedge	lighthouse
heredity	perhaps
hot	rehash
hoard	somehow

Sound Omission   Occasionally, the [h] will be omitted from contextual speech. This may occur because the phoneme lacks voice and is often lost in rapid conversation. Some words in particular stand out as those which may confuse speakers.

- *Herb* is spelled with the letter "h" but the phoneme [h] is not used with it, [ɝb]. However, in derivatives of this word, the phoneme [h] can be used if the speaker wishes. These words are *herbaceous, herbage, herbal, herbality, herbicide, herbivore.*

- Although the word *heir* is spelled with the letter "h," the phoneme is not used and the word is pronounced [ɛr].

- The word *hermit* pronounces the [h], but the proper noun *Hermitage* may not.

- *Honesty* and *honor* are words that are spelled with the letter "h," but the [h] is not pronounced.

The important point to remember about this sound is that it is *usually* produced in words containing it.

Drill Sentences
1. Harry behaved as though he had no handicap.
2. Heredity can have an effect on the health of your heart.
3. It was Harriet's habit to lie in a hammock by the hedge.
4. He inhabited his house behind the health club.
5. Somehow the rehearsal ended in a heated dispute.
6. Perhaps you can house me here in your house.
7. Heat hit Ohio in the summer.
8. When hungry, he ate ham and dehydrated fruit.
9. Please help me learn to behave in a heroic manner.
10. I hope that the redhead will understand my incoherencies.
11. Herb has inherited a whole hockey team.
12. Who can rehearse in the hall?
13. It is unhealthy to inhale without exhaling.
14. We can hydrate and reheat half of the dehydrated food.
15. Her behavior prevented Harriet from being rehired.
16. We heard hail hitting behind the hothouse.
17. Get in the habit of withholding a hundred dollars each month.

18. Hazel rehashed her plans for the Hawaiian trip.
19. He wasn't very humble about his height.
20. History has been high on the lists of his professors.

Additional Drill

Poets make extensive use of alliteration, which is the repetition of consonant sounds in the initial position in words. The following poems and poetry excerpts will give you additional drill material for most of the consonants you have studied.

1. You spotted snakes with double tongue,
     Thorny hedgehogs, be not seen;
   Newts, and blind-worms, do no wrong;
     Come not near our fairy queen.

—William Shakespeare

2. Philomel, with melody,
   Sing in our sweet lullaby;
   Lulla, lulla, lullaby; lulla, lulla, lullaby:
     Never harm,
   Nor spell, nor charm,
   come our lovely lady nigh;
   So good night, with lullaby.

—William Shakespeare

3. Hear the sledges with the bells,
     Silver bells!
   What a world of merriment their melody foretells!
     How they tinkle, tinkle, tinkle,
   In the icy air of night!
   While the stars, that oversprinkle
     All the heavens, seem to twinkle
       With a crystalline delight;
     Keeping time, time, time,
     In a sort of runic rhyme,
   To the tintinnabulation that so musically wells
     From the bells, bells, bells, bells,
       Bells, bells, bells—
   From the jingling and the tinkling of the bells.

—Edgar Allan Poe

4. We are the music-makers,
     And we are the dreamers of dreams,
   Wandering by lone sea-breakers,
     And sitting by desolate streams;

World-losers and world-forsakers,
   On whom the pale moon gleams:
Yet we are the movers and shakers
   Of the world forever, it seems.

                          —Arthur William O'Shaughnessy

5. All hushed and still within the house;
   Without, all wind and driving rain;
But something whispers to my mind,
Wrought up in rain and wailing wind:
Never again? Why not again? Never again!
   Memory has power as well as wind!

                          —Emily Brontë

6. . . . Summer is come, for every spray now springs;
The hart hath hung his old head on the pale;
The buck in brake his winter coat he flings;
The fishes float with new prepared scale;
The adder all her slough away she slings;
The swift swallow pursueth the flies smale;
The busy bee her honey now she mings.

                          —Henry Howard

7. The sound of her silk skirt has stopped.
On the marble pavement dust grows.
Her empty room is cold and still.
Fallen leaves are piled against the doors.
   Longing for that lovely lady
How can I bring my aching heart to rest?

                          —Li Fu-jen

8. We were young, we were merry, we were very very wise,
   And the door stood open at our feast,
When there passed us a woman with the West in her eyes,
   And a man with his back to the East.

                          —Mary Coleridge

Chapter Ten Checklist

C O N S O N A N T S

The following passage includes words that contain consonants in the sequence in which they appeared in this chapter with three or four words containing each phoneme. (It is not comprehensive insofar as it contains all consonants juxtaposed with all other possible consonants.) IPA letters are written above the alphabetical letters that are underlined to help you

to identify sounds. To the left of the passage is a checklist column for consonants. Use this checklist as you did the vowel checklist. Read the passage over several times using the assistance of audio/video equipment or a friend and check off those consonants for which you require additional drill.
(*See pages 279–280 for a tear-out version of this form.*)

p _____

         p   p p p   b   b   b   p   b b
Perhaps people who have been abroad are better at pricing baubles,

b _____

    b   m   hw
bangles, and other goods, or just think they are. It may be that when

m _____

   w   m   m   m   w
one has made the time to examine goods around the world, one is not

hw _____

   w   w   hw   f
swept away where a less traveled person might be. For example,

w _____

        f   f   f
some finely crafted goods may be found in the Orient if you are

f _____

         f v f   v   v   ð
willing to go so far. Very few people inevitably are, of course. Others

v _____

   θ   θ   d   θ   ð   t ð
think nothing of spending thousands on that kind of trip, though.

θ _____

     t   d   t   dt t   tt   t
Sometimes you no doubt spend ten to fifty times as much on an item

ð _____

       t t   d   t   d
in the States as you would in the place in which it is manufactured.

t _____

   z   s   z   s   s   z
Zealous shoppers often go to great lengths to search out bargains,

d _____

 s   s   s z   s   n   n
starting with discount stores and extending to Europe. Never under-

s _____

         n   n   l   l
estimate seasoned hunters. Lower prices are their goal. Nothing could

z _____

     l   l   l
be more pleasing than a lovely deal.

n _____

   ʃ   ʃ   ʒ
Oceans and nations are no barrier. Conversion rates are no problem.

l _____

     ʃ   ʒ   s   r
Europe should have it! Asia should have it—a bargain! "Born to

ʃ _____

    ʃ   r   r   r   r
shop!" some say. A fair warning is in order here. One may not be able

ʒ_____   to ex<u>ch</u>ange a <u>j</u>ar, <u>j</u>ade broo<u>ch</u>, or other <u>j</u>ewel bought in <u>Ch</u>ina. Yes,

r_____   that's the u<u>s</u>ual case. F<u>ew</u> things <u>c</u>an be ta<u>k</u>en ba<u>ck</u> to Tur<u>k</u>ey. Good-

tʃ_____   ness knows, it comes down to this. <u>G</u>oing away doesn't get you better

ʤ_____   <u>g</u>oods. <u>G</u>ood thi<u>ng</u>s begin at <u>h</u>ome. Shoppi<u>ng</u> and buyi<u>ng</u> in the States

j_____   some<u>h</u>ow <u>h</u>elps the economy. So stay <u>h</u>ere to become a worldly wise

k _____   shopper.

g_____

ŋ _____

h _____

Chapter Ten Review

Review the following concepts:

- Consonants: characteristics/classifications
- Terms: affricates, alveolar, bilabial, blends, cognates, continuant, dental, fricatives, glides, glottal, labio, laterals, lingua, nasal, palatal, plosives, velar

Respond to the following:

1. Identify all of the consonant cognates. Write sample words.
2. List the nasal consonants. Write sample words.
3. With what phonemes is the letter "x" sounded?
4. Consonants are classified according to what three things?
5. Why do some consonants need to sound "crisper" than others?

APPLICATION

1. Which consonants do you easily produce?

2. Which consonants are more problematic for you?

3. Are you substituting one consonant for another, such as a [t] or [d] for [θ] and [ð]?

4. Are you using voice and voicelessness properly?

5. Is your production of consonants sharp and clear?

FOCUS MESSAGE

1. *ESL:* There are some primary considerations for you with regard to consonants. First there will be consonant sounds with which you may not be familiar. Chances are, the "th" sounds are your biggest challenge. Spend more time drilling on those sounds. Another confusion for you might be that English spelling and sounds are not always consistent. The pronunciation lists in Appendixes Two and Three contain several of these more difficult words.

2. *Acting:* Whether on stage or screen your command of consonant sounds is vital to message clarity. Granted, slurred speech can characterize (like Marlon Brando in *The Godfather*), but you first need a mastery of sound in order to violate it. You might also want to begin to observe the sound substitutions of people with dialects in order to prepare yourself for the creation of stage dialects.

3. *Broadcasting:* Consonants can play havoc with your microphone. You must learn to control the "popping" effect of plosives and fricatives and the "hissing" effect of sibilants. Additionally, as you read copy on the air, be aware that the words as spelled may be pronounced quite differently than you might suppose. You must continue to extend your pronunciation vocabulary. The pronunciation lists in Appendixes Two and Three can help. Do not just read these. Say the words and integrate them into your speaking vocabulary.

NOTE

1. Douglas R. Hofstader, *Metamagical Themas* (New York: Bantam Books, 1986), p. 44.

A FINAL WORD

Although the body of the textbook ends here, your work must continue. You initiated a program for voice improvement, because you recognized a need for information. You were motivated to develop your voice and diction skills, but it is important that you continue to develop those skills.

Over the period of your study you: (1) learned how the voice is produced; (2) were introduced to the various concepts of pitch, loudness, rate, and quality; (3) were presented with a brief discussion of the American English language; and (4) received instruction on the production of the vowels, diphthongs, and consonants of this language. No doubt you spent time drilling and exercising to acquire improved speech skills, and by now may be conscious of competently demonstrating your improved voice and clearer articulation. That is to say, when you make an effort to think about it, you can effect the sound of voice you want with the degree of clarity you need, but you have not yet achieved the ability to perform unconsciously. This is not the time to stop practicing; indeed, this is exactly the time when you should begin to practice more rigorously.

Refer periodically to exercises in this text that have helped you reach your goals. Set aside time each day to refresh skills with drillwork. If you continue exercising toward your goals, it won't be long before you will be able to use your new voice unconsciously.

APPENDIX ONE

IPA Pronunciation Guides

Vowel Pronunciation Guide

Sample word	IPA
eat	i
it	ɪ
ate	eɪ*
pet	ɛ
pat	æ
pat	ɑ†
about	ə
cut	ʌ
rather	ɚ
bird	ɝ
father	ɑ
law	ɔ
oat	oʊ*
look	ʊ
school	u
ice	aɪ
out	aʊ
oil	ɔɪ
Tuesday	ɪu
Tuesday	ju

*These diphthongs are more commonly used and recognized than the short versions, [e] and [o] respectively.

†[a] Most linguists and phoneticians consider this phoneme to be a vowel used primarily in New England as a substitute for [æ]. It is also used as the initial phoneme in some diphthongs.

Consonant Pronunciation Guide

Sample word	IPA
pay	p
been	b
met	m
whether	hw
weather	w
feather	f
voice	v
think	θ
the	ð
ten	t
den	d
see	s
zebra	z
no	n
lip	l
shoe	ʃ *or* š
persuasion	ʒ *or* ž
check	tʃ *or* tš
jar	ʤ *or* dž
read	r *or* ɭ*
yes	j
keep	k
get	g
sing	ŋ
help	h

*This chart includes changes effected at the 1989 IPA convention.

APPENDIX TWO

100 Commonly Mispronounced Words

The following list represents some words that are often mispronounced. Each word is followed by the current standard pronunciation written in the International Phonetic Alphabet. This pronunciation is based on the Tenth Edition of *Merriam-Webster's Collegiate Dictionary* and the *Pronunciation Dictionary* of J. C. Wells.[1] The syllabic stress mark is placed in front of the stressed syllable in multisyllabic words.

Remember that language changes constantly, and many variations occur as change takes place. An example of this is the word *educate*. The 1956 dictionary indicates the pronunciation of this word to be [ɛdjukeɪt], but the 1993 dictionary (used for this list) indicates the more current pronunciation to be [ɛdʒəkeɪt].

A dialect or accent will also produce a variation. To avoid confusion, IPA here represents current pronunciations. We have changed the [e] and [o] to [eɪ] and [oʊ], but continue to use the [r].

1.	actual	ˈæktʃəwəl	20.	collegial	kəˈlidʒəl
2.	aegis	ˈidʒəs	21.	collegiate	kəˈlidʒət
3.	aesthetic	ɛsˈθɛtɪk	22.	comparable	ˈkɑmprəbəl
4.	almond	ˈɑmənd	23.	contact	ˈkɑntækt
5.	antidote	ˈæntɪdoʊt	24.	contemptuous	kənˈtɛmtʃəs
6.	architect	ˈɑrkətɛkt	25.	corps	kɔr
7.	arctic	ˈɑrktɪk	26.	couldn't	ˈkʊdnt
8.	ask	æsk	27.	data	ˈdeɪtə
9.	asterisk	ˈæstɚɪsk	28.	deluge	ˈdɛljuʒ
10.	athlete	ˈæθlit	29.	didn't	ˈdɪdnt
11.	balk	bɔk	30.	diphtheria	dɪfˈθɪrɪə
12.	buoy	ˈbuɪ	31.	diphthong	ˈdɪfθɔŋ
13.	business	ˈbɪznəs	32.	drowned	draʊnd
14.	calm	kɑm	33.	educate	ˈɛdʒəkeɪt
15.	carafe	kəˈræf	34.	electoral	ɪˈlɛktrəl
16.	casualty	ˈkæʒəltɪ	35.	entertain	ɛntɚˈteɪn
17.	chic	ʃik	36.	environment	ɪnvaɪrənˈmɛnt
18.	cinnamon	ˈsɪnəmən	37.	err	ɛr
19.	climactic	klaɪˈmæktɪk	38.	escape	ɪsˈkeɪp

[1]Merriam Webster's Collegiate Dictionary. Tenth Ed. 1993. J. C. Wells, 2000. Longman Pronunciation Dictionary. Second edition. Harlow: Pearson Education Limited.

39.	et cetera	ɛt'sɛtərə	70.	pretty	'prɪtɪ
40.	evening	'ivnɪŋ	71.	probably	'prɑbəblɪ
41.	film	fɪlm	72.	realtor	'rɪəltɚ
42.	gesture	'ʤɛstʃɚ	73.	recognize	'rɛkɪgnaɪz
43.	grievous	'grivəs	74.	regular	'rɛgjələ
44.	grimace	'grɪməs	75.	respite	'rɛspət
45.	haute	oʊt	76.	salve	sæv
46.	heinous	'heɪnəs	77.	sarcasm	'sɑrkæzəm
47.	herb	ɝb	78.	schism	'sɪzəm
48.	hundred	'hʌndrəd	79.	secretary	'sɛkrətɛrɪ
49.	incongruous	ɪn'kɑŋgrəwəs	80.	similar	'sɪmələ
50.	inquiry	ɪn'kwaɪrɪ	81.	sophomore	'sɑfmɔr
51.	iron	'aɪɚn	82.	southern	'səðɚn
52.	larynx	'lærɪŋks	83.	specific	spɪ'sɪfɪk
53.	library	'laɪbrɛrɪ	84.	statistics	stə'tɪstɪks
54.	magnanimity	mægnə'nɪmətɪ	85.	strength	strɛŋθ
55.	mauve	moʊv	86.	suave	swɑv
56.	mischievous	'mɪstʃəvəs	87.	sword	sɔrd
57.	momentous	moʊ'mɛntəs	88.	tact	tækt
58.	monstrous	'mɑnstrəs	89.	taupe	toʊp
59.	nuclear	'nɪuklɪə	90.	temperature	'tɛmpɚtʃɚ
60.	nuptial	'nʌpʃəl	91.	terror	'tɛrɚ
61.	orange	'ɑrɪnʤ	92.	theory	'θɪərɪ
62.	pathos	'peɪθas	93.	tour	tʊr
63.	perform	pɚ'fɔrm	94.	tremendous	trɪ'mɛndəs
64.	picture	'pɪktʃɚ	95.	turbot	'tɝbət
65.	poem	'poəm	96.	twenty	'twɛntɪ
66.	prefer	prɪ'fɝ	97.	wanton	'wɔntən
67.	preferable	'prɛfrəbəl	98.	wash	wɑʃ
68.	prelude	'prɛljud	99.	wonderful	'wəndɚfəl
69.	prescribe	prɪ'skraɪb	100.	wouldn't	'wʊdnt

Vocabulary Builders

Use the following list of words to build vocabulary. Some words here might be mispronounced because these words are unkknown to the user or infrequently used. Pronunciations, identified by IPA symbols, are based on *Merriam-Webster's Collegiate Dictionary*, Tenth Edition, and the *Pronunciation Dictionary* of J. C. Wells.

abeyance	ə'beɪjəns	amateur	'æmətə˞
abhor	əb'hɔr	amicable	'æmɪkəbəl
abrupt	ə'brʌpt	amity	'æmətɪ
abscond	æb'skɑnd	anachronism	ə'nækrənɪzəm
absorb	əb'zɔrb	analogy	ə'nælədʒɪ
abstemious	æb'stimɪəs	analysis	ə'næləsəs
abyss	ə'bɪs	anathema	ə'næθəmə
acacia	ə'keɪʃə	ancient	'eɪnʃənt
academe	ækədim	anomalous	ə'nɑmələs
accept	æk'sɛpt	antidote	'æntɪdot
accompanist	ə'kʌmpənəst	aplomb	ə'plɑm
accrue	ə'kru	apropos	æprə'pou
acetic	ə'sitɪk	arboretum	ɑrbə'ritəm
acoustic	ə'kustɪk	archipelago	ɑrkə'pɛləgo
acumen	ə'kjumən	archive	'ɑrkaɪv
ad hoc	'æd'hɑk	artifice	'ɑrtəfəs
adjective	'ædʒɪktɪv	ascetic	ə'sɛtɪk
advocate	'ædvəkeɪt (verb)	askance	ə'skæns
	'ædvəkət (noun)	askew	ə'skju
aerobic	ær'oʊbɪk	assailed	ə'seəld
aesthetic	ɛs'θɛtɪk	assistive	ə'sɪstɪv
affluent	'æfluənt	augur	'ɔgə˞
aggregate	'ægrɪgət	aura	'ɔrə
albeit	ɔl'biət	austere	ɔs'tɪr
alchemy	'ælkəmɪ	autonomy	ɔ'tɑnəmɪ
alkali	'ælkəlaɪ	azure	'æʒə˞
allay	ə'le		
altruism	'æltruɪzəm	baccalaureate	bækə'lɔriət
aluminum	ə'lumənəm	balsam	'bɔlsəm
alumna	ə'lumnə	bankrupt	'bæŋkrəpt
alveolar	al'viələ˞	barometer	bə'rɑmətə˞
Alzheimer's	'æltshaɪmə˞z	baroque	bə'rok

basil	'bæzəl	chalet	ʃæ'leɪ
beatific	biə'tɪfɪk	chamois	'ʃæmɪ
beaux arts	bo'zɑr	charisma	kə'rɪzmə
beige	beɪʒ	chary	'tʃærɪ
benign	bɪ'naɪn	chasm	kæzəm
bereave	bɪ'riv	chaste	'tʃeɪst
bereft	bɪ'rɛft	chauvinism	'ʃovənɪzəm
bewildered	bɪ'wɪldə-d	chiaroscuro	kiɑrə'skjʊroʊ
bias	'baɪəs	chignon	'ʃɪnjɑn
bier	bɪr	chimera	kaɪ'mɪrə
bifurcate	'baɪfə-ket	chromatic	kro'mætɪk
bilabial	'baɪlebɪəl	chrysalis	'krɪsələs
bilge	bɪlʤ	cipher	'saɪfə-
bisque	bɪsk	civilization	sɪvələ'zeɪʃən
bludgeon	'blʌʤən	coalition	koə'lɪʃən
bombard	bɑm'bɑrd	codicil	'kɑdəsəl
boor	bʊr	cogent	'koʊʤənt
bore	bɔr	cognizant	'kɑgnəzənt
borough	'bɝoʊ	cohere	ko'hɪr
borrow	'bɑroʊ	colloquy	'kɑləkwɪ
boudoir	'budwɑr	columnar	kə'lʌmnə-
bourgeois	'bʊrʒwa	compromise	'kɑmprəmaɪz
brioche	bri'oʃ	concede	kən'sid
bronchial	'brɑŋkɪəl	conceit	kən'sit
bureau	'bjʊroʊ	concoct	kən'kɑkt
bureaucracy	bjʊ'rɑkrəsɪ	concussion	kən'kʌʃən
bury	bɛrɪ	condominium	kɑndə'mɪniəm
		congregation	kɑŋgrɪ'geɪʃən
cabal	kə'bɑl	congruent	kən'gruənt
cable	'keɪbəl	connote	kə'noʊt
caesura	sɪ'ʒʊrə	conscience	'kɑntʃəns
calk or caulk	kɔk	conscious	'kɑntʃəs
calliope	kə'laɪəpɪ	consequences	'kɑnsəkwɛnsəs
calve	kæv	conservator	kən'sɝvətə-
capacious	kə'peɪʃəs	contemporaneity	kəntɛmprə'niətɪ
caprice	kə'pris	controversial	kɑntrə'vɝʃəl
caricature	'kærɪkətʃʊr	convenient	kən'vinjənt
cataclysm	'kætəklɪzəm	corpus	'kɔrpəs
catarrh	kə'tɑr	coterie	'koʊtə-ɪ
catastrophe	kə'tæstrəfɪ	countenanced	'kaʊntənənst
catechism	'kætəkɪzəm	coup de grace	kudə'gras
causal	'kɔzəl	cricoid	'kraɪkɔɪd
causality	kɔ'zælətɪ	crustacean	krəs'teɪʃən
cavalry	'kævalrɪ	culture	'kʌltʃə-
celestial	sə'lɛstʃəl	cumulative	'kjumjələtɪv
cerebral	sə'ribrəl	curiosities	kɪʊrɪ'asətiz
chafe	'tʃeɪf		
chaff	'tʃæf	daunt	dɔnt
chagrin	ʃə'grɪn	debacle	dɪ'bakəl
chaise	ʃeɪz	debauch	dɪ'bɔtʃ

debt	dɛt	ethereal	ɪ'θɪriəl
decisive	dɪ'saɪsɪv	exacerbate	ɪg'zæsə·beɪt
default	dɪ'fɔlt	exam	ɪg'zæm
deficit	'dɛfəsət	exclusion	ɪks'kluʒən
deify	'diəfaɪ	exigency	'ɛksədʒənsɪ
deign	deɪn	expletive	'ɛksplətɪv
demise	dɪ'maɪz		
demonstrable	dɪ'manstrəbəl	facade	fə'sad
demur	dɪ'mjʊr	facetious	fə'siʃəs
denouement	denu'ma	facile	'fæsəl
depraved	dɪ'preɪvd	factual	'fæktʃwəl
deprivation	dɛprɛ'veɪʃən	farther	'farðə·
depth	dɛpθ	fascia	'feɪʃə
descry	dɪ'skraɪ	fauces	'fɔsiz
desperate	'dɛsprət	fault	fɔlt
despot	'dɛspət	February	'fɛbrəwɛrɪ
deter	dɪ'tə·	feign	feɪn
device	dɪ'vaɪs	felon	'fɛlən
devise	dɪ'vaɪz	fidelity	fɪ'dɛlətɪ
diaphanous	daɪ'æfənəs	fiduciary	fə'djuʃɪɛrɪ
dinghy	'dɪŋɪ	finality	fɪ'nælətɪ
disaster	diz'æstə·	flaccid	'flæsəd
discern	dɪs'ɜ·n	flagellate	'flædʒəlet
disdain	dɪs'deɪn	flagrant	'fleɪgrənt
district	'dɪstrɪkt	flaunt	flɔnt
docile	'dasəl	flux	flʌks
domicile	'damɪsaɪəl	forage	'fɔrɪdʒ
dyad	'daɪæd	foray	'fɔreɪ
		forensic	fə'rɛnsɪk
eccentric	ɪk'sɛntrɪk	forfeit	'fɔrfət
echelon	'ɛʃəlan	fracas	'freɪkəs
ecology	ɪ'kalədʒɪ	franc	'fræŋk
economic	ɛkə'namɪk	fugue	fjug
economy	ɪ'kanəmɪ		
ecstasy	'ɛkstəsɪ	gait	geɪt
efficacy	'ɛfɪkəsɪ	gamble	'gæmbəl
egalitarian	ɪgælə'tɛrɪən	gambol	'gæmbəl
eke	ik	gaudy	gɔdɪ
elevation	ɛlə'veɪʃən	gauge	geɪdʒ
elude	ɪ'lud	gawk	gɔk
emboldened	im'boldənd	genre	'ʒanrə
empathy	'ɛmpəθɪ	genial	'dʒinjəl
enigma	ɪ'nɪgmə	gentian	'dʒɛntʃən
enormous	ɪ'nɔrməs	gherkin	'gɜ·kən
ephemeral	ɪ'fɛmrəl	gnaw	nɔ
epitome	ɪ'pɪtəmɪ	gradient	'greɪdɪənt
epoch	'ɛpək	gradual	'grædʒwəl
equitable	'ɛkwətəbəl	graduate	'grædʒəweɪt (verb)
escape	ɪs'keɪp		'grædʒəwət (noun)
eschew	ɪs'tʃu	gratuity	grə'tjuətɪ

gregarious	grɪˈgærɪəs	intact	ɪnˈtækt
grievance	ˈgrivəns	inter	ɪnˈtɝ
grizzled	ˈgrɪzəld	intravenous	ɪntrəˈvinəs
guarantee	gɛrənˈtɪ	inundate	ˈɪnəndeɪt
guardian	ˈgɑrdɪən	inveigle	ɪnˈveɪgəl
guile	ˈgaɪəl	iridescent	ɪrəˈdɛsənt
gyp	ʤɪp	irony	ˈaɪrənɪ
		isolation	aɪsəˈleɪʃən
halcyon	ˈhælsɪən	issue	ˈɪʃu
halve	hæv	isthmus	ˈɪsməs
harass	həˈræs		
harmony	ˈhɑrmənɪ	jacquard	ˈʤækɑrd
haughty	ˈhɔtɪ	jaeger	ˈjeɪgɚ
hawk	hɔk	jewelry	ˈʤuəlrɪ
heir	ær	jocund	ˈʤɑkənd
hiatus	haɪˈeɪtəs		
hierarchy	ˈhaɪrɑrkɪ	kindred	ˈkɪndrəd
Hoosier	ˈhuʒɚ	kinesics	kənˈnisɪks
horrible	ˈhɔrəbəl	kitsch	kɪtʃ
horror	ˈhɔrɚ	knave	neɪv
hors d'oeuvre	ɔrˈdɝv	knell	ˈnɛl
hosiery	ˈhoʊʒrɪ		
hostile	ˈhɑstəl	laconic	ləˈkɑnɪk
hovel	ˈhʌvəl	languor	ˈlæŋgɚ
hymn	hɪm	laryngeal	ləˈrɪnʤəl
hyperbole	haɪˈpɝbəlɪ	lathe	leɪð
		laud	lɔd
icon	ˈaɪkɑn	lecture	ˈlɛktʃɚ
identical	aɪˈdɛntɪkəl	length	lɛŋθ
idiom	ˈɪdɪəm	leviathan	lɪˈvaɪəθən
idyllic	aɪˈdɪlɪk	lexical	ˈlɛksɪkəl
ignominy	ˈɪgnəmɪnɪ	liaison	ˈliəzɑn
illusive	ɪlˈusɪv	libertine	ˈlɪbɚtin
immensity	ɪmˈɛnsətɪ	libido	ləˈbido
immobile	ɪˈmoʊbəl	licentious	laɪˈsɛntʃəs
impugn	ɪmˈpɪun	lieu	lu
inane	ɪnˈeɪn	lineage	ˈlɪniɪʤ
inclinations	ɪnkləˈneɪʃənz	literature	ˈlɪtɚətʃʊr
incomparable	ɪnˈkɑmprəbəl	lithe	laɪð
increment	ˈɪŋkrəmənt		
indigent	ˈɪndɪʤənt	machination	mækəˈneɪʃən
indignant	ɪnˈdɪgnənt	machineries	məˈʃɪnərɪz
indistinct	ɪndɪsˈtɪŋkt	magnate	ˈmægneɪt
infamous	ˈɪnfəməs	magnitude	ˈmægnətɪʊd
ingenious	ɪnˈʤinjəs	magus	ˈmeɪgəs
ingenuous	ɪnˈʤɛnjəwəs	maillot	ˈmaɪo
ingrate	ˈɪngreɪt	malign	məˈlaɪn
ingratiate	ɪnˈgreɪʃɪeɪt	marquise	mɑrˈkiz
innumerable	ɪnˈɪʊmrəbəl	masonry	ˈmeɪsənrɪ

maturation	mætʃə'reɪʃən	penchant	'pɛntʃənt
mature	mə'tʊr	peony	'piənɪ
memoir	'mɛmwar	perceive	pə·'siv
metaphor	'mɛtəfɔr	perfidy	'pɝfədɪ
metastasize	mə'tæstəsaɪz	perfunctory	pə·'fʌŋktrɪ
micrometer	maɪ'kramətə·	pernicious	pə·'nɪʃəs
microscopic	maɪkrə'skapɪk	perpetually	pə·'pɛtʃwəlɪ
mien	min	perpetuate	pə·'pɛtʃəweɪt
miraculous	mə'rækjʊləs	persevere	pə·sə'vɪr
mirage	mə'raʒ	persona	pə·'soʊnə
miscellany	'mɪsəleɪnɪ	phantom	'fæntəm
miscreant	'mɪskriənt	physiology	fɪzɪ'alədʒɪ
misogynist	mə'sadʒənəst	picaresque	pɪkə'rɛsk
misshapen	mɪ'ʃeɪpən	picturesque	pɪkʃə'rɛsk
mnemonic	nɪ'manɪk	plateau	plæ'toʊ
motif	mo'tif	poor	pʊr
motive	'moʊtɪv	pore	pɔr
moustache	'mʌstæʃ	potpourri	poʊpʊ'rɪ
myriad	'mɪriəd	pour	pɔr
mystified	'mɪstəfaɪd	precede	prɪ'sid
		precis	'preɪsi
naive	na'iv	prejudice	'prɛdʒədəs
negotiations	nɪgoʃi'eɪʃənz	preoccupied	prɪ'akjəpaɪd
neural	'njʊrəl	prerogative	prɪ'ragətɪv
nihilism	'naɪəlɪzəm	privilege	'prɪvlɪdʒ
nodule	'nadʒuəl	pseudo	'sudoʊ
nonpareil	nanpə'rɛl	punctuate	'pʌŋtʃəwet
nouveau riche	nuvo'riʃ		
nuance	'nɪuans	quaff	kwaf
nullified	'nʌləfaɪd	qualm	kwam
		query	'kwɪrɪ
obfuscate	'abfəsket	queue	kju
obliviously	ə'blɪviəslɪ	quiche	kiʃ
obviate	'abvieɪt	quintessence	kwɪn'tɛsəns
oceanic	oʃɪ'ænɪk	quivered	'kwɪvə·d
ombudsman	'ambʊdzmən	quixotic	kwɪk'satɪk
ominous	'amənəs		
opaque	oʊ'peɪk	radically	'rædɪkəlɪ
		raffish	'ræfɪʃ
palate	'pælət	ragout	ræ'gu
palette	'pælət	ramie	'reɪmɪ
pallet	'pælət	rampant	'ræmpənt
pallette	pæ'lɛt	raucus	'rɔkəs
papal	'peɪpəl	recitative	rɛsətə'tiv
paradoxical	pærə'dɔksɪkəl	reclamation	rəklə'meɪʃən
paragon	'pærəgɔn	recluse	'rɛklus
paralyzing	'pærəlaɪzɪŋ	recompense	'rɛkəmpɛns
Parmesan	'parməzan	recoup	rɪ'kup
parquet	par'keɪ	refuge	'rɛfjudʒ

regime	rɪˈʒim	tedious	ˈtidɪəs
relevance	ˈrɛləvəns	temperate	ˈtɛmprɛt
remoteness	rɪˈmoʊtnəs	thwart	θwɑrt
remunerate	rɪˈmjunɚeɪt	tissue	ˈtɪʃu
renaissance	rɛnəˈsɑns	topiary	ˈtoʊpɪɚɪ
residual	rɪˈzɪʤəwəl	torpor	ˈtɔrpɚ
restrict	rɪˈstrɪkt	tout	taʊt
revocable	ˈrɛvəkəbəl	toward	tɔrd
rhythm	ˈrɪðəm	tract	trækt
rickety	ˈrɪkətɪ	treatise	ˈtritəs
riotous	ˈraɪətəs	tribulation	trɪbjəˈleɪʃən
		Tuesday	ˈtɪuzdeɪ
saboteur	sæbəˈtʊɚ		
sachet	sæˈʃeɪ	ubiquitous	juˈbɪkwətəs
sanctuary	ˈsæŋtʃəwɚɪ	umbrage	ˈʌmbrɪʤ
sanguine	ˈsæŋgwɛn	usurp	jʊˈsɝp
satchel	ˈsætʃəl	uxorious	əkˈsorɪəs
satiate	ˈseɪʃɪeɪt (verb)		
scholar	ˈskɑlɚ	vacuity	væˈkjuətɪ
scourged	ˈskɚʤd	vagary	ˈveɪgərɪ
sculptor	ˈskʌlptɚ	vanishing	ˈvænɪʃɪŋ
scythe	ˈsaɪð	vegan	ˈvigən
secrecy	ˈsikrəsɪ	vehement	ˈviəmənt
seethe	sið	vehicle	ˈvihɪkəl
segue	ˈsɛgweɪ	venue	ˈvɛnju
serene	səˈrin	victual	ˈvɪtəl
serious	ˈsɪrɪəs	vignette	vɪnˈjɛt
sheath	ʃiθ		
sheathe	ʃið	wash	wɑʃ
siege	ˈsiʤ	whorl	hwɔrl
sieve	sɪv	wieldy	ˈwildɪ
skeptical	ˈskɛptɪkəl	wraith	reɪθ
skew	ˈskju	wrath	ræθ
societal	səˈsaɪətəl	wretched	ˈrɛtʃəd
solder	ˈsɑdɚ		
solemn	ˈsɑləm	xenophile	ˈzɛnəfaɪl
sphere	sfɪr		
stalk	stɔk	yacht	jɑt
stolid	ˈstɑləd	yeoman	ˈjoʊmən
stratagems	ˈstrætəʤəmz	yore	jɔr
strictest	ˈstrɪktəst	your	jʊr
subtle	ˈsʌtl		
succinct	səkˈsɪŋkt	zeal	zil
succor	ˈsʌkɚ	zealot	ˈzɛlət
sumptuous	ˈsʌmtʃuəs	zoology	zoˈɑləʤɪ
surfeit	ˈsɝfət		
taut	tɔt		
technical	ˈtɛknɪkəl		

APPENDIX FOUR

Sound Recognition Practice

Name: _____

Date: _____

I. Below you will find words that are written in IPA. Practice sounding out the phonemes, and write the word that is represented in the blank. Your insructor should supply answers.

1. æk'sɛpt_____

2. ædʒɪktɪv _____

3. artʃ_____

4. ə'skju _____

5. bɔk _____

6. beɪʒ_____

7. bɪlʤ _____

8. 'baðɚ_____

9. 'bɪʊroʊ_____

10. kæv_____

11. 'kɔzəl _____

12. 'sɛntʃrɪ_____

13. ʃeɪz _____

14. kloʊð _____

15. kən'kakt _____

16. 'kantʃəns_____

17. dɛt _____

18. dɪs'deɪn _____

19. ɪ'kaləʤɪ _____

20. ɪs'keɪp _____

21. 'farðɚ _____

22. flɔnt _____

23. geɪt_____

24. nɔ _____

25. dʒɪp _____

26. aɪ'dɛntɪɪkəl_____

27. ɪn'tækt _____

28. 'ʤuəlri_____

29. 'lærɪŋks _____

30. 'mægnət _____

31. na'iv _____

32. 'oʊkɚ, _____

33. 'peɪpəl _____

34. pʊr _____

35. 'rɪəltɚ_____

36. 'rɪðəm _____

37. 'sarkæzəm_____

38. 'skju _____

39. tækt _____

40. 'tɪʃu_____

Name: _____

Date: _____

II. Below are words easily recognized as written orthographically. Say the word properly to yourself, and write the word in IPA in the blank. Your instructor should supply answers.

1. ache _____
2. aegis _____
3. alveolar _____
4. arctic_____
5. benign _____
6. bias _____
7. bore _____
8. bureaucracy _____
9. business_____
10. cable_____
11. cereal _____
12. chamois _____
13. cohere _____
14. concede _____
15. conscious_____
16. depth _____
17. discern _____
18. district _____
19. empathy _____
20. exam _____

21. fault _____
22. folk _____
23. gaudy _____
24. gyp _____
25. halve _____
26. incomparable _____
27. issue _____
28. knell_____
29. later _____
30. metaphor_____
31. nuclear_____
32. ought _____
33. phantom _____
34. plateau_____
35. recoup _____
36. restrict _____
37. seethe_____
38. suite _____
39. taut_____
40. tract _____

Name: _____

Date: _____

III. The lists that follow may be used in two ways. Your instructor may elect to pronounce the words, and will instruct you to transcribe the word into IPA. Use this sheet for your transcription. Another way to use the practice sheet is to pronounce each word yourself and write the word in IPA. Work with your instructor for answers.

List A

1. cup _____
2. pass_____
3. knob_____
4. among _____
5. magic _____
6. aim _____
7. what_____
8. away_____
9. after _____
10. free _____
11. of_____
12. vow _____
13. thin_____
14. breadth _____
15. that_____
16. breathes_____
17. fate _____
18. oat_____
19. dawn _____
20. crude _____
21. smell_____
22. casts _____

List B

1. nose _____
2. drives _____
3. book_____
4. lips _____
5. shoe _____
6. ocean _____
7. beige_____
8. massage _____
9. dream_____
10. brown _____
11. church _____
12. judge _____
13. yes _____
14. amuse_____
15. exercise _____
16. chronic_____
17. began _____
18. vogue _____
19. single _____
20. young_____
21. help _____
22. who _____

Evaluation Forms

Name: _____

Date: _____

Chapter One Vocal Profile

(Complete following Chapter One)

Directions: Answer the questions below to assist your instructor in understanding your voice and your objectives for this course.

Place of birth:

List places you have lived for over a year (until age 10 or 12):

Parents' language or linguistic heritage:

Your age:

List any physical or health considerations (include dental work) that would apply to speech:

Describe your professional goals:

Describe the way your voice sounds to you (nasal, high pitched, clear, etc.):

Describe how others have described your voice:

List at least three things you hope to learn or wish to change:

Name: _____

Date: _____

Chapter One Evaluation

Voice and Diction Overview

Directions: Using this form, pinpoint any special areas of voice and diction needing improvement. Place a checkmark at the appropriate descriptor and then write your observations in the space provided.

_____

PITCH: Too high: _____   OK: _____   Too low: _____

General observations:

_____

VOLUME: Too loud: _____   OK: _____   Too soft: _____

General observations:

_____

RATE: Too fast: _____   OK: _____   Too slow: _____

General observations:

_____

_____

QUALITY:

Describe how your voice sounds:

Do you have any special difficulties?

General observations:

_____

ARTICULATION: Muffled: _____   Clear: _____   Dialect: _____

Special articulation features:

General observations:

_____

GENERAL OVERVIEW: Monotonous: _____   Varied: _____

General observations:

_____

YOUR GOALS:

YOUR PLAN FOR ACHIEVING THOSE GOALS:

_____

Name: _____

Date: _____

Chapter Four Evaluation

Pitch

(Complete following Chapter Four)

Directions: Assess the factors below. Circle the number that best indicates your pitch level (as determined by your instructor or estimated by you). Respond to the other questions.

USUAL PITCH LEVEL:

_____ 1 _____ 2 _____ 3 _____ 4 _____ 5 _____
 Very high   Somewhat high   Just right   Somewhat low   Too low

My usual pitch level and my best pitch level are about the same:

yes _____   no _____

INTONATION:

_____ 1 _____ 2 _____ 3 _____ 4 _____ 5 _____
 Monotoned   Patterned   Slightly varied   Varied   Too varied

PITCH RANGE: _____ (Number of notes)

General observations:

Instructor's comments:

Objectives:

Name: _____

Date: _____

Chapter Five Evaluation

Volume

(Complete following Chapter Five)

Directions: Assess the loudness and force factors of your voice by circling the descriptor that fits you. Add other pertinent information.

LOUDNESS LEVEL:

_____ 1 _____ 2 _____ 3 _____ 4 _____ 5 _____
Too loud Somewhat loud Adequate Somewhat soft Too soft

_____ 1 _____ 2 _____ 3 _____ 4 _____ 5 _____
Too varied Somewhat varied Adequate Somewhat monotonous Monotonous

BREATH-SUPPORT:

_____ 1 _____ 2 _____ 3 _____ 4 _____ 5 _____
Too thin Sometimes thin Somewhat breathy Very breathy Effective

SYLLABIC STRESS:

_____ 1 _____ 2 _____ 3 _____ 4 _____ 5 _____
Usually incorrect Sounds awkward Sometimes OK Generally appropriate Very good

Problem words:

WORD EMPHASIS:

	1		2		3		4		5	
	Wrong stress often		Sounds awkward		Sometimes OK		Generally appropriate		Very good	

General observations:

Instructor's comments:

Objectives:

Name: _____

Date: _____

Chapter Six Evaluation

Rate

(Complete following Chapter Six)

Directions: Assess your voice for the factors listed below, with the aid of your instructor. Circle or check the appropriate response. Be sure to write down observations.

Conversational words per minute: _____

Public Speaking words per minute: _____

Reading words per minute: _____

Your average: _____

RATE:

_____ 1 _____	2 _____	3 _____	4 _____	5 _____
Too fast	Somewhat fast	Average	Somewhat slow	Too slow

	Yes	*Some*	*No*
Hesitant	_____	_____	_____
Staccato	_____	_____	_____
Jerky	_____	_____	_____
Steady	_____	_____	_____
Lacked pause	_____	_____	_____
Variety	_____	_____	_____

General observations:

Instructor's comments:

Objectives:

Name: _____

Date: _____

Chapter Seven Evaluation

Quality

(Complete following Chapter Seven)

Directions: Assess the quality factors of your voice. Place a checkmark at the point(s) you and your instructor determine as descriptive of your voice. Respond to the other parts of the form.

Nasal   _____

Denasal   _____

Breathy   _____

Guttural   _____

Strident   _____

Thin   _____

Hoarse   _____

Harsh   _____

Raspy   _____

Clear   _____

Strong   _____

Full   _____

Describe the sound of your voice:

Instructor's comments:

Objectives:

Name: _____

Date: _____

Chapter Eight Evaluation

Articulation

(Complete following Chapter Eight)

Directions: Assess your articulation in general by circling or checking the appropriate descriptors. Respond to questions below.

OVERALL ARTICULATION:

_____ 1 _____ 2 _____ 3 _____ 4 _____ 5 _____
             Garbled   Somewhat garbled   Fair   Clear   Overdone

Respond to the following questions:

1. Are you opening your jaw?   Yes _____   No _____

2. Do you use active lip movement?   Yes _____   No _____

3. Is your tongue remaining on the bottom of your
   mouth for sounds that require movement?   Yes _____   No _____

4. Are your teeth fairly aligned (top teeth slightly
   over bottom teeth)? Does that affect clarity?   Yes _____   No _____

5. Are you raising your velum appropriately?   Yes _____   No _____

6. Does your dialect affect clarity?   Yes _____   No _____

   If yes, specify: _____

List below specific sounds with which you seem to have difficulty:

List below words with which you seem to have difficulty:

Instructor's comments:

Objectives:

Name: _____

Date: _____

Chapter Nine Checklist

Vowels/Diphthongs

(Complete following Chapter Nine)

Directions: The following passage includes words that contain front vowels, back vowels, mid vowels, and diphthongs in the sequence in which they appeared in this chapter. There are at least three or four words containing each phoneme.

An IPA symbol above letters and underlining will aid you in identifying sounds. To the left of the passage is a checklist column for vowel/diphthong phonemes.

Use an audio or video recorder or a partner to assist you in your evaluation. Make a checkmark beside any phoneme for which you require additional practice.

i _____ Each of us thinks it is easy enough to believe in important issues. In

I _____ the city even dreams exist. So that begins the story.

e _____ The name of the game is to get what you can, a friend had said. I was

ε _____ afraid that wasn't ethical, and I cared to stay in the trade business. Is

æ _____ that so bad? Perhaps! Still there was a chance to challenge my values.

ɑ _____ After all, my father called it honor.

ɔ _____ "Be honest," he always said. That was his argument, his talk, what he

o _____ taught me.

ʊ _____ That was long ago when I was open and willing to grow. Though he

u _____ stood for good, the school of hard knocks proved many exceptions to

ə _____ the rule, told me that no matter where you stood on issues you could ʌ _____   lo͡se. (u above lose)

ɚ _____   A͡bove the͟ advice and am͡ong any u͟lterior motives, I have co͡me to

ɝ _____   treasu͟re his rathe͟r te͟rse wo͟rds. I have ru͟n for pu͟blic office and have

aɪ _____   beco͡me a soldie͟r, pe͟rhaps, for the͟ governme͟nt. No͟w, I͟ realize ho͟w

aʊ _____   po͟wer bu͟ys ti͟me in cities and to͟wns. So, the bo͟y becomes the man

ɔɪ _____   and jo͟ins the vo͟ices which went before him. There is jo͟y and some

ɪu _____   be͟auty in that. There is a ne͟w sense of u͟niversal du͟ty.

Name: _____

Date: _____

Chapter Ten Checklist

Consonants

(Complete following Chapter Ten)

Directions: The following passage includes words that contain consonants in the sequence in which they appeared in this chapter with three or four words containing each phoneme. (It is not comprehensive insofar as it contains all consonants juxtaposed with all other possible consonants.) IPA letters are written above the alphabetical letters that are underlined to help you to identify sounds. To the left of the passage is a checklist column for consonants. Use this checklist as you did the vowel checklist. Read the passage over several times using the assistance of audio/video equipment or a friend and check off those consonants for which you require additional drill.

p _____   Perhaps people who have been abroad are better at pricing baubles,

b _____   bangles, and other goods, or just think they are. It may be that when

m _____   one has made the time to examine goods around the world, one is not

hw _____   swept away where a less traveled person might be. For example,

w _____   some finely crafted goods may be found in the Orient if you are

f _____   willing to go so far. Very few people inevitably are, of course. Others

v _____   think nothing of spending thousands on that kind of trip, though.

θ _____   Sometimes you no doubt spend ten to fifty times as much on an item

ð _____   in the States as you would in the place in which it is manufactured.

t _____   Zealous shoppers often go to great lengths to search out bargains, d _____   starting with di**s**count **s**tore**s** and e**x**tending to Europe. **N**ever u**n**der-

s_____   estimate seaso**n**ed hu**n**ters. **L**ower prices are their goa**l**. Nothing could

z_____   be more p**l**easing than a **l**ovely dea**l**.

n _____   O**c**eans and na**ti**ons are no barrier. Conver**si**on rates are no problem.

l_____   Europe **sh**ould have it! A**si**a **s**hould have it—a bargain! "Bo**r**n to

ʃ_____   **sh**op!" some say. A fair wa**r**ning is in o**r**der he**r**e. One may not be able

ʒ_____   to ex**ch**ange a **j**ar, **j**ade broo**ch**, or other **j**ewel bought in **Ch**ina. Yes,

r_____   that's the **u**s**u**al case. F**ew** things **c**an be ta**k**en ba**ck** to Tur**k**ey. **G**ood-

tʃ _____   ness knows, it comes down to this. **G**oing away doesn't get you better

dʒ_____   **g**oods. **G**ood thi**ng**s begin at **h**ome. Shoppi**ng** and buyi**ng** in the States

j_____   some**h**ow **h**elps the economy. So stay **h**ere to become a worldly wise

k _____   shopper.

g_____

ŋ _____

h _____

GLOSSARY

Accent (1) Refers to the degree of stress or emphasis given a syllable in a word; (2) Also used interchangeably with *dialect,* as in "he has a southern accent."

Acoustic Refers to the science of sound and its properties.

Affricate A combination of two approximate consonant sounds that results in a new sound.

Allophone A variation of a sound, or phonemic variance, dependent on the context of that sound.

Alveolar Consonant sounds made against the upper gum ridge or alveolar ridge.

Amplitude Refers to the degree of air pressure during sound production. The result is the perceived volume of a sound.

Articulation The positioning of the articulators (jaw, lips, tongue, teeth, alveoli, palate, and velum) in order to create the individual sounds of any given language.

Arytenoids Two small cartilages at the rear of the larynx to which the vocal folds attach.

Assimilation Changes, modifications, or omissions in sound as a result of placement in connected speech, often considered to be negative.

Back channeling Communication feedback that regulates communication.

Bilabial Refers to consonant sounds produced with two lips.

Blend Refers usually to two or more consonant sounds produced together; for example, *bl* in *blend.*

Breathiness A vocal quality characterized by excessive release of air during speech.

Breathing The process of inhaling and exhaling air and utilizing that air for producing voice.

Coarticulation Articulation as it occurs in connected speech, which alters the primary place of articulation.

Cochlea Organ of the inner ear.

Code switching As used in this text, the ability to shift from one dialect or accent to another. It is directly applied to language.

Cognates Two consonants produced in the same place in the mouth; one is voiced and one is voiceless.

Concha Shell-like portion of the outer ear.

Consonant Phonemes that are produced by setting up an articulatory obstruction to either the vocalized or unvocalized breath stream.

Continuant Consonants that are produced with continuousness as opposed to being interrupted.

Cricoid cartilage Rings of cartilage at the base of the larynx. The arytenoids sit on the top edge of the cricoid cartilage.

Decibel (db) The unit of measurement of the intensity of sound and thus its loudness. Ordinary conversation is about 65 to 70 db.

Denasal Lack of appropriate nasality in speech. Ordinarily caused by nasal blockage.

Dental Teeth. Refers to consonant sounds that are produced in conjunction with the teeth.

Diacritical markings Symbols, such as accent marks, tilde, etc., that indicate phonetic values. Usually found in dictionaries.

Dialect A variation of articulated language characterized by differences from the overall language in vocabulary, grammar, phonemic, inflections, stress, and rhythms.

Diaphragm Dome-shaped muscle situated just beneath the lungs; aids in respiration.

Diction (1) Production of the sounds of a language, synonymous with articulation and enunciation; (2) choice of words in oral or written communication.

Diphthong Vowel combinations that result from a continuous glide from one approximate vowel position to another.

Duration The time spent producing a given sound or silence.

English   With varying dialects, the most widely used language in the world.

Epigiottis   A blade of cartilage that covers the glottis during swallowing.

Frequency   The measurement in hertz (Hz) of cycles per second of a sound wave. Frequency is perceived as pitch.

Fricatives   Consonants produced by forcing the vocalized or unvocalized breath stream through a narrow passage created by the articulators resulting in a frictionalized sound.

Glide   Consonants continuously produced while articulators move from one position to another.

Glottal   Refers to consonants or sounds produced through the glottis. The consonant [h] is an example.

Glottis   The space between the vocal folds.

Guttural   A quality of voice that is produced low in the oro-pharyngeal cavity or throat.

Harshness   A quality of voice frequently perceived as dry and raspy.

Hertz   The unit of measurement of frequency.

Hoarseness   A quality of voice perceived as wet and irregular, often associated with vocal nodes.

Inflection   An upward or downward change in pitch usually on a single vocalization, sometimes with a slight break in vocalization.

International Phonetic Alphabet (IPA)   A means of representing with symbols all of the sounds in all languages.

Intonation   The overall pitch movement that characterizes a language or a person's speech.

Labio   Lips. Refers to consonants produced primarily with the lips.

Larynx   Structure at the top of the trachea that houses the vocal folds. Colloquially termed "voice box."

Lateral   Refers to consonants produced around the sides of the tongue.

Laxness   Refers to the relaxation of muscular tension that is characteristic of some vowels.

Lingua   Tongue. Refers to consonants produced with the tongue against or pointed toward another articulator.

Linguistics   The study of language.

Loudness   The perception of amplitude or the degree of force with which a sound is produced.

Malleus   Small bone in the middle ear.

Meatus   Ear canal.

Nasal   Nose. Consonants emitted solely through the nose.

Nasality   Refers to excessive nasal resonance.

Organ of Corti   Membrane in the inner ear containing nerve endings.

Palatal   Refers to consonants produced with the tongue against the hard palate.

Palate   Can refer to either the hard palate (roof of the mouth) or soft palate (situated in the high rear of the mouth).

Paralinguistic   Refers to the use of voice to convey messages or meaning beyond the word or words used.

Pause   A break in speech characterized by silence.

Pharynx   Throat.

Phonation   The vibration of the vocal folds.

Phoneme   An individual sound in any given language.

Pitch   Frequency defines the number of vibrations of a sound wave. Pitch is the perception of frequency as "high or low."

Plosive   Consonants produced by first blocking the vocalized or unvocalized breath stream and then releasing it suddenly.

Projection   Increasing loudness of voice to adjust to one's audience and space.

Pronunciation   The proper utterance of orthographic depictions (writing) of sound and syllabic stress, the correct way to produce a given word.

Quality   Refers to the uniqueness of a voice based on pitch, loudness, and general resonance of that voice.

Raspiness   A quality of voice that appears irritated and results in a grating sound.

Rate   Refers to the speed with which a speaker utters words, measured in words per minute (wpm).

Resonation   The amplification or modification of vocalized sound that takes place in the pharynx and oral and nasal cavities.

Retroflexed   Refers to sounds produced with the tip of the tongue curled toward the hard palate.

Schwa   The most common sound in American English. A mid-mouth vowel that is usually unstressed. Symbolized both in the dictionary and in IPA as [ə].

Speech phrasing Forming a group of spoken words that constitute a meaningful unit and are surrounded by pauses.

Stapes Small bone in the middle ear.

Stress The emphasis given a word or syllable by means of increased loudness or a change in pitch.

Stridency A quality of voice perceived as high pitched and tinny.

Syllabic stress The emphasis given a syllable by increasing loudness or changing pitch.

Syllable A unit of language that consists of at least one vowel but may consist of more than one vowel and be combined with consonants. Constitutes a word or part of a word.

Tensiveness The degree of tension that characterizes some vowels.

Thinness A quality of voice characterized by lack of breath support and weak resonation.

Timbre Quality of voice.

Trachea Tube between the larynx and bronchial tubes; the windpipe.

Typanic membrane Diaphragmatic tissue at the end of the ear canal.

Variety Refers to the employment of upward or downward pitch changes in order to avoid monotone or a narrow pitch range. May also be applied to varying the other vocal properties of rate, loudness, and quality.

Velar Consonants that are produced with the back of the tongue against the velum.

Velum The projection of the soft palate that is seen in the rear of the mouth, the tip of which is the uvula.

Vocal folds Two thin bands of muscular tissue that are edged by ligaments and are located in the larynx. Vibration of the folds creates sound.

Vocal nodes Irregular growths on the vocal folds caused by irritation and causing the voice to sound hoarse or raspy.

Voice Vocal fold vibration. Used in reference to consonants and vowels.

Voicelessness Used in reference to consonants; lack of vocal fold vibration.

Vowel Phonemes that are produced with continuous vocalization and with no obstruction to the breath stream.

INDEX